THE ZONE GARDEN

3·4·5

Cynthia
Margaux
7/97

Books by Charlotte M. Frieze
Social Gardens
The Zone Garden 3 • 4 • 5
The Zone Garden 5 • 6 • 7
The Zone Garden 8 • 9 • 10

THE ZONE GARDEN

3·4·5

A SUREFIRE GUIDE TO GARDENING IN YOUR ZONE

CHARLOTTE M. FRIEZE

Illustrations by Joel Barkley

Photographs by Michael H. Dodge from the White Flower Farm Collection

A High Tide Press Original
A Fireside Book
Published by Simon & Schuster

FIRESIDE
Rockefeller Center
1230 Avenue of the Americas
New York, NY 10020

Designed by Doris Straus

Edited by Lisa MacDonald

Manufactured in Hong Kong

10 9 8 7 6 5 4 3 2 1

Library of Congress Cataloging-in-Publication Data
The zone garden : a surefire guide to gardening in your zone / Charlotte M. Frieze ;
illustrations by Joel Barkley ; photographs by Michael H. Dodge from the White Flower Farm Collection.
p.   cm.
"A High Tide Press original." "A Fireside book." Includes indexes. Contents: [1] 3-4-5 -- [2] 5-6-7 [3] 8-9-10.
1. Gardening--United States. 2. Plants, Cultivated--United States. 3. Gardening. 4. Plants, Cultivated.   I. Title.
SB453.F76 1997
635'.0973--DC20   96-46057
CIP

ISBN 0-684-82465-5

ACKNOWLEDGMENTS

The author wishes to express her gratitude to Doris Straus, who conceived of the idea for this project and designed it brilliantly; to Roger Straus III for his undeviating support; to my editor Lisa MacDonald, who always kept the books on track with her intelligence, organization and enthusiasm; to Anne Yarowsky for acquiring this project and bringing it to fruition; to illustrator Joel Barkley, principal photographer Michael H. Dodge, and photographers Peter Cummin, William B. Harris, Saxon Holt, Peter C. Jones, Claudia A. Palmer, Allan Mandell, Erik Simmons, Roger Straus III and Eliot Wadsworth II for their exquisite images; to Shepherd and Ellen Ogden, Alex and Carol Rosenberg, John Saladino and Sally Tappen for sharing their gardens; to Elizabeth Scholtz for her encouragement; to Alexander A. Apanius, Mary Palmer and Hugh Dargan, Niki Ekstrom, Bill Evans, Mike Graham, Doyle Jones, Jack Lieber, Scott Ogden, Greg Piotrowski, and Adam Lifton-Schwerner for their expert advice; to Susan Goldberger for her insightful recommendations; to Mary Dearborn, who made the complicated simple; to Christine S. Shaw, who kept the hard drive spinning; to Sheila White, without whose assistance I would still be writing the first draft; to Lynne Duffy of White Flower Farm for her thorough and thoughtful picture research; to Katherine Powis and The Horticultural Society of New York for their excellent library; to Robert A. M. Stern for his support and the time in which to write these books; to Frank Lipman, who kept me going; to my parents for giving me my first garden; and to my husband, Peter C. Jones, whose love and devotion have carried me through the many challenges of writing these books.

Additional Photography Credits

Peter Cummin: pages 47; 54: top right, center, bottom; 56: center, bottom right; 58: top left, center, bottom left; 98: center; 136: top left, top right, bottom; 138: center; 162: top right; 164: top left; *William B. Harris*: page 164: center; *Saxon Holt*: page 195; *Peter C. Jones*: pages 11; 18; 24; 39; 56: bottom left; 60; 80: center; 82; 96: top left, center, bottom left, bottom right; 100: top left, bottom left; 114; 122; 130; 140; 166-167; 168; 169; 194; 204; 206: left; 207; 214-215; *Allan Mandell:* page 200; *Claudia A. Palmer:* page 74: top left; *Erik Simmons*: pages 112-113; 162: bottom; *Roger Straus III:* pages 70; 102; 155; *Eliot Wadsworth II:* pages 22-23.

TABLE OF CONTENTS

TABLE OF CONTENTS

Michael H. Dodge

1
THE ZONE GARDEN

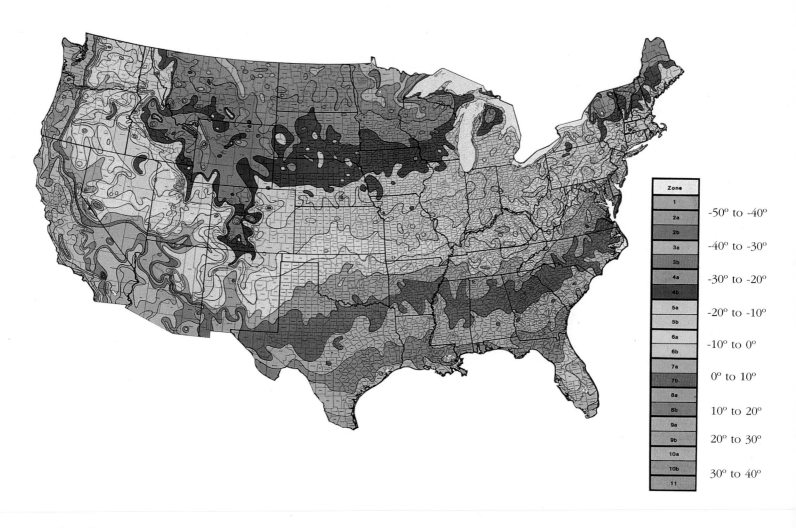

Zone	
1	
2a	−50° to −40°
2b	
3a	−40° to −30°
3b	
4a	−30° to −20°
4b	
5a	−20° to −10°
5b	
6a	−10° to 0°
6b	
7a	
7b	0° to 10°
8a	
8b	10° to 20°
9a	
9b	20° to 30°
10a	
10b	30° to 40°
11	

Agricultural Research Service, USDA

I
THE ZONE GARDEN

Temperature
Altitude
Frost
Snow
Rainfall
Humidity
Sunlight

Papaver somniferum

Wind
Soil
Soil Types
Compost
Soil pH
Soil Fertility
Saline Soil

When the plant and seed catalogs arrive in January, the photographs are so beautiful that it's easy to be tempted to buy one of everything. However, like all gardeners, I'm sure you have experienced the disappointment of plants that have inexplicably failed and realize that gardening is about more than selecting plants for color, shape and size.

Climate is at the heart of the garden. By tailoring your gardening practices to where you live, *The Zone Garden* helps take the guesswork out of plant selection, placement and care. With an understanding of the elements at work in your own backyard, you can choose plants targeted for your unique microclimates to achieve peak performance in your garden.

PLANT HARDINESS AND THE ZONE MAP
For years gardeners have relied on the United States Department of Agriculture's Hardiness Map, which illustrates eleven different climate zones delineated by average minimum annual temperatures. Using this zone system, plants are rated by their ability to survive the winter. For example, a plant rated as hardy to Zone 5 will survive temperatures to -20° Fahrenheit but not Zone 3's minimum temperature of -40°. Locate your county on the map to determine your zone.

Zone 3 — orange — minimum temperatures of -30° to -40°
Zone 4 — purple — minimum temperatures of -20° to -30°
Zone 5 — spring green — minimum temperatures of -10° to -20°

Think of the USDA map as a cold-weather survival guide. But survival alone will not lead to a bountiful garden. Instead, use the Zone Map as a starting point to understanding the needs of your plants.

Getting To Know Your Zone

Zones 3, 4 and 5 stretch across the country, beginning in northern New England, traveling down through New York, then crossing through the High Plains and Western Mountains to the Pacific Northwest and Alaska.

Gardeners in these zones experience all four seasons, including the crisp beauty of a fall day as well as the welcome breath of spring. However, gardeners in Zones 3, 4 and 5 must also work within the constraints of a short growing season and many must also contend with a roller coaster of extreme changes in temperature — occasionally as much as a 40° plummet in an afternoon! (As Mark Twain said about New England, "If you don't like the weather, just wait a while.") Spring and fall tend to be somewhat moderate, but the winter and summer months can bring severe weather, including extreme cold and blistering heat and drought.

The limits of the short growing season and long cold winters are particularly felt in the Adirondacks and northern New England. For many plants, these long periods of cold temperatures cause greater damage than short, icy blasts because extended cold penetrates into the bark and wood cells of a plant.

In addition to long, cold winters, the northern prairie states also have bitter winds. During extended cold periods, the ground freezes to a deep level and may cause plants to "heave" their root systems out of the ground. This leaves them vulnerable to the wind, which dries out plant cells, especially those with exposed roots. Sudden hot or cold winds can come up, often one right after another. And summers can be intolerably hot and dry with severe storms.

The Upper Midwest shares the cold winter, but has a shorter cold season and brutal freeze-thaw activity in late winter and early spring. An excessive freeze-thaw cycle is especially tough on plants as a plant's metabolism quickens during a thaw, then is suddenly halted when a freeze occurs. Plants must be carefully winterized to minimize damage from these temperature changes. Midwestern summers also put plants to the test; heat and wind with little rain often create a lethal combination.

As you can see, climatic conditions vary widely within the same zone (Zone 5 runs through parts of Alaska, Arizona, Michigan and Massachusetts), and even in your own backyard. To help your garden flourish, understand your local climate and then zero in on the growing conditions in your own garden.

Zeroing In On Your Microclimate

A microclimate is a small area where growing conditions differ from the overall climate. Microclimates occur when climatic, natural and man-made elements converge; a multitude can exist within your property.

Savvy gardeners in your cold climate exploit warm pockets to extend the growing season, grow more tender or sun-loving plants, and protect against brutal winters. Cold pockets are reserved for the hardiest plants; wet spots for thirsty plants and dry areas for drought-tolerant plants.

Walk around your property during the different seasons. Mark on a plan where you feel warmest in a winter wind and coolest on a blistering hot summer day. Look for late-winter sun traps and low spots of pooling water. Work with the following elements to find the perfect spot for that favorite rose.

TEMPERATURE

All plants have a minimum temperature below which they can't survive, a maximum temperature above which they can't survive and an optimum temperature. Heat as well as cold control plant growth and influence the following critical plant processes:
PHOTOSYNTHESIS   The process in which leaves, using the sun's energy, convert carbon dioxide from the air and nutrients found in water into carbohydrates.

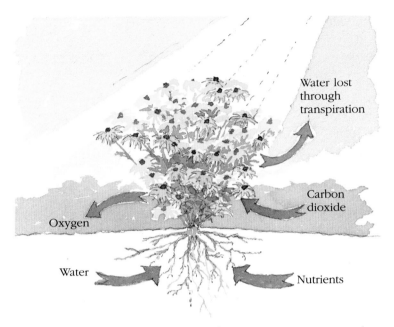

Through photosynthesis, leaves, using the sun's energy, convert carbon dioxide, from both air and the nutrients in water, into carbohydrates, which are necessary for plant growth.

TRANSPIRATION   The process in which leaves lose water vapor and oxygen through evaporation.
RESPIRATION   The process in which carbohydrates are broken down to create energy, carbon dioxide and water.

The Growing Season
While hardiness zones are based on the average annual minimum temperature in a given zone (see "Plant Hardiness And The Zone Map," p.11), the growing season is based on the average number of days above 43° Fahrenheit, the lowest temperature at which grass grows.

Here's how it works. Air temperature controls the soil temperature. Together these temperatures influence dormancy (the slowing down of plant processes and temporary halting of growth), which determines the length of your growing season. The average length is as follows:

Zone 3: 165 days
Zone 4: 195 days
Zone 5: 210 days

To determine the growing season in your area (which may significantly differ from these general guidelines), as well as a record of the first and last days of frost, contact your local Agricultural Cooperative Extension Service (see p.218).

Temperature Moderators And Boosters
Hampered by the short growing season, gardeners in colder zones must pay close attention to how wind can affect temperature. A garden enclosed by hedges or walls can raise the temperature within the garden; conversely, wind blowing over the surfaces of pools and other water features will lower temperatures. Utilizing the microclimates created by these garden factors will allow you to experiment successfully with plants beyond your zone.

Extreme Cold
Extreme cold is the central issue for gardeners in Zones 3, 4 and 5. Brutal cold can cause winterkill unless plants are carefully selected, properly sited and winterized. Winterizing will also help protect the plants from the devastating effect of repeated hard freezes and rapid thaws.

Extreme Heat
The dog days of summer can be just as tough on plants as the dead of winter. The harsh sun and drought can combine forces, sending plants into false dormancy for survival. Water drought-intolerant plants often during extended heat waves.

ALTITUDE

Altitude can be a major factor in determining your microclimate. For every 250 feet above sea level, the temperature drops about 1° Fahrenheit. With only a 10° difference between zones, a high site may well be in the next colder zone. To determine your altitude, refer to a local U.S. Geological Survey map or a survey map of your property. The contour numbers represent the altitude in feet.

> HINT: As higher altitudes often mean higher light intensities, some sun-loving plants will grow well in partial shade in high-altitude locations such as the Rocky Mountains.

FROST

An untimely frost can severely damage a garden. A late spring frost can sneak up totally without warning, turning fresh young leaves brown and killing buds before they've had a chance to flower.

Frost is frozen moisture. It forms on plants when air temperatures drop below 32° Fahrenheit and in the soil when ground temperatures drop below freezing. The last day of frost determines the earliest sowing dates for tender plants. The first frost sadly signals the end of the growing season. For a record of the frost dates in your area, call your local nursery or contact your Agricultural Cooperative Extension Service (see p.218), and start to keep a record in your own garden.

The duration of frost and its depth are important to gardeners. Frozen ground means water is not available to roots. While deep-rooted trees are unaffected by frost, shallow-rooted plants, plants with borderline hardiness and evergreen shrubs, such as *Rhododendron* spp., need winter protection. (See "Winterizing" in each chapter.)

Beware of frost pockets, particularly if your home is on a hillside. Cold air naturally flows downhill like water, and if blocked

Cold air naturally flows downhill like water, and if blocked by a hill, wall, building or even a tight hedge, it will spread out and up, forming damaging frost pockets.

by a hill, wall or building will spread out and up, forming airpools or frost pockets that, like water, can freeze and damage roots. To minimize frost damage, keep cold air moving through the garden, and avoid planting in any known frost pockets.

> HINT: If your garden is prone to late spring frosts, select plants that flower later in the season to prevent frosting of the blooms.

SNOW

Gardeners welcome a winter blanket of snow as it provides excellent insulation from often dramatic temperature fluctuations, and, with the spring thaw, the melting snow replenishes the soil's water supply. Snow can also prevent excessive frost heaving, which can push shallow-rooted plants out of the ground.

However, some snows can be damaging. If snow is followed by frigid temperatures, it will freeze on the limbs before it has had a chance to melt or fall off. This can cause severe damage to woody plants, evergreens and hedges. Don't allow heavy snow to accumulate on trees and shrubs; brush it off as often as necessary. And in areas with heavy snowfall and gusting winds, consider a temporary snow fence or plant an evergreen windbreak to reduce damage from drifting snow. An early snow can come as a surprise; make sure you have properly winterized your garden before the first snowfall.

HINT: If you live on the High Plains, warm winter winds can melt the protective snow cover. Protect your garden by applying a heavy winter mulch in the fall.

RAINFALL
Water is the lifeblood of plants. Through transpiration, plants draw water and nutrients from the soil up into their leaves where it is then vaporized by the sun. When the water supply is interrupted, plant growth slows down and may even stop.

Farmers worry about rainfall and you should too. If you live near the ocean or the Great Lakes you generally enjoy increased rainfall and a more moderate climate. But for those living further inland, rainfall may be irregular. Dry climate gardeners should select drought-tolerant plants (see "The Drought-tolerant Garden," p.209), or install an irrigation system. In all climates, if you are away from the garden for long periods, make provisions with a neighbor to ensure adequate water should an unexpected dry spell arise.

Drainage
Adequate drainage is just as important as a steady supply of water. Deep roots are promoted by a low watertable or deep-watering. Too much water, or "waterlogging," decreases the amount of air in the soil. Air provides oxygen and insulation for the roots. Only specialized plants, such as some *Asclepias* (butterfly weed), can survive long periods without it. A high water table will keep roots up at the surface where they are susceptible to cold; deep roots are well insulated from frost.

Good drainage is especially important for many plants, such as *Nepeta* x *faassenii* (catmint), during their winter months of dormancy. They will not survive the winter in soggy soil, but with adequate drainage, they are perfectly hardy. Keep an eye out for wet spots in your garden. While roses may hate them, these are great places for plants that like wet feet, like *Nasturtium officinale* (watercress).

Xeric Landscaping
Xeric landscaping is a term many people are using to describe water-efficient gardening, which incorporates selecting plants compatible with the microclimate and natural level of rainfall. This is a good practice for all gardeners. First, look for natives, as many are naturally adapted to the microclimate and have survival mechanisms such as deep root systems and leaves with protective wax coating. However, not all native plants are xeric plants. Look for plants from other areas that are adapted to long periods of drought and poor soils.

HUMIDITY
Humidity is water vapor in the air and moisture in the soil. Humidity levels are measured as a percentage of total saturation; coastal areas and areas with heavy rainfall will have higher levels. Humidity is beneficial to plants such as ferns, but it can cause severe fungal growth on others. If your garden is in a humid area, allow good air circulation in and around the garden and select plants that are adapted to humidity. Mildew-resistant strains of many popular perennials, such as *Phlox paniculata* and *Monarda didyma*, are now available.

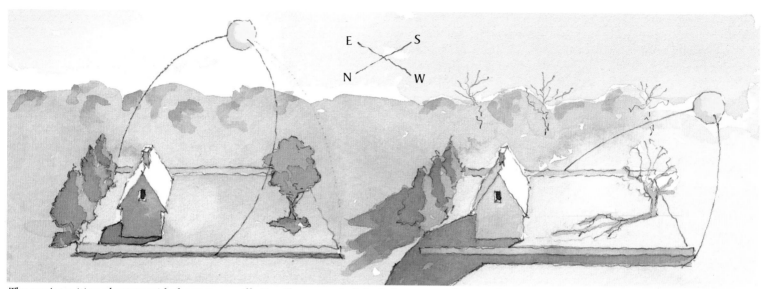

The sun's position changes with the seasons, affecting the amount of shade in your garden. In the summer (left), it is high and creates short shadows. In the winter (right), the sun is low and produces long shadows.

SUNLIGHT

The sun provides the radiant energy and warmth necessary to raise the temperature of the soil and the air to stimulate plant growth and flower and fruit production. All plants have specific needs for sunlight, which is quantified as follows:

FULL SUN At least six hours of intense sun between 10 A.M. and 6 P.M.

PARTIAL SHADE Dappled sun or shade from the hottest sun.

BRIGHT SHADE Reflected, not direct sunlight.

FULL SHADE No direct or reflected sunlight.

The intensity of the sun varies at different times of the day. The midday sun is the hottest, followed by the afternoon, then the morning sun. Remember, light requirements may be affected by climatic conditions; a plant that requires partial shade in Zone 5 may perform better in full sun in Zone 3.

When planning a garden it's important to know where and when the sun hits your yard and for how long each day. Make a map of your yard showing which areas have full sun, partial, bright or full shade at different times of the day. Pay attention to the seasons; the sun's position changes and deciduous trees come into leaf. You may be surprised to find that the corner you thought was so sunny back in February is in partial shade come June. A shady garden requires a vastly different selection of plants than a sunny one.

With a short growing season and cooling air currents, northern gardeners need to site their gardens for optimum sun exposure. To extend the growing season, or establish a spring garden, locate it on the south side of the house, but beware of the drying western sun — your plants may require additional water.

The winter sun can also be very hot. It can dehydrate broadleaf evergreens, and even burn the bark, causing "sun scald." And in deciduous trees, unprotected by their seasonal foliage, the hot winter sun can thaw the sap, causing the bark to split.

WIND

We appreciate a cooling breeze on a hot summer day, and plants do too! It disperses their pollen and seeds, prevents pockets of stagnant air in the garden, and dries off the morning dew, preventing fungal growth. However, wind can dehydrate leaves just as it dries laundry on a line. A plant on a windy hilltop, on the open plains or along the coast will have to work harder to provide a steady supply of water to the leaves. This may result in diminished growth.

Trees exposed to continuous winds can become one-sided. Avoid planting in wind tunnels created by hills, masses of trees or buildings. Never locate fragile plants such as *Delphinium* in windy spots unless you have a wind barrier. Select only salt-tolerant plants such as *Rosa rugosa* for coastal gardens exposed to salt-laden winds.

Storms with high-velocity winds are a gardener's nightmare. High winds can break limbs, defoliate stems, uproot trees and loosen root systems. A gardener's only defense is a good tree-maintenance program that includes regular pruning, cabling when necessary and the prompt removal of dead trees.

If you do lose a tree that stands close to another, the chances are good that the root system of the second tree has also been damaged. Keep an eye on it and take precautions if necessary.

Windchill

Wind can also lower temperature. If your home is on a windy hillside, your garden may be a Zone 4, while your friend's protected garden down the road may be a Zone 5.

Cold northerly and westerly winds can prolong the winter by preventing your garden from warming up. Conversely, in late summer, a cold wind can stop heat-loving vegetables, such as tomatoes, from ripening. To counter cooling winds, gardens should be placed for optimum sun exposure. The best site is one that is slightly sloping and facing the southeast.

Shelter From The Wind

You may wish to shelter windy locations with a windbreak, which can be created by planting a hedge, hedgerow, or stand of trees, or by erecting a fence or wall. To prevent strong winds from toppling a windbreak or creating a downward draft on the leeward side, allow 50 percent of the air to flow through the barrier. To reduce a steady wind, a hedge or fence should be 12' high; but in small areas windbreaks need be no higher than the plants requiring protection.

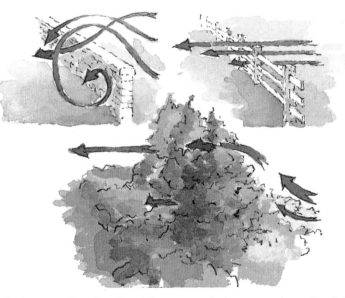

The best windbreaks allow 50 percent of air to pass through. Solid walls can create damaging downdrafts on the leeward side.

Soil: The Common Denominator

A friend once referred to good soil as "black gold," and she's right. Good soil can greatly increase the riches of your garden. Soil is composed of mineral particles, organic matter, air, water and beneficial living organisms, such as earthworms, bacteria and fungi. It is divided into three layers: topsoil, which contains most of the nutrients needed to stimulate plant growth; subsoil, which is less fertile; and the lower layer, which is derived from the underlying parent rock. Soil provides plants with anchorage, sustenance and insulation. In each zone there is the possibility of every kind of soil, and it can change right within the bounds of your property. The good news is, if you don't have the rich soil you need, you can improve it. But first, know what you have to work with.

SOIL TYPES

Soil type is determined by its texture or the size of the mineral particles. Sand is the largest, followed by silt and then clay. So it follows that the percentage of each particle size in a soil determines its type. For example, if a soil is over 50 percent sand, it is categorized as a sandy soil. The general soil types are as follows:

SANDY OR LIGHT SOIL   Coarsely textured with little organic matter.

SILTY SOIL   Medium fine textured sediment, medium density.

CLAY OR HEAVY SOIL   Finely textured, dense.

LOAM   Good mix of about 40 percent sand, 40 percent silt, 20 percent clay.

Soil has many important functions: water percolation and retention, aeration, temperature control, nutrient supply, storage and release. The particle size or soil type influences how these processes function.

At one end of the spectrum is heavy or clay soil, which drains poorly, heats and cools slowly, but is often fertile. In summer, clay soil stays hot longer and can bake the roots; in winter it retains the cold and can freeze the roots. At the other end of the soil spectrum is sandy soil, which drains quickly and thus requires more irrigation and fertilization. However, both sandy soil and loam soil (with high organic content) have mini air pockets that insulate the roots from temperature extremes much as double-paned glass windows do.

Loam: The Ideal Soil

Different plants require different kinds of soil. *Cosmos* love a sandy soil, while roses thrive in a soil rich in organic matter. However, the ideal soil for most gardens is a loam soil, which is a mixture of sand, silt and clay with ample amounts of decayed organic material called humus. (See "Compost," below.) Loam is porous, yet spongy enough to retain moisture, and rich in nutrients, which encourages soil bacteria activity.

What Kind Of Soil Do You Have?

The percentage of sand, silt and clay determines what type of soil you have. To determine your soil type, try these simple tests:

The *squeeze test* is the easiest and quickest. Take a handful of moistened soil and squeeze it in your hand. If it feels gritty and falls apart when released, there is a large amount of sand in your soil. If it feels gritty but clings together, it is a loamy sand soil. Clay soil will make a smooth smear, while sandy clay will make a gritty smear.

The *shake test* takes a little longer. Fill a quart jar about two-thirds full of water. Slowly add soil from one spot in your garden until the jar is almost full. Close the jar and give it a good shake. After several hours, different layers will have settled out. Sand weighs the most and will sink to the bottom; silt will settle in the middle with clay on top. Compare the amount of each. The highest percentage determines your soil type.

Amending Soil

Improve your soil with organic soil amendments. See the Organic Amendments chart (p.181) for additional information.
SANDY SOILS Manure, compost, clay-rich soil.
CLAY SOILS Manure, compost, sharp sand (washed and screened quartz sand is best).

In the shake test, the minerals in your soil are separated out in layers, helping you determine your soil type.

COMPOST

Compost is the Cinderella of the garden. What begins as waste products from your kitchen or garden is magically transformed into a garden elixir, rich in nutrients. You can make compost anywhere; a friend makes it in a small bucket on her Brooklyn fire escape.

Make compost by layering organic matter, soil, lime and manure or fertilizer. Keep it moist, but in heavy rains do cover it to prevent the leaching of nutrients. Make sure you turn it every two weeks or so. It's ready for use when the ingredients have broken down and are no longer recognizable. Use compost at the rate of one shovelful to about one square yard.

Add To Your Compost Pile

Vegetative kitchen refuse such as vegetable and fruit scraps, coffee grounds, tea bags and clean eggshells; garden debris such as leaves, faded blossoms, grass clippings, straw or hay; household waste such as pet fur, human hair, sawdust, wood ashes (only if you have acid soil), and shredded newspaper.

Do Not Add To Your Compost Pile

Woody garden debris (takes too long to break down); invasive vines and grasses; noxious weeds; meat, bones, butter, oils, bread or any food derived from grains such as pasta; anything that might attract unwelcome vermin to your garden; used kitty litter or droppings from other carnivorous pets, such as dogs, as they can carry disease.

SOIL pH

Good soil also contains the nutrients necessary for healthy plants. The quantity of nutrients released by the soil and made available to plants depends on the soil's pH, or the amount of acidity or alkalinity. The soil pH scale ranges from 1 to 14 as follows:

Acid soil: 1 to 7
Neutral soil: 7
Alkaline soil: 7 to 14

The amount of calcium, an alkaline element, influences the pH of soils. In areas of heavy rainfall such as the Pacific Northwest and the Northeast, calcium usually leaches out of the soil, resulting in lower pH levels. Soils derived from calcium-rich limestone generally remain alkaline, while sandy soils tend to be more acid.

Although most ornamentals are tolerant of a wide pH range, most are happiest around 6.5. Some, however, do require a particular pH for healthy growth. These plants are good indicators of your soil's pH. If you find healthy *Tsuga* (hemlocks), *Rhododendron* spp. or blue hydrangea on your property, you have acid soils. Beech and ash trees are indicators of alkaline soils. If you plan to grow vegetables, you will maximize production with a neutral pH. For specific pH recommendations, see "Soil" in each chapter.

Testing pH

Determine the pH of your soil with an electronic pH meter or soil testing kit. Or send soil samples to your local Agricultural Extension Service. Be sure to take samples from several spots in the garden, as levels may vary. Remember to tailor your soil amendments to the plants in your garden.

> HINT: To avoid too much adjusting, select plants that are compatible with your soil type and pH.

Adjusting pH

Amend your soil after you have determined the pH needs of your plants. If your soil is too acid, add lime to neutralize the soil. Good sources of lime include: finely ground Dolomitic limestone, calcium carbonate and mushroom compost. The amount of lime you add depends on the texture of your soil. But do not add lime when adding manure, because the combination will produce ammonia, which could hurt your plants.

If your soil is too alkaline, add elemental sulfur, cottonseed meal or an acid mulch such as pine needles, sawdust or peat to neutralize the soil.

> HINT: Tap water varies greatly across the country and could affect some plants. Add vinegar to neutralize alkalinity.

SOIL FERTILITY

A soil rich in nutrients is like a refrigerator full of healthy food. Plants flourish when properly nourished. Fertility is measured by the levels of nitrogen (N), phosphorus (P) and potassium

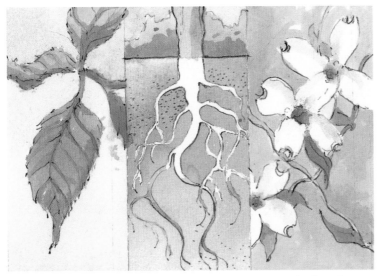

Soil Fertility: (Left to right) Nitrogen (N) encourages leaf and stem growth; phosphorus (P) stimulates root growth; potassium (K) benefits the plant's overall health.

(K) in a given soil sample. Nitrogen encourages leaf and stem growth; phosphorus, root growth, flowering and fruiting; potassium, overall health.

The secondary nutrients (calcium, magnesium and sulfur) and micronutrients (boron, chlorine, copper, iron, manganese, molybdenum and zinc) are also important for a plant's health. Commercial fertilizers will provide a great many of these nutrients; seaweed and compost supply them all. Refer to the Organic Amendments chart on p.181 for specific recommendations.

Soil inadequacies can cause leaf discoloration. A general yellowing indicates a lack of nitrogen. But if the veins remain green, the cause is chlorosis, an iron deficiency possibly brought about by poor drainage, improper pH, or overfertilization. Overfertilization can also weaken a plant.

Testing For Soil Fertility

This test can be done with a testing kit or by sending a sample of your soil to your local Agricultural Extension Service. The following table will help you read the results of your test:

	Fertility Levels		
	Low	Medium	High
N:	0 to 20	20 to 50	over 50
P:	0 to 12	12 to 25	over 25
K:	0 to 50	50 to 100	over 100

If your soil is in the mid range, you're doing everything just right. If levels are low, add nutrients at the recommended rate for your plants and soil. If levels are high, do not add more nutrients, but retest later in the season and adjust if necessary. Soil amendments do leach out of the soil and must be replenished.

SALINE SOIL

Salts normally percolate through the soil, moving away from the root zone, where they do the most damage. In dry climates, however, there may not be enough rainfall to leach the salts through the soil. In coastal regions, the culprit is salt spray.

Testing For Salts

Soil laboratories can also test your soil for salt content. This is done with an electrical conductivity test. If the results are:

0 to 2: Low salt; no damage to plants
2 to 4: Elevated salts; may affect sensitive plants
4 to 8: High salt; will kill most plants

If you have elevated levels of salt, select salt-tolerant plants. Correct soils with high salt levels before planting by applying gypsum or using furrow irrigation, which does not allow the salts to remain near plant root systems. Prevent raising salt levels in your garden by using non-saline de-icers when thawing icy roads, driveways and paths.

Eliot Wadsworth

II
YOUR
GARDEN

Peter C. Jones

II
YOUR GARDEN

Echinacea purpurea

Armed with information on your zone, microclimates, soil and water, you can have a beautiful garden with less effort than you think. Even a small amount of planning will help you move toward the garden of your dreams. First, take a good look at the big picture. How do you want to use your house and land? What kind of garden do you want? Perhaps an entrance garden to welcome your friends at the front door; a terrace surrounded by colorful flowers on which to entertain; a kitchen garden filled with vegetables and herbs; or even a hedge to hide a neighbor's unsightly addition.

Gardens nurture body and soul. Imagine surrounding yourself with rustling leaves and lovely fragrances. Imagine inviting birds and butterflies with a colorful, mixed perennial and shrub border. Imagine serving your friends vegetables from your own garden. Imagine a lush bed of roses that blooms all summer long. Now, make a wish list.

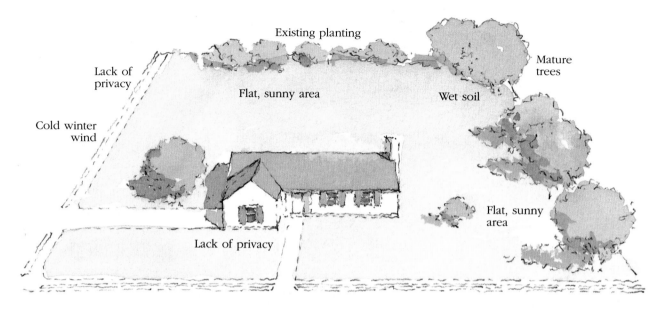

Before you begin, analyze your property for different climatic conditions as well as noise and good and bad views.

Labels on image:
Existing planting
Mature trees
Lack of privacy
Flat, sunny area
Wet soil
Cold winter wind
Flat, sunny area
Lack of privacy

KNOW YOUR PROPERTY

Before you make your garden dreams a reality, it's time to step back and assess your property. Each site is unique with its own personality, strengths and weaknesses. So before you begin, understand what you have to work with.

Make a sketch of your property noting the location of your house, property lines and existing conditions, including all micro-climate considerations (see Chapter 1). Add the street, driveway and paths up to and around your house, any terraces or decks, and locate all trees, shrubs, hedges and gardens on the plan.

Look out your windows and walk around your property marking your sketch with different colored arrows representing the views you want to emphasize or disguise. Look toward the neighboring houses and determine if you need more privacy.

Amend, add or delete items from your wish list according to what you discover from your plan and what you think you can realistically afford.

> *HINT: If you have a new home, you may want to wait and see what comes up in the yard throughout the course of a year.*

LANDSCAPE DESIGN IN A NUTSHELL

Good design is at the heart of every successful landscape. While planting a beautiful garden is a source of great pride, the design of your property is just as important. Consider the following concepts when working with your landscape:

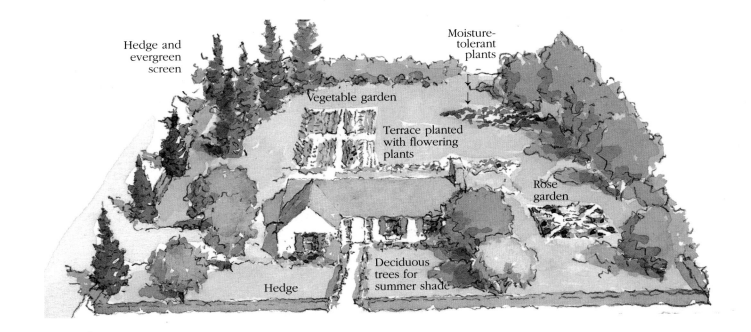

Hedge and evergreen screen

Moisture-tolerant plants

Vegetable garden

Terrace planted with flowering plants

Rose garden

Deciduous trees for summer shade

Hedge

UNITY   To create harmony, all elements of the landscape should feel part of a larger whole. The repetition of elements such as shrubs or trees or the enclosure of spaces with walls, hedges or fences can create a unified landscape.

SCALE   The comparative size of plants is integral to creating a pleasing sense of proportion. Plantings should be designed in scale with the overall landscape.

BALANCE   Like a seesaw, a balanced garden can be achieved in more than one way: the symmetry of a formal planting can come from the repetition of similar plants, while a large tree in an informal planting can be offset by a mass of shrubs.

MASS   Similar plants planted in large masses form a bold, uncluttered statement in the landscape.

HINT: In a small property it is best to use one planting style to create a unified garden.

CHOOSING A SITE
Examine your sketch and look for the best locations for each item on your list. You will find some instant answers. There might be only one flat, sunny area big enough for a vegetable garden and you may discover that the corner set aside for a shade garden receives hot, western afternoon sun. Remember, while it is essential to meet the climatic needs of the plants, the impact of the garden on your overall landscape is equally important.

Site Planning At A Glance

When choosing a site, there are many things to consider:
- Orientation (north, south, east and west)
- Location of property lines, utility lines, septic fields and water source
- Microclimate considerations:
  Sun/shade map of your site (See p.16.)
  Drainage problems and wet spots
  Frost pockets
  Windy spots
- Slope (both flat and steep areas)
- Circulation for people, pets and cars
- Views: both good and bad
- Need for sun/shade
- Need for buffers: for privacy, sound, wind, or dust
- Local building codes (if you plan on building structures)
- Energy and water conservation
- Fire hazards
- Impact on overall landscape

The resulting master plan will give you a garden agenda that you can implement and modify over time. Having a plan will prevent you from making frustrating mistakes like erecting a swing set in the perfect spot for a rose garden. If you have a difficult property or find yourself completely perplexed, you may wish to consider hiring a design professional.

HINT: Wind can shorten the growing season by cooling the air and soil. Lengthen your growing season by planting your garden in a warm, sunny spot, adding wind barriers where necessary.

START SMALL

With your master plan in hand, decide on a project. But start small! Once you figure out how much time and money your new garden requires, you can determine how much more you can handle. Don't be overly ambitious. Nothing is more frustrating than seeing a once carefully tended garden engulfed in weeds. Instead, work on your garden in stages, adding to it as you have the time.

HINT: A general rule of thumb for determining how large a garden you can handle is to decide what you want and cut it in half.

DESIGNING YOUR GARDEN

The best garden design complements the architecture, develops from an understanding of the natural character of the land, works with the climate and reflects you! The choice of garden styles is endless. A garden can be rustic or formal; modern or traditional. As Zones 3, 4 and 5 span the country, you might find gardens in rustic styles in Montana or Colorado, French or English gardens in Wisconsin, colonial gardens in New England. Look around your neighborhood; notice the plant selections and how they work with the different styles of architecture. What will look best with your home?

Think of your own garden as a garden room. The ceiling can be of tree branches, wood, or canvas; the floor of grass, groundcovers, decking, stone or brick. Form the enclosure with shrubs, trees, stone walls or fences. Decorate it with flowering plants. Furnish it, light it and control the sound in it just as you would your living room.

CHOOSING PLANTS

Slender and elegant, short or round, some raise their branches high, while others swoop down to touch the ground. Workhorses such as *Cornus alba* 'Siberica' (red-twig dogwood) look best when massed together; others are so beautiful they can stand alone. Plant color; size; need for sun, shade and water; time of bloom . . . so many things to consider, it really is the great challenge of gardening. But it is also the most fun. Don't feel you have to use every plant right from the start; half the fun is seeing how the garden grows and fine-tuning it from season to season. Remember, gardens don't happen overnight; they evolve.

Plant Design In A Nutshell

FORM The plant's mature shape. A tree may be vase-shaped or rounded, shrubs upright or spreading. A perennial may produce mounds of flowers or a glorious single, tall stem.

SIZE Plant, leaf and flower size are essential ingredients for scale and balance.

COLOR Leaf color as well as flower color are useful in altering space and mood. When selecting colors, think first of the purpose of the garden. Pick up the red from your front door or plant soft lavenders, pinks and whites in front of a weathered shingled house.

TEXTURE Leaf as well as flower texture creates the personality of the plant. Leaves can be rounded or sword-like, feathery, coarse or needle-like. Fine-textured plants soften hard surfaces; large-leafed plants add a bold accent.

Remember, leaves are just as important as flowers in planting design. For a lush look, include lots of greenery and vary the leaf textures for visual excitement. Emphasize a choice specimen by contrasting it with plants of a different color, texture or form. But, above all, when selecting plants, think climate, climate, climate!

Climate Considerations

Your garden will flourish with the least amount of effort if you match the plant's needs to your site and microclimate. So, gather information. Peruse catalogs for plants hardy to your zone. Try calling your local Agricultural Cooperative Extension Service and consider joining a horticultural society or garden club. Visit nurseries and nearby gardens. See what thrives and what struggles. Take advantage of your neighbors' successes, while avoiding their failures.

The weather in Zones 3, 4 and 5 is one of extremes. (See "Getting To Know Your Zone" on p.12.) Blistering heat, frigid winter temperatures, late and early frosts, damaging freeze-thaw cycles . . . buy only the plants that can tolerate these extremes unless you have discovered a protective microclimate to satisfy the plants' needs.

With a short growing season, growing a traditional flower border in Zones 3 and 4 can be a challenge. Some areas experience summers with too little heat for some plants to mature. Other perennials bloom later than normal and are out of sync with their normal companion plants. Gardeners new to cold-climate gardening need to shift gears and plan a mixed border of annuals, perennials, ornamental grasses and shrubs to provide a colorful, summer-long display. Use deciduous and evergreen shrubs such as *Viburnum* spp., *Picea glauca* 'Conica' (dwarf Alberta spruce), and *Juniperus* spp. to form the backbone of the garden and then fill in with annuals, perennials and grasses for seasonal color. But remember, when selecting any perennials for Zones 3, 4, and 5, think hardy!

Genus, Species, Varieties And Cultivars

Plants have two different types of names: a botanical name, which is in Latin and universally accepted, and a common name, which may differ from region to region. The Latin name consists of two words. The first is the genus; the second the species. As a species is a subdivision of the genus, you'll find that all plants of a certain genus share common characteristics but differ in at least one habit. For instance, *Lilium auratum* is a gold band lily and *Lilium candidum* is a Madonna lily. Calling black-eyed Susan *Rudbeckia* might take some getting used to, but it is more accurate and it will soon become second nature.

Today there are thousands of cultivars from which to choose. Although they retain most of the characteristics of the species, they may differ slightly in their drought or temperature tolerance, disease resistance, color or fruit size. Some are open pollinated and reproduce by means of the wind or animals (such as birds and bees); these are never exactly alike. Many heirloom plants are reproduced this way. Breeders simply select the best plants for next year's seed crop. Hybrids are man-made forms and have more consistent qualities. Have fun choosing your plants. Experiment! You're likely to find one that's just right for your climate.

Environmental Considerations

Planting design is more than just a pretty picture. It is a means with which to conserve our natural resources and, in especially dry climates, reduce fire hazard.

To lower energy consumption:

- Locate evergreen trees and hedges on the north side to block bitter winter winds.
- Position deciduous shade trees on the south side of the house to cool it and provide shelter from summer heat.

To reduce water evaporation and conserve water:

- Group plants of similar water needs together to prevent water waste.
- On windswept or hot, dry sites use native plants, which are better adapted to the existing conditions.
- Design garden enclosures to reduce evaporation due to wind.
- Select drought-tolerant plants.
- Use mulch.
- Contour the land to trap rainfall.

To reduce risk of fires:

- Plant buffers of low-growing, fire-retardant plants around the perimeter of your property.

Garden Design Checklist

Use the following checklist to plan a garden that's right for where you live:

- Style of your house
- Purpose, style, shape and size of the garden
- Microclimate
- Soil
- Water supply
- Local plant palette
- Mature plant size, color, texture and form
- Year-round interest
- Bloom sequence
- Energy and water conservation
- Fire safety in dry microclimates

ESSENTIAL TOOLS

Just as an artist prepares the canvas before applying the paint, you should carefully prepare your site before planting. If you don't have the basic tools, it's time to outfit yourself. Select the right basic tools and make sure you buy good ones! Using the right tool for the job will make difficult garden tasks easier and leave you with more time to smell the flowers.

To get your plants into the ground as soon as possible, be sure that you are fully equipped, and that the planting beds are dug, soil amended and mulch available, before bringing your plants home from the nursery.

Digging And Planting

SPADE for straight-sided holes, cuts easily through sod and is ideal for edging and transplanting.
ROUND-POINT SHOVEL for digging and mixing soil, compost and fertilizer.
TROWEL for hand digging; all gardeners need more than one trowel; be sure to vary the blade widths.

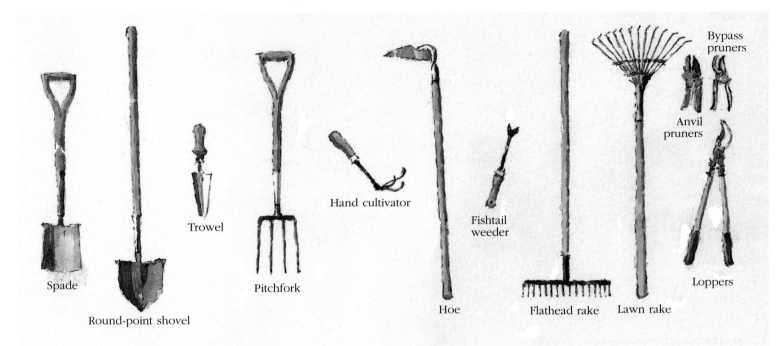

Spade
Round-point shovel
Trowel
Pitchfork
Hand cultivator
Fishtail weeder
Hoe
Flathead rake
Lawn rake
Bypass pruners
Anvil pruners
Loppers

Good tools make working in the garden a pleasure.

Cultivating And Lifting

PITCHFORK for working heavy soil, lifting root vegetables, dividing perennials and turning over the compost pile.
HAND FORK for loosening soil in tight spaces and lifting small plants.
HAND CULTIVATOR for loosening the soil and weeding. (Less precise, but faster than a dandelion weeder or trowel.)

HINT: If your back isn't what it used to be, buy tools with long handles to reduce bending.

Weeding

HOES for surface weeding, aerating and hilling up soil.
FISHTAIL WEEDER (also known as an asparagus fork or dandelion weeder) for deeply rooted weeds.

Raking

FLATHEAD RAKE for removing debris; breaking up and leveling soil and gravel. (Twelve teeth are standard; sixteen are good for vegetable gardens and gravel terraces.)
LAWN RAKE for gathering fallen leaves, twigs, grass clippings and debris.

Pruning

PRUNERS for cutting herbaceous stems, rose or berry canes, woody twigs and branches up to 1/2". (Bypass pruners have two sharp blades and a scissors-like action, which make a clean, precise cut; anvil pruners have a sharp upper blade that cuts against a flat, lower anvil.)

LONG-HANDLED LOPPERS for cutting thick or high branches.

PRUNING SAWS for cutting branches over 1" thick.

HEDGE SHEARS for shaping hedges or topiaries, and cutting back herbaceous plants.

GRASS SHEARS for trimming grass and plants with soft stems.

If you're left-handed, pruners made especially for you are now available through catalogs and garden centers. And if you have arthritis or would like to reduce hand stress, select hand pruners with rotating handles or ratchet pruners (with each squeeze of the handles, the ratchet moves up a notch, while maintaining pressure on the branch, until the blades cut cleanly through the wood).

HINT: Pruners with bright handles won't get lost in the foliage. Some gardeners prefer bright blue handles, as they stand out against colorful fall leaves.

Hauling

BARROW a basket on wheels for collecting weeds and carrying light loads.

WHEELBARROW a one-wheeled cart for hauling heavier loads; great to use along narrow paths.

TWO-WHEELED CART for hauling large or heavy loads. Easier to maneuver than a wheelbarrow.

HINT: Remember you can always rent rarely used equipment such as rototillers and shredders.

BUYING TOOLS

This is not the place to skimp, but don't worry, good tools are not always the most expensive. Tools are a personal decision, so test them all out before buying them. First grasp the handle. Does it feel comfortable in your hand? A good tool should feel solid and well balanced. Pruners must be sharp, well aligned and securely bolted; shafts on digging tools must be strong enough to defeat the inevitable rock.

High-end stainless steel tools, available through catalogs and garden centers, are strong, durable and rust-resistant and make digging easier because soil doesn't stick to the working surface. Carbon steel tools, usually found at the hardware store, are much less expensive, but are subject to rust and therefore require more care. Avoid stamped sheet metal tools, which can bend or break under pressure.

MAINTAINING TOOLS

Good tools that are well cared for can last a lifetime. So, whenever possible, clean tools after use. For carbon steel tools, use an oiled rag to prevent rusting. Experienced gardeners keep a bucket of sand saturated with a quart of motor oil in the garden shed to clean and oil tools simultaneously. Remember to lubricate all movable metal parts and sharpen blades regularly. Remove sap from pruners with steel wool and oil.

HINT: Keep anvil pruners sharp so they cut through the stems instead of crushing them.

GARDEN LAYOUT

Laying out the planting beds can be a very satisfying task. If you haven't determined the shape, decide what is appropriate for your garden: rectangular, circular or free-form. For geometric beds, you will need heavy string, stakes, a 50' to 100' long metal tape measure, and a hammer. Pound stakes into the corners of rectangular beds and stretch the string between them. For circles, drive a stake at the center, attach a string to the stake, and use it as a compass to mark the edge. The easiest way to lay out a free-form curve is with a garden hose. When you have finalized the shape of the bed, go around its edge nicking out a line of sod with a spade. This will set the guidelines for digging your new bed.

REMOVING SOD

If you are digging a new bed in a lawn area, it will be necessary to eradicate the grass roots completely, and this takes time. Grass, especially perennial quack grass, can be deep-rooted. Use an environmentally safe herbicide or strip the sod, then till the soil repeatedly at two- to three-week intervals until the soil is free of grass shoots. Prior to sowing seed or planting, level and rake the soil until it is finely pulverized. If you do opt to use an herbicide like Roundup, allow three weeks in your gardening schedule between the last application and planting or seeding. Take special care in selecting your herbicide; some will "sterilize" the soil for up to a year.

HINT: When digging out the planting beds, protect the lawn by placing the soil on a dropcloth.

PLANTING BEDS

Ideally, planting beds should be prepared the previous fall, which gives them time to settle over the winter and gives you a head start in the garden come spring. If this is not possible, prepare the beds in the spring, just prior to planting.

First, check the condition of your soil. If the soil is too wet, it will stick to your tools, making digging extra hard. You also risk compacting the soil with your footsteps, damaging the soil's texture. On the other hand, if it is too dry, it will be difficult to get a spade into the ground.

The preparation of planting beds varies depending on what is to be planted. Annuals are shallow-rooted and require less preparation than perennials. A shrub border requires more depth to accommodate the large root balls. Vegetable, herb and rose gardens require excellent drainage. For specific planting recommendations, see "Bed Preparation" in each chapter.

DIGGING THE BED

Time to dig the bed! There are three different types of digging, each requiring more work than the previous: simple, single and double digging. How you dig depends on how particular you are about the results. The better the beds are prepared, the better your plants will perform. But don't go in for overkill; there's no sense double digging an annual garden. For specific depth recommendations, see "Bed Preparation" in each chapter.

SIMPLE DIGGING Best for working in established or irregularly shaped beds. Lift each spadeful of soil and turn it over before returning it to the hole, bringing the bottom layer of soil to the top. Break up all lumps and remove all rocks, weeds or debris. Work in organic matter, soil amendments and fertilizers as required.

SINGLE DIGGING An efficient and effective method for most new beds. Mark your bed in 1' strips along its width. Dig a trench 1' wide, removing the soil and setting it aside. With a fork, loosen the soil at the bottom of the trench and add soil amendments. Remove the soil from the next strip and turn it into the first trench. Continue this process until you reach the end, then amend and fill the last trench with the soil previously set aside.

Double digging shifts the soil in a perennial bed, improving drainage and soil structure to get perennials off to the best start.

DOUBLE DIGGING Double digging is a lot of work but some gardeners believe the results make the extra effort well worth their while, especially for herbaceous and perennial borders. This method improves drainage, but is only possible in deep soils, as the trenches are dug two spade blades, or "spits," deep.

Divide your planting area into 1' strips along its width. In the first strip, make a trench by removing the soil from the upper and bottom spits and set it aside in separate identifiable piles. (If your topsoil is shallow, it is especially important to keep soil from the upper and lower spits separate.) Then remove the soil from the top of the second strip and set it aside. Transfer the soil from the bottom spit of the second trench into

the bottom of the first and cover it with the top spit from the third trench. Continue this process until the end, using the soil from the first spit to fill in the last two.

TILLING

Tilling, or working the soil, provides aeration, improves soil structure and drainage and is critical to a successful garden. For large areas, it is often necessary to use a rototiller, but in small areas you can work to a greater depth by tilling by hand. Spades and forks are the best tools for tilling the soil. To dig efficiently, push the spade or fork into the ground for the entire length of the blade, maintaining a 90° angle, and then lift and turn the blade over. Thoroughly till annual beds and vegetable gardens in the fall or before planting.

RAISED BEDS

Raised beds are your best bet in cool climates and areas with inadequate drainage or poor or shallow soils. Raised beds heat up faster in the spring and hold heat to help plants continue to grow on cool or cloudy days. In addition, by raising the soil level above the existing grade with amended soil, you will improve the texture and fertility of the soil while also increasing its depth and drainage. But raised beds are not for every garden. In hot, dry climates they dry out more quickly, requiring additional water. In cold weather, raised beds freeze earlier and deeper than the surrounding ground, so they aren't the best choice for more cold-sensitive crops such as strawberries.

PLANTING TIMES

When it comes to gardening, timing is everything. In cold climates most trees, perennials, roses, and deciduous and evergreen shrubs are planted while they are dormant in the early spring. This gives them a chance to set new roots before the heat of summer and the freezing temperatures of winter.

However, if you move into a new house in the fall and are eager to get started, planting of all easily grown shrubs, excepting broadleaf evergreens, can be successful if completed by mid-October. Fall-flowering bulbs are planted in the early fall; spring-flowering bulbs are planted in the fall. Plant summer-blooming annuals as soon as the ground is warm and the nights are frost free.

PLANTING
For specific recommendations, see "Planting" in each chapter.

MAINTENANCE
A well-maintained garden allows plants to flourish. When you plan your garden, consider how much time you can spend each week tending it. Weeding, fertilizing and watering continue throughout the gardening year. Deadheading, pruning and mulching are seasonal. If you have a flower or vegetable garden, picking is not only time-consuming but essential for a healthy garden.

TIME AND ENERGY SAVERS
1. Select the right plants for your microclimate.
2. Select disease-resistant plants.
3. Avoid high-maintenance plants.
4. Use groundcovers, not grass, in shade, on slopes or in other difficult spots.
5. Use edging to keep grass and groundcovers in place.
6. Use high-quality tools.
7. To avoid too much watering, select plants compatible with your rainfall.
8. Use good irrigation equipment, especially drip irrigation.
9. Mulch to reduce weeding and watering.
10. Mow more frequently so you don't have to pick up the clippings.
11. Keep an eye out for insects and diseases. The faster they're controlled, the less work fighting them.

WATERING
Water the garden when it is dry! With your short growing season, you want to make sure your plants don't slow down for a lack of water, especially during the long growing days of June and July. If your mulch is concealing the soil, look at your plants. They will tell you when they're thirsty.

WILTING The most obvious sign. But be sure to check the soil, as wilting can also be a symptom of too much water or a response to root damage. Dig down into the soil around the root area. If it is dry, water! If it is wet, wait and let it dry out before watering again.

FOLDING OR CUPPING Plants like *Impatiens wallerana* will fold their leaves when they're dry for self-preservation. Less exposed leaf surface means less evaporation.

COLOR CHANGES When plants are dry, leaves lose their rich color and turn dull.

There are several things to keep in mind when you water your garden:

Watering in the morning is preferable. It provides plants with a good reserve to make it through hot summer days and allows excess water to evaporate before nightfall. Evening watering allows water to sit on the leaves, encouraging mildew on flowers and disease on lawns. But, if your plants are desperate, water them *immediately* no matter what time of day. In a dry spell, it may be necessary to water twice a day.

Water deeply to encourage deep root growth. Soak the soil thoroughly, then allow it to dry moderately before watering again. In this way you will encourage your plants' roots to grow downward toward the moist soil. The deeper the roots, the less susceptible they are to drought.

Water the soil, not the foliage or blossoms. Use a watering wand on the end of your hose to get in under the foliage. Use drip irrigation or soaker hoses for flower beds to prevent damage to the blossoms from overhead sprinklers.

Conserving Water
Water conservation is critical in dry climates and a good practice for all gardeners. To conserve water in the garden:
- Use irrigation appropriate for each kind of plant: trees, shrubs, flowers, vegetables.
- Use drip irrigation whenever possible. Remember, sprinklers lose water to evaporation; drip irrigation is more efficient.
- Use mulches to prevent the soil from drying out.

HINT: Wind is just as drying as sun. If your garden is on an exposed site, you may have to water more often.

WEEDING
A weed is any plant that is not meant to be in the planting bed. A maple seedling may be welcome in the woods, but is an eyesore in your perennial border or rose garden. Weeds always seem out of place, diluting the desired impact of the design. In dry climates it's especially important to remove these interlopers, as they compete intensely with garden plants for water and nutrients.

I like to weed by hand first thing in the morning, while the sun is still cool and the soil is slightly moist. When the soil is very wet it sticks to the roots, making extra work. If the soil is so dry it has become hard, you risk breaking the stems off the weeds, leaving the roots behind. Cultivate large areas with a hoe when the soil is dry but loose.

You can pull many weeds by hand, but never break off the weed in the process! Like pinched seedlings, weeds will bound back stronger and bushier than ever. A fishtail fork is a real help for stubborn, deep-rooted weeds like dandelions or weeds in tight spaces. Position the fork right next to the weed, push it straight into the soil, then push the fork handle away from the weed to lever it out of the ground. Be sure to go as deep as you can so as to remove as much root as possible, but stay well clear of the roots of your garden plants. Water your garden when you finish; weeding can loosen the soil and a good watering will help settle it.

Weed the beds at least once a week. Annual weeds are easily removed when they are seedlings, and you certainly don't want them to go to seed! There's a lot of truth in the old farmer's adage: "One year's seeding makes seven years' weeding."

HINT: If you are removing nettles, be sure to wear gloves. The sting can last for hours.

MULCH
Mulch is the soil's protective blanket and invaluable to a successful garden, particularly in the cold zones. Mulches can be organic (composted leaf mold, bark, sawdust, woodchips, composted grass clippings, buckwheat or cocoa hulls, composted salt marsh hay, straw, corn cobs, evergreen boughs, pine needles or cones) or inorganic (gravel, washed stones, oyster shells or black plastic). Mulches vary in texture and color. Carefully match the mulch to the garden setting.

Apply a light mulch 2" deep during the summer months and augment as necessary. On windy sites, use bigger mulch chips; they won't blow away as easily.

For extra winter protection, layer your mulch beginning with two inches of compost, then add a few inches of a bulkier mulch such as salt marsh hay or straw. In very cold areas you may consider topping the mulch off with evergreen boughs, but don't put them down too early. Small critters won't be able to resist building their nests in your garden. In the spring the heavier mulches should be removed, while the compost should remain to enrich the soil.

HINT: If you want to use maple leaves as a mulch, be sure to shred them first. Shredded maple leaves decompose quickly; whole maple leaves tend to pack down, allowing little water to penetrate.

Use mulch to:
- Protect plants from temperature fluctuations.
- Protect plants from extreme cold or heat.
- Winterize your plants.
- Reduce weeds.
- Conserve soil moisture.
- Reduce soil erosion and runoff on slopes due to wind and rain.
- Reduce soil compaction from intense rains.
- Improve soil structure and fertility.
- Prevent seed from washing away during heavy spring rains.
- Prevent seed such as grass or wildflowers from blowing away (light mulches only).
- Create garden paths.
- Prevent fungi from splashing up on plant leaves.

Never mulch when:
- Your soil is waterlogged.
- Young seedlings are smaller than the mulch is thick.

Black Plastic Mulch

Black plastic can be an effective mulch in out-of-the-way places such as vegetable gardens. It should be overlapped 4" to 6" to prevent weeds from sneaking up through the seams.

Use black plastic mulch:
- Away from the entertaining areas in your garden where it is not an eyesore.
- Only in areas with good drainage, since it inhibits evaporation.
- In vegetable gardens to lengthen the season by warming the soil in spring and fall.

HINT: In the summer, the black plastic can become too hot. Cover it with straw or another light-colored mulch to reflect the radiant energy.

LEAF REMOVAL

Most fallen leaves make excellent mulch, especially in shrub beds, but in humid and very dry areas leaves should be removed. In humid climates fallen leaves can promote disease. Leaves should be removed from the beds and added to the compost pile. Diseased leaves, however, should be discarded altogether.

In dry climates the accumulation of fallen leaves can present a fire hazard in late summer and early fall. If you live in a fire hazard zone, the clearing of potential fire fuels such as brush and dry fallen leaves should be part of your annual maintenance program.

COLD WEATHER IN THE GARDEN
The Short Season

Cool-climate gardeners need all the help they can to extend their short growing season.

To lengthen the growing season:
- Start seeds early indoors.
- Only sow outdoors fast-growers suited to your climate.
- Whenever possible, buy larger plants.
- Prepare your beds in the fall.

- Plant your garden in a heat trap facing south, protected from cooling winds.
- Use raised beds.
- Warm the soil in your vegetable garden in early spring by covering it with black plastic.
- Warm the soil in flower gardens with more attractive mulch.
- Cover new transplants with hot caps made of old plastic jugs, fiberglass cones or translucent plastic.
- Surround your plants with "Walls-O-Water," commercially available polyethylene tepees containing water, which moderate the temperature within their enclosure.
- Water regularly.
- Protect your plants from frost.

Preparing For Winter Temperatures

One never knows what to expect come winter: record warm temperatures; brutal, deep freezes; lots of snow or none at all. Many plants in Zones 3, 4, and 5 need protection from the cold and fluctuating temperatures. See "Winterizing" in each chapter for appropriate winterizing techniques.

Surprise Frosts

For cold-climate gardeners, late-spring and early-fall frosts can further shorten an already challenging, short growing season. A gentle sprinkling of water in the early morning to wash the frost off the leaves can help prevent damage caused by the rapid drying and burning of leaves when morning sun hits full force.

Keep an old sheet or a roll of plastic handy to protect favorite tender plants from unusually cold winter nights. But don't forget to remove the plastic when the day warms up. Unlike burlap or sheets, it will magnify the heat and burn the leaves.

Assessing Damage From A Late Frost

An unexpected deep freeze in late spring after plants have begun to grow can wreak havoc on a cold-climate garden. But never prune or discard any plant until it has had a chance to make a comeback. The following guidelines will help you assess the damage:

ASSESSING FOLIAGE DAMAGE

Slimy brown foliage: Remove and discard foliage.

Bronzed or brown-edged: Allow to drop off naturally; they'll be replaced in the spring.

Crispy, brown leaves: Very little hope for recovery.

ASSESSING WOOD DAMAGE

Do a scrape test: If the scraping reveals green tissue beneath, you have reason to be optimistic.

Split bark: Prune the limb back in late February to an inch below the split.

Pests And Intruders

Your garden is a prime target for inconsiderate, hungry pests who dig, munch and crunch with abandon. They come from all angles: chipmunks and voles come from below; squirrels dig down from above; rabbits and deer waltz right in on ground level while birds zoom in from the sky. It's easy to feel defenseless, but there are ways to protect your garden.

Deer

In many areas in Zones 3, 4, and 5 deer have gone from being a beloved wild animal to a gardener's greatest enemy. Where gardeners once erected deer statues in the garden, they now install deer fencing! Deer populations have outgrown their bounds, and they have begun looking to greener gardens for their dinners. Deer generally prefer a bland diet, staying away from the stronger, more pungent plants with lemon, mint or sage-like aromas (see "The Deer-resistant Garden," p.213). But remember, if deer are starving they will nibble on almost anything! The best defense is often an electric fence.

Electric fencing can now be done with electric tape. Three strips attached to 9' posts will do the job. Paint the strips black to make them blend into the setting. Police the fence for several weeks looking for breakage; deer will soon become familiar with the barrier and stay away.

Chewing Pests

Caterpillars and cutworms munch on leaves during the day while slugs and snails are more discreet; they do their damage in the dark of night. Nematodes, small eel-like worms, work underground on the root systems of plants. To prevent damage, rotate vegetables with nonsusceptible plants or control them with plants such as *Tagetes* (marigold), which have roots that entrap nematodes. Always destroy infected plants.

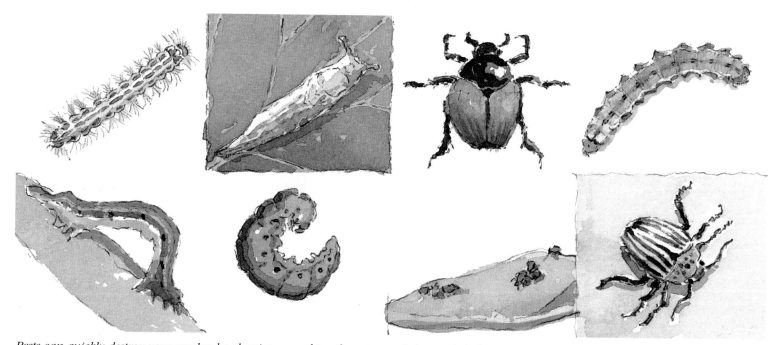

Pests can quickly destroy your garden by chewing or sucking the sap out of plants. (Clockwise from top left) Tent caterpillar, slug, Japanese beetle, corn earworm, Colorado potato beetle, aphid, cutworm and cabbage looper.

Sucking Pests

Sucking pests include aphids, leaf miners, mealy bugs, spider mites, whiteflies, thrips and scale. As voracious as chewing pests, they suck the sap and cell contents from plants, leaving behind a trail of yellow leaves or deformed foliage, buds, flowers and fruit. To reduce damage, sucking pests such as spider mites can be removed by spraying the undersides of leaves with cold water. Mealy bugs can be removed with alcohol. Whiteflies and aphids are attracted to and trapped by oil applied to painted yellow boards laid in the garden.

Disease

There are three causes of plant disease: fungi, bacteria and viruses. Your best bet in preventing the occurrence of bacteria and viruses is the use of resistant plants. Some of the most common and easiest to control fungal diseases include:

BLACKSPOT Black spots appear on plant leaves, gradually growing together, killing the leaf and defoliating the plant. The best prevention is good air circulation. Keep the interiors of plants thinned out and do not crowd plants. Discard or burn all infected leaves to control its spread.

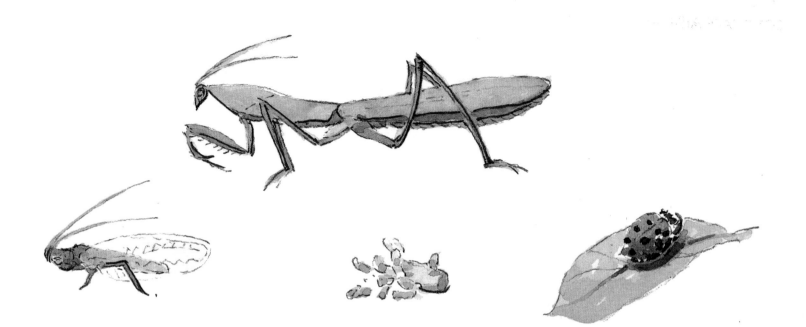

Safe pest control includes introducing natural predators into the garden. (Clockwise from top): Praying mantid, ladybug, trichogramma wasp and green lacewing.

DOWNY MILDEW The development of powdery, white, mold-like fungus on leaves, buds and stems. To prevent, buy mildew-resistant cultivars, do not overcrowd plants, avoid overhead irrigation and provide good air circulation and drainage.

DAMPING OFF The rotting at soil level of young seedlings and cuttings. Prevention is the best control. When propagating new plants, use sterilized soil, treat seeds with a fungicide, provide good air circulation and avoid overwatering.

What Is Integrated Pest Management?

Integrated Pest Management (IPM), although it may include selective use of toxic sprays, advocates the following methods of safe pest control: natural predators, hand-picking insects, crop rotation, using insect diseases and traps, and the release of sterile male insects to mate but not reproduce.

> *HINT: If your neighbor uses toxic sprays, suggest safe alternatives and that they spray on windless days.*

SOME SAFE ALTERNATIVES AND PRECAUTIONS

When Planning Your Garden
- Avoid plants most attractive to pests.
- Select disease-resistant plants.
- Interplanting or companion planting: The planting of plants that repel insects among the plants the insects find most attractive. Especially effective in vegetable gardens.
- Rotate your crops.
- Be sure your garden has good air circulation.
- If moles or gophers are a problem, use raised beds and line the beds with 1/2" wire before filling them with topsoil. For shrubs, line the planting hole.

Keep A Clean Garden
- Keep weeds under control.
- Remove diseased leaves after they've fallen to prevent spread.
- Keep your garden tools clean.
- Wipe your pruners with alcohol when moving to a new species to avoid the spread of disease.

Invite Good Predators
- Invite beneficial predators, such as birds and bats, into your garden for twenty-four-hour insect patrol.
- Place martin houses in sunny, open areas in late March prior to arrival of the scout birds who fly ahead of the migrating colonies.
- Place bat houses that can accommodate twenty to fifty bats near the garden. Although you may think bats are scary, remember a single bat can eat up to five hundred mosquitoes an hour.

HINT: If you invite birds into your garden, be sure to protect your ripening berries with netting, mylar streamers or other deterrents.

Create Barriers
- Use barriers such as paper cups set into the soil to protect seedlings from cutworms.
- Wrap aluminum foil around the base of your plants to deter spider mites, Mexican bean beetles, striped cucumber beetles, leafhoppers and squash bugs.
- Protect the bases of tree trunks from rabbits and mice with plastic shields or hardware cloth.
- Cover the soil's surface with sharp-edged diatomaceous earth to deter soft-bodied slugs and cabbage worms.
- Enclose your garden with chicken wire that extends 12" below grade to frustrate rabbits, woodchucks and other small critters.
- Install an electric fence or electric tape at raccoon height — 18" high — around your vegetable garden; at 9' high or more around your yard to deter deer.

If You Find Pests
- Place low containers of beer set into the soil to lure slugs to their death.
- Pick off bugs such as Japanese beetles and drop them in a jar of kerosene or soapy water.
- Destroy the nests of insects such as tent caterpillars.
- Pour a kettle full of hot water down ant hills to rid your garden of ants.
- Some gardeners use traps containing pheromones (sex attractants) to lure insects to their death. These do attract insects and should be placed away from the garden.

- Use a garden hose, adjusted to have enough force to knock insects off plants without damaging the leaf structure, to control aphids and spider mites. Don't forget to spray the undersides of the leaves, too!
- Use homemade sprays made of water and garlic or hot pepper puree to deter pests.
- Sprinkle garlic powder around your plants — said to deter deer from roses.
- Place mothballs around but not touching your plants to discourage chipmunks. Replace as they lose their smell.
- Tuck clumps of dog fur out of sight under leaves to deter rabbits.
- Spray a solution of one tablespoon of baking soda with a few drops of horticultural oil in one gallon of water to control mildew.
- Control the reproduction of apple maggots by hanging a sticky red, apple-like ball in your apple trees. The maggot eggs laid on it won't hatch.

In An Emergency
- Use horticultural oils, which smother rather than poison insects such as aphids, scale, spider mites, and whiteflies.
- Use commercially available insecticidal soaps to control aphids, earwigs, leaf miners and leaf rollers.
- Apply natural, organic poisons such as Neem, Pyrethrum and Rotenone. While they are not toxic to humans, some organic poisons can be harmful to beneficial insects and fish. Always apply with great care.
- Homemade "bug spray" is unappetizing to make but quite successful. To make it, pick abnormal and normal caterpillars off your plants, pulverize them in a blender with a cup of nonchlorinated tepid water, add more water, let sit several days and then dilute again and spray on plants. You will have spread the infection carried by the abnormal caterpillars and curtailed their munching.
- Use biological pesticides to control bagworms, cabbage worms, gypsy moths and tent caterpillars, among others. BT (*Bacillus thuringiensis*), commercially available as Dipel and Thuricide, is a naturally occurring bacterium. Read instructions carefully and apply it at the right time for maximum effect.

And don't forget, not all insects are detrimental to the garden. Some insects actually eat the bad guys, but insecticides don't discriminate. Try to steer clear of toxic sprays and dusts, choosing Integrated Pest Management, a safer means of pest control. Yes, a flower or head of lettuce is more attractive without little holes nibbled out of it, but the long-term damage done by pesticides can be far-reaching. In the end, the decision to use pesticides is yours, but first identify the pest, then seek the advice of your nurseryman or local Agricultural Cooperative Extension Service and use toxins with the greatest of care.

Michael H. Dodge

III
THE
FLOWERS

Annuals
Perennials
Roses
Bulbs, Etc.

ANNUALS

Temperature
Sun/Shade
Soil
Water
Bed Preparation
Seeds Or Plants?
Seeds
Plants
Cultivating

Fertilizing
Mulch
Thinning
Pinching
Deadheading
Cut Flowers
Fall Cleanup
Best Bets For Your Garden

Zinnia elegans

Annuals are plants that complete their life cycle in one season. With little care, many grow quickly from seed sown in the late spring, producing a profusion of flowers from midsummer until frost. Available in a wide variety of colors, shapes and sizes, annuals are wonderfully diverse flowers. Some grow tall, while others climb and trail. Some thrive in hot, dry sunny areas, while others are at home in the cool shade. But, to me, the greatest advantage of annuals is their impermanence. You can change your color schemes from year to year, and even season to season. A handful of annual seed packets is like having a box of Crayolas to color your garden. And, unlike perennials, the more you pick or pinch them, the more flowers they produce.

Both beautiful and practical, annuals are the perfect flowers with which to decorate house and garden. In the garden large masses of annuals can be focal points, or fillers in borders after the perennials have passed. As cut flowers, they are cheerful, plentiful and often fragrant. Annuals can come to your rescue when you have new plantings and need to cover the soil between plants. A container of colorful annuals will brighten your terrace or deck; low annuals will beautifully edge a path. For every spot in the garden or home, there's an annual to suit your needs.

Grow Annuals:
- As fillers in mixed borders
- To edge a path
- To hide yellowing bulb foliage
- To fill in bare spots
- For temporary splashes of color
- To brighten dark corners
- To add color to shrub borders
- To fill in around young shrubs, tying the mass together
- In your cutting garden
- In pots and planters
- In beds for quick, long-lasting color
- As accents in borders against a fence, wall or hedge

TEMPERATURE

Cold weather usually signals the end of an annual's life cycle. Annuals are extremely sensitive to climatic conditions and are categorized by their cold and heat tolerance, so be sure to keep both in mind when making your selections. The different types of annuals are:

HARDY ANNUALS Can survive some frost. Are successful when sown directly outdoors, even while cool temperatures prevail. Includes *Lathyrus odoratus* (sweet pea), *Consolida ambigua* (annual larkspur), *Lobularia maritima* (sweet alyssum).

HALF-HARDY ANNUALS Will take some frost, but not as much as hardy annuals. Includes *Cleome hasslerana* (spiderflower) and *Petunia* x *hybrida*.

TENDER ANNUALS Cannot tolerate frost. Many tender annuals need several weeks in order to reach flowering size, and thus should be sown early indoors, in cold frames, or outdoors as soon as the danger of frost has past. They can also be purchased as greenhouse-grown seedlings or rooted cuttings. Includes *Ageratum houstonianum*, *Salvia* and *Zinnia*.

WARM-SEASON ANNUALS Half-hardy or tender annuals that prefer warm temperatures and warm soil. They may show no growth until the soil warms sufficiently. Includes *Verbena* x *hybrida* and *Helianthus* (sunflower).

COOL-SEASON ANNUALS Hardy annuals and some half-hardy annuals that can tolerate cool weather. Includes *Viola* x *wittrockiana* (pansy), *Brassica oleracea* (ornamental cabbage and kale), *Antirrhinum majus* (snapdragon) and *Matthiola incana* (stock).

Consider the following when choosing annuals:
- The last date of frost in the spring
- The first date of frost in the fall
- The highest expected temperatures in the summer

In your cold climate, include annuals that are hardy or half-hardy to lengthen the time of bloom. If you live in an area with extended hot spells, look for warm-season annuals.

SUN/SHADE

Most annuals thrive in full sun. Thankfully, there are a number of lovely annuals that prefer shade, including *Impatiens*, *Begonia* and *Coleus*.

SOIL

A good garden loam with a pH ranging from 5.5 to 7.0 is excellent for most annuals. However, some native annuals, such as *Coreopsis tinctoria,* are tolerant of varying soil conditions.

WATER

If your garden is on a windswept site or in an area prone to seasonal droughts, your annuals will be fuller and more floriferous with additional water. And remember, freshly sown seed and seedlings should be kept moist until they are established.

BED PREPARATION

Good bed preparation always pays off with an abundance of flowers. As annuals have shallow roots, the beds need only be prepared to a depth of 8"-12". Enrich the soil with compost or well-rotted manure in the fall or early spring to promote the early growth of healthy plants. Annual blooms are so prolific they require a healthy plant system to nourish them.

SEEDS OR PLANTS?

Carefully consider the growth rate of the annuals you've selected. With your short growing season, the best annuals for your climate grow quickly from seed to full bloom. And remember, if you opt for a bed of just annual seeds, the gardening season will be well under way before the annuals begin to bloom. To enjoy an extended season of bloom, start annual seeds indoors several weeks before your last frost date, or buy plants. Fast growers, like *Tropaeolum majus* (nasturtium), *Ipomea purpurea* (morning glory) and *Lathyrus odoratus* (sweet pea), can be sown directly in the garden.

> *HINT: If you have clay soil, which is slow to warm up in the spring, use seedlings instead of seed whenever possible for earlier bloom.*

SEEDS
Buying Seeds

Annual seeds can be purchased from your local garden center or from a variety of mail-order sources (see "Sources"). They are available as loose seeds in seed packets or in a more limited selection, as seed tapes. Seed tapes are actually soluble tapes with seed imbedded in them for perfect planting in rows!

Growing from seed is more work, but there are advantages. There is an enormous selection of annuals, including many improved and old-fashioned varieties, available through mail-order catalogs. Look for All-American selections that will work well within your growing season. When buying seedlings you often have to buy mixed colors; with seeds, you can grow a particular color. But perhaps the greatest advantage of all is price! Seeds are the best bargain in the garden.

Time To Sow

Get the best results possible by planting annual seeds at the right time and right temperature:

HARDY ANNUALS Sow outside from mid- to late spring when the soil temperature has risen to 45° Fahrenheit. Some seeds like *Papaver* (poppy) and wildflowers can be sown in the fall.

HALF-HARDY ANNUALS Sow indoors in containers in the spring, maintaining a temperature range of 55° to 70° Fahrenheit or sow outdoors from late spring to midsummer.

TENDER ANNUALS Sow indoors in containers in spring, maintaining a temperature of 55° to 70° Fahrenheit, or sow outdoors after all threat of frost.

Germination

Seeds need warmth, water, oxygen and light to germinate. Sow seeds indoors in flats or plastic trays filled with a sterile, lightweight soil mix. Soilless mixes containing vermiculite and peat moss also provide excellent results. Place them in a warm sunny location or under fluorescent lights. Most seeds will respond within a few days. To speed up seeds with hard shells, such as *Lathyrus odoratus* (sweet pea) and *Ipomea purpurea* (morning glory), chip or soak them before sowing. This allows moisture to penetrate the surface, stimulating growth. When the seedlings have developed two sets of leaves, carefully "prick out," or transplant to larger containers.

Damping Off

During germination, seedlings are susceptible to "damping off," a soil-borne disease that causes them to wilt. It spreads most easily in warm, moist conditions with poor air circulation.

To avoid damping off:
- Use clean pots or trays.
- Use sterilized potting soil.
- Keep seeds moist, but do not overwater.
- Do not crowd seeds; thin them out as necessary.

Hardening Off Seedlings

Before transplanting seedlings into the garden, they must be gradually acclimated or "hardened off." Harden off seedlings by first moving them to a cold frame (a box with a light permeable cover that can be opened and closed depending on the temperature) or a shady, protected spot outdoors for a few hours. Gradually increase the time outdoors to build up their tolerance. When the temperature is right, transplant them into the garden.

Sowing Outdoors

To plant in rows, first stretch a string between two stakes marking the center of the row. Use the corner of a hoe to form deep furrows directly beneath the string. For shallow furrows use the tip of a trowel. Distribute the seeds evenly, then firm the soil over the furrow using the flat side of a rake. Gently sprinkle the beds, taking care not to wash the seeds away. Keep the soil moist but not waterlogged until the seeds sprout.

When seeding a large area, broadcasting is your best bet. Broadcast the seeds, using a drop or rotary spreader, first in one direction across the entire area, then repeat it, walking in a direction perpendicular to the first. This will give you the most even results.

Seedling Packs (clockwise from top left): Seedlings are available in flats, individual pots and cell-packs.

PLANTS
Buying Plants

Buying annual plants is an easy way to have instant color in the garden and extend your short season. Plants are usually available in flats, cell-packs and individual pots.

SEEDLING FLATS Seedlings sold in a large box or flat. Roots tend to be intertangled, so not the best choice.

CELL-PACKS Four to twelve seedlings in individually molded plastic container. Minimal transplant shock since plants are grown individually.

INDIVIDUALLY POTTED Transplants sold in 2" to 6" pots. Plants retain all roots so are easily re-established in your garden. Larger plants give you a head start on the growing season, provide a big splash fast and require less pampering.

When buying seedlings or larger plants, look for:
- Plants that are pest-free.
- Plants that have a good shape with healthy leaves.

and avoid:
- Plants that are leggy or have yellow leaves.
- Plants that are potbound. (Check to see if roots are growing out of the bottom of the pot.)

Planting Time

Many annuals are killed by frost, so no matter how eager you are to get the plants in the ground, be cautious. Some guidelines:

HARDY ANNUALS Plant from early spring through midsummer.

HALF-HARDY ANNUALS Plant from midspring through midsummer.

TENDER ANNUALS Plant in late spring, when temperatures are reliably warm and all threat of frost has passed, through midsummer.

HINT: The general planting time for annuals in Zone 4 is just after Memorial Day. But do keep coverings available to protect them from late frosts.

Planting

Dig a hole slightly bigger than the root ball, and set the plant in the hole at the same level as it was growing in the container. Gently replace the soil around the roots, and tamp down carefully to remove all air pockets and allow the roots to make good contact with the soil.

When you remove a plant from a container, you inevitably injure a few roots, which may cause a slight setback in plant growth. Your goal when planting is to reduce stress. Here are some suggestions:
- Transplant on a cloudy day or in the early morning before the heat of the day.

- Water the seedlings before transplanting, gently spraying the leaves to reduce wilting.
- Water transplants thoroughly after planting.
- Shade plants if necessary.
- Pinch back to reduce surface area of leaves and to promote branching.

Be ready to plant when you bring your annuals home from the nursery. If you can't plant right away, put your plants in a shady spot and give them lots of water.

CULTIVATING

Breaking up the soil to encourage air and moisture penetration is called cultivation. Soil should never be allowed to form a hard crust! If your annuals are planted in rows, cultivate them using a hoe to loosen the soil around the base of the plants, being careful not to break the stems or injure the roots. A three-pronged fork is excellent for hand-cultivating small areas. Begin prior to mulching, once the seedlings are a few inches high. Cultivate weekly, if you do not mulch.

FERTILIZING

Most sun-loving annuals benefit from an application of liquid fertilizer two weeks after seed germination and monthly thereafter. Fertilize shade annuals, such as *Impatiens*, less frequently. To encourage flowering, use a complete fertilizer with a high middle number, representing phosphorus, such as 5-10-10. Avoid high-nitrogen fertilizers for annuals such as *Tagetes* (marigold) and *Ipomea purpurea* (morning glory); high nitrogen would produce an abundance of leaves and no flowers. But if you are growing annuals such as *Coleus* for their foliage, you'll get good results using an equally balanced fertilizer, such as 8-8-8. In areas with high rainfall and sandy soils, try controlled-release fertilizers, which don't leach through the soil as quickly.

MULCH

Mulch annual beds when the seedlings are several inches high. Spread a 2"-3" layer of a light mulch, such as shredded leaves, spent hops, buckwheat or cocoa hulls.

To avoid damaging your more fragile plants, first spread the mulch, then insert the small plants in it. If you are mulching just one or two tender transplants, cover them with an upturned pot and spread the mulch. When the pot is removed, the mulch will gently fall into place around, but not on, the small plants.

THINNING

When sowing, seeds are often so small it's difficult to space them just right. Several seeds may begin to develop right next to each other. To develop into a full, healthy plant, a seedling needs enough space in which to grow. Look over your seedlings. Decide which look the most vigorous, then make room for them by thinning out, or pulling out, the less vigorous plants. To prevent disturbance to the remaining seedling, press down on the soil around it with your fingers, while simultaneously pulling out the other. The general rule of thumb for spacing annuals is to allow one-half their mature height between plants. Look at the seed packets for more specific directions.

Pinching, the removal of the growing tip (left), encourages bushy, new growth (right).

PINCHING

Most annuals grow naturally into a full, bushy plant or tall spire. Other annuals, such as *Viola* spp. (pansy), *Petunia* x *hybrida* and *Antirrhinum majus* (snapdragon), need a little help developing into pleasing and productive shapes. "Pinching back" prevents the plants from becoming leggy and encourages them to fill out. To pinch back a plant, remove the terminal bud or tip of the plant after several sets of leaves have developed along the main stem. It is sometimes necessary to pinch back the side shoots as well. Two or more branches will grow from each pinched stem.

DEADHEADING

Deadheading is the wonderfully descriptive term for the removal of faded flowers. Use pruning clippers or your fingers to deadhead. Use shears to deadhead large masses of flowers with upward-growing blossoms like *Tagetes* (marigold) or *Iberis (*candytuft). Be sure to make a clean cut and don't tear the stem.

Deadhead after flowering to:
- Maintain the appearance of the flower bed.
- Discourage disease.
- Prolong flower production by preventing annuals from going to seed.

To save time in the garden, plant flowers that naturally drop their petals, such as: *Begonia, Impatiens, Lobularia* (sweet alyssum), *Ageratum, Lobelia, Salvia,* and *Catharanthus* (annual vinca).

CUT FLOWERS

There are few things more satisfying than walking out to the garden early in the morning to pick flowers for your home or friends. But annuals come on later in the spring and die back early in the fall, so to extend your cutting garden, do consider including perennials. See "The Cutting Garden," p.211.

> HINT: *Growing your own flowers from seed gives you control over the selection.*

Picking Annuals

1. Cut flowers early in the morning when they are most turgid.
2. Cut stems at an angle using a sharp knife or oriental shears.
3. Take as long a stem as possible without removing future flower buds.
4. Plunge freshly cut flowers immediately into a bucket of warm water you've carried into the garden.

Prolonging The Life Of Cut Annuals

1. Recut the stems under water and place them in deep, warm water for at least ten minutes.
2. Remove all leaves below the water level.
3. Keep the vase filled with water.
4. Change the water in the vase daily to prevent buildup of bacteria in the water.
5. Mist the flowers and foliage to prevent wilting.
6. To restore wilted flowers, give the stems a clean cut and place them in a mixture of a half a cup of vinegar to one quart of cold water.

Special Hints

CALLISTEPHUS CHINENSIS (CHINA ASTER) To make flower heads stand upright, soak stems in a solution of one teaspoon sugar to one quart water.

CHRYSANTHEMUM (DAISY) AND *TAGETES* (MARIGOLD) Add several drops of peppermint oil to water. Also prevents water from smelling.

CONSOLIDA (ANNUAL LARKSPUR) Crush stems and plunge into solution of one-half teaspoon peppermint oil to one quart water.

LATHYRUS ODORATUS (SWEET PEA) Place in solution of one tablespoon alcohol to one quart of water.

HELIANTHUS (SUNFLOWER) Freshly cut sunflowers emit oil into the vase water, causing an unpleasant smell. To neutralize the oil and control the smell, fill the vase three-quarters full with water, add household bleach until you can just smell it, then add water to fill the vase.

FALL CLEANUP

As annuals perform for only one season, they should be removed as soon as they have been killed by the frost, and added to your compost pile.

Annuals

Best Bets For Your Garden

above left: Calendula officinalis

above right: Callistephus chinensis

left: Begonia x semperflorens

below: Catharanthus roseus

Botanical Name / Common Name	Color	Height / Spacing	Sun/ Shade
Ageratum houstonianum Ageratum	White, pink, blue	6-18" *6-12"*	○
Antirrhinum majus Snapdragon	Many colors, except blue and lavender	1-3' *15"*	○
Begonia x *semperflorens* Wax begonia	White, pink, rose, red	8-18" *12"*	○ ◑
Brassica oleracea Ornamental cabbage	White, yellow	12" *12"*	○
Calendula officinalis Pot marigold	Orange, yellow	12-15" *12"*	○
Callistephus chinensis China aster	White, pink, red, purple	10-36" *12"*	○
Catharanthus roseus Annual vinca	White, pink, rose, light purple	6-18" *10"*	○ ◑
Centaurea cyanus Bachelor's button	White, pink, blue, purple	24-30" *2'*	○
Cleome hasslerana Spiderflower	White, pink, light purple	3-4' *15"*	○
Consolida spp. Annual larkspur	White, pink, blue, lilac	2-3' *6"*	○
Coreopsis tinctoria Golden coreopsis	Orange, yellow, maroon	2-4' *6-15"*	○ ◑
Cosmos bipinnatus Mexican aster	White, pink, red	3-5' *18-24"*	○ ◑
Dahlia hybrids Dahlia hybrids	All colors, except blue	1-5' *3-4'*	○ ◑
Eschscholzia californica California poppy	Pink, red, orange, yellow	12" *8"*	○

Annual Key: Hardy annual (HA); Half-hardy annual (HH); Tender annual (T)

Microclimate	Planting Time / Bloom Time	Comments
HH; warm-season; drought- and seashore-tolerant	Sow or plant after frost / *Late spring until frost*	Edging, cut flowers; attracts butterflies; self-seeding, but not always true from seed; rich, well-drained soil; alkaline-tolerant; deer-resistant
HA; cool-season	Spring / *Summer - fall*	Borders, mass plantings, cut flowers; attracts butterflies; pinch out terminal bud when transplanting; deadhead to prolong bloom; rich, well-drained soil; alkaline-tolerant; deer-resistant
HH; warm-season; seashore-tolerant	Anytime after frost / *Summer until frost*	Bedding, hanging baskets, containers; well-drained soil; deer-resistant
HA; cool-season; freeze-resistant	Fall / *Fall*	Good for fall color; rich, well-drained soil, tolerates alkaline and moist soils
HA; cool-season; best in areas with cool summers; resists light frost; seashore-tolerant	Sow in early spring / *Summer*	Borders, containers; any well-drained soil; tolerates poor, sandy, moist and alkaline soils
HH; warm-season; water during drought	After last frost / *Summer*	Bedding, cut flowers; does not rebloom; requires several sowings; rich, well-drained soil; tolerates moist and alkaline soils; deer-resistant
HH; warm-season; drought- and heat-tolerant	Transplant after last frost / *Summer - fall*	Bedding, edging, containers; rich, well-drained soil
HA; cool-season	Spring / *Summer*	Borders, cut flowers; thin for larger plants and flowers; sow seed every 2 weeks for continuous bloom; any well-drained soil, tolerates poor, sandy soils
HH; warm-season; drought-tolerant	Spring or summer / *Summer*	Borders, cut flowers; easy to grow; self-sows; rich, well-drained soil
HA; cool-season	Sow in late spring / *Summer*	Bedding, cut flowers; self-sows; requires cool soil to germinate; rich, well-drained soil; space 1' apart in humid areas; fertilize frequently; deer-resistant
HA; warm-season; heat-tolerant	Early spring / *Summer*	Borders; attracts butterflies; feathery foliage; do not thin; prefers crowding; any well-drained soil, tolerates poor, sandy soil
HH; warm-season	Sow in spring / *Summer until frost*	Borders, cut flowers; attracts butterflies; self-sows; well-drained soil; tolerates poor, sandy and alkaline soils
T; warm-season	Late spring / *Summer until frost*	Perennial grown as annual; tuber; borders, cut flowers; pinch early for bushier, stronger plant; well-drained soil; plant 6-8" deep; fertilize regularly; lift/store annually
HA; cool-season	Sow in fall / *Summer - fall*	Naturalizes well; transplants poorly; tolerates poor, sandy and alkaline soils

Annuals

Best Bets For Your Garden

above Gomphrena globosa 'Strawberry Fields'

left: Lavatera trimestris 'Mont Blanc'

below left: Helianthus annuus

below right: Impatiens wallerana

Botanical Name / Common Name	Color	Height / Spacing	Sun/ Shade	
Gaillardia pulchella / Blanket flower	Cream, orange, yellow	12-18" / *12"*	○	
Gomphrena globosa / Globe amaranth	White, pink, rose, reddish purple	10-18" / *6-10"*	○ ◑	
Helianthus annuus / Sunflower	Yellow, gold	3-7' / *12"*	○	
Iberis umbellata / Candytuft (annual)	White, red, lilac	12-18" / *12"*	○	
Impatiens balsamina / Balsam	White, pink, rose, red, salmon, lilac	12-18" / *6-8"*	◑	
Impatiens wallerana / Impatiens	White, pink, salmon, red, lilac, magenta	12-18" / *18"*	●	
Ipomea alba / Moonflower	White	20-30" / *8-12"*	○	
Ipomea purpurea / Morning glory	White, pink, blue, purple	10-15' / *8-12"*	○	
Lathyrus odoratus / Sweet pea	White, pink, blue, lavender	4-6' / *12"*	○	
Lavatera trimestris / Annual mallow	Pink, rose, red, white	12" / *18"*	○	
Lobelia erinus / Lobelia	Blue	4-10" / *4-6"*	○	
Lobularia maritima / Sweet alyssum	White, lilac	2-6" / *6"*	○ ◑	
Matthiola incana / Stock	White, pink, yellow, purple	15-30" / *15"*	○	
Nicotiana alata / Flowering tobacco	White to scarlet	12-18" / *18-24"*	○	

Annual Key: Hardy annual (HA); Half-hardy annual (HH); Tender annual (T)

Microclimate	Planting Time Bloom Time	Comments
HH; warm-season; drought- and seashore-tolerant	Early spring *Summer*	Cut flowers; attracts butterflies; dry sandy soil; tolerant of poor, sandy and alkaline soils
HH; warm-season; drought-tolerant	Sow in early spring *Summer*	Cut or dried flowers; rich, well-drained soil; tolerates clay and alkaline soils
HA; warm-season; drought-tolerant	Sow in spring* *Summer*	Cut flowers; well-drained soil; tolerates poor, sandy and clay soils; *start indoors for best results in Zone 3
T; cool-season	Fall or spring *Spring*	Cut flowers; rock gardens; well-drained soil; deer-resistant
HA; warm-season; seashore-tolerant	Anytime after frost *Summer until frost*	Bedding, hanging baskets, containers; attracts butterflies; rich soil; tolerates poor, sandy and moist soils; deer-resistant
HH; warm-season	After frost *Summer until frost*	Perennial treated as annual; bedding, containers; hanging baskets; moist soil; deer-resistant
T; warm-season	Sow after frost* *Midsummer until frost*	Twining vine; rich, well-drained soil; tolerates clay soil; *for best results in Zones 3 and 4 start indoors, then transplant to spot with hot afternoon sun; deer-resistant
HA; warm-season	Spring* *Summer - fall*	Twining vine; rich, well-drained soil; tolerates clay soil; *for best results in Zones 3 and 4 start indoors, then transplant to spot with hot afternoon sun; deer-resistant
HA: cool-season	Sow in spring *Summer*	Bush or tendril climber; cut flowers; fragrant; rich, fertile, well-drained soil
HA; cool-season; drought-tolerant	Sow 2 weeks before last frost *Summer - early fall*	Borders; fast-growing; dry, moderately rich soil
HA; cool-season; dry climates; seashore-tolerant	Spring *Summer until frost*	Bedding, edging, containers; sandy soil; deer-resistant
HH; prefers cool-season; seashore-tolerant	Sow in early spring or plant in spring *Summer - early fall*	Borders, hanging baskets; fragrant; tolerates poor, sandy and alkaline soils; keep spent flowers removed by shearing for succession of bloom; deer-resistant
HH; cool-season; seashore-tolerant	Sow in early spring *Summer*	Cut flowers, bedding; fragrant; sow seed thickly and do not thin to force early bloom; loamy soil; tolerates moist and alkaline soil; deer-resistant
HH; warm-season; seashore-tolerant	Transplant after last frost *Summer until frost*	Borders; night-blooming; fragrant; attracts butterflies; moist, alkaline soil

Annuals

Best Bets For Your Garden

above left: Tagetes 'Discovery'

above right: Nigella damascena

left: Tropaeolum majus

below left: Thunbergia alata

below right: Verbena x hybrida 'Silver Anne'

Botanical Name Common Name	Color	Height Spacing	Sun/ Shade
Nigella damascena Love-in-a-mist	White, pink, blue	18" *8"*	○
Papaver rhoeas Shirley poppy	White, red	3' *8"*	○
Pelargonium spp. Geranium	White, pink, red, salmon, light purple	12-15" *12"*	○
Petunia x hybrida Petunia	White, pink, red, yellow, purple	12-18" *12"*	○
Salvia spp. Salvia	Red, blue	10-24" *15-20"*	○
Scabiosa atropurpurea Sweet scabious	White, pink, purple	18-24" *8-12"*	○
Tagetes spp. Marigold	Orange, yellow, brown, many shades	6-36" *12"*	○
Thunbergia alata Black-eyed Susan vine	Orange-yellow	10' *8-12"*	○
Tithonia rotundifolia Mexican sunflower	Orange, yellow	4-6' *12"*	○
Tropaeolum majus Nasturtium	Shades of yellow to mahogany	12" *15"*	○
Verbena x hybrida Verbena	Pink, red, blue, lilac	8-18" *18"*	○
Viola tricolor Johnny jump-up	Purple with white, yellow	4-6" *6"*	○ ◑
Viola x wittrockiana Pansy	All colors	6" *6-8"*	○ ◑
Zinnia elegans Zinnia	White, pink, red, orange, yellow	1-3' *12"*	○

Annual Key: Hardy annual (HA); Half-hardy annual (HH); Tender annual (T)

Microclimate	Planting Time / Bloom Time	Comments
HH; cool-season	Sow in early spring *Summer*	Borders, cut and dried flowers; fast-growing; use peat pots if starting indoors; transplants poorly; deadhead to extend bloom; average, well-drained soil
HA; cool-season; drought-tolerant	Sow in early spring *Early summer*	Borders, cut flowers; moist, well-drained soil; tolerates poor, sandy soils
HH; warm-season; seashore-tolerant; humidity-intolerant	Plant after last frost *Late spring until frost*	Can bring indoors for winter; well-drained soil, do not overfertilize, neutral to alkaline soil
HH; warm-season	Spring *Late spring until frost*	Containers, borders; feed and pinch regularly; rich, moist soil; does not like water-logged soil in cool weather; deer-resistant
T; warm-season; tolerates heat and humidity; thrives in hot but not dry conditions; seashore-tolerant	Plant after last frost *Summer until frost*	Perennial grown as annual; bedding; rich, well-drained soil; deer-resistant
HH; warm-season; seashore-tolerant	Sow in spring or plant after last frost *Summer - early fall*	Borders, cut flowers; attracts butterflies; average soil
HH; warm-season; seashore-tolerant	Plant after last frost *Summer until frost*	Bedding, edging; attracts butterflies; used in companion planting to dissuade pests; all soils; tolerates poor, sandy and alkaline soils; deer-resistant
T; warm-season	Start seed indoors; plant when warm *Summer - early fall*	Perennial grown as annual; twining vine; hanging baskets; window boxes, trellises; rich, well-drained soil; tolerates moist soils
HH; warm-season; drought-, heat- and seashore-tolerant	Sow in late spring *Summer until frost*	Borders; attracts butterflies; best in rich, well-drained soil; tolerates poor, sandy and alkaline soils; deadhead regularly; deer-resistant
HA; cool-season	Sow after last frost *Spring or fall*	Bush or vine; bedding, containers, cut flowers; train on poles; prefers poor soil; poor flowering in rich soil; do not overfertilize; deer-resistant
HH; warm-season; heat- and seashore-tolerant	Plant after frost *Summer - early fall*	Borders, containers, cut flowers; fragrant; attracts butterflies; compact and spreading varieties; rich, well-drained soil; tolerates poor, sandy soils
HH; cool-season	Plant after last frost *Late spring - fall*	Perennial treated as annual; borders, containers; pick regularly; rich, moist soil; self-seeding
HH; cool-season	Plant after last frost *Late spring - fall*	Biennial grown as annual; fragrant; borders, containers; pick frequently; rich, moist soil
HH; warm-season; thrives in heat with water; good air circulation; to avoid mildew, do not wet leaves	Sow/plant when soil is warm *Midsummer until frost*	Cut flowers; attracts butterflies; sow every 2 weeks for continuous bloom; well-drained soil; alkaline-tolerant

Peter C. Jones

APPENDIX

VII

PERENNIALS

Iris ensata

Perennials are plants you can depend on year after year to bring life to your garden. Although perennial foliage usually dies back in the fall, their roots carry them through the winter, enabling the plants to make a reappearance each spring. Many families have become so attached to their perennials that they are handed down from generation to generation or transplanted when the family moves. As most can be propagated by division, many gardeners take great pleasure in sharing their favorites with friends.

Perennials are grown for their decorative foliage as well as their colorful blooms. They are traditionally grown in borders, cottage gardens and mass plantings, and as groundcovers and for cutting. The English have made perennials famous with their exquisite, beautifully choreographed perennial borders. Try them with bulbs in the spring garden, under shrubs and trees, along the edge of a pond or in a shade garden. Plant perennials at the base of a vine to cool its roots or edge a rose bed with perennials such as *Nepeta* x *faassenii* (catmint). With so many to choose from, there's a perennial for any location in your garden.

PERENNIALS VS. ANNUALS

To help you determine whether perennials are right for your garden, consider some of the differences between perennials and annuals:

ANNUALS CAN BLOOM ALL SEASON LONG. Some perennials, such as *Scabiosa* 'Butterfly Blue,' bloom for up to four months, while others, such as *Astilbe*, often bloom for just a few weeks each year.

ANNUALS REQUIRE WARM TEMPERATURES TO BLOOM; MANY PERENNIALS THRIVE IN COOLER TEMPERATURES. With carefully selected perennials your garden can begin blooming early in the spring and continue into the late fall.

ANNUALS MUST BE REPLANTED EVERY YEAR, which is fun for variety, but time-consuming.

PERENNIALS REQUIRE MORE MAINTENANCE THAN ANNUALS. A perennial must be healthy and vigorous to persist from year to year.

Grow Perennials:

- In herbaceous borders against a fence, wall or hedge
- In mixed perennial and shrub borders
- In mass plantings
- In shade, rock or water gardens
- As groundcovers
- To edge rose gardens
- To hide yellowing bulb foliage
- To fill in bare spots between shrubs
- To fill in around young shrubs, tying the mass together
- To brighten dark corners
- In your cutting garden
- In pots and planters

HINT: A garden all in white will glow in the moonlight.

TEMPERATURE

Perennials are sensitive to both cold and warm temperatures, although the primary concern for gardeners in Zones 3, 4 and 5 is the cold. Look for plants that are cold-hardy in your zone, and since the growing season is short, consider the bloom time for each perennial. There are many favorites that thrive in your cold climate: *Lupinus* explodes in meadows in the late spring; *Delphinium* achieves great heights in New England; alpine plants excel in the mountains.

But late bloomers like *Aster* and some *Chrysanthemum* may not have a chance to put on their splendid displays. In Zone 3, select aster varieties such as 'Alma Potsche' and 'Hella Lacy' that bloom in early September. *Phlox paniculata* and *Echinacea purpurea* (coneflower) will ignore light frosts without coverings.

Most areas in Zone 3 rarely see hot summers, but as we near the close of the century, extended periods of heat are becoming more common in Zones 4 and 5. With many perennials, you may find the hotter the summer, the shorter the bloom period. If you experience windy, hot summers, opt for hardy, drought-tolerant perennials such as *Achillea* and *Coreopsis*.

When selecting perennials, take into account the following:

- First and last dates of frost
- The coldest expected winter temperature
- The highest expected summer temperature

SUN/SHADE

Although most perennials prefer a sunny location, there is a wide selection of perennials that grow in light shade, including *Heuchera* x *brizoides* (coral bells), *Aquilegia* (columbine) and *Alchemilla mollis* (lady's mantle). *Dicentra* (bleeding heart), *Hosta* and *Convallaria majalis* (lily-of-the-valley) are among those that thrive in full shade.

SOIL

Most perennials require a humus-rich, well-drained but moist soil. A good balance of clay, sand and silt will provide the necessary drainage, yet retain moisture. If you have sandy or clay soil, amend your soil or select perennials that tolerate your conditions. A slightly acid soil, with a pH of 5.5-6.6, will suit most perennials.

WATER

Regular moisture is important for most perennials during the growing season. If your summers bring hot winds and drought, be sure to monitor your soil carefully. When the top two inches have dried out, and rain is not on the horizon, it's time to water. Always water deeply and thoroughly when planting new perennials. But avoid using sprinklers; they will damage the blossoms and wet the leaves, attracting mildew. Don't stop watering in winter; if the soil is dry, but not frozen, your perennials may need additional moisture.

> *HINT: To control mildew on* Phlox paniculata, *spray the foliage with Wilt Pruf during the growing season.*

PLANNING A PERENNIAL BORDER

Planning a perennial border is like composing a symphony. Perennials, like violins, trumpets and drums, perform at specific times to create a harmonious whole. As each instrument contributes a different sound to the orchestra, each perennial offers the garden a different form, silhouette, color and texture.

The Planting Bed

First, set the stage. If possible, locate your border on either side of a walk, or in a garden enclosed by walls, fences or hedges. Flowers often show off to their best advantage against a solid background. If you do site your bed in front of a solid background, make a narrow path behind the bed. This will provide easy access for tending the plants and prevent you from compacting the planting bed with your footsteps.

The bed should be in scale and proportion to its location in your landscape. Small perennial borders should be at least 5' to 6' wide; 10' to 12' is an ideal depth for long beds. Stay clear of any trees that may have invasive roots.

The Plant List

Next, decide whether the border will be devoted solely to perennials or whether it will be mixed, and include bulbs, annuals, biennials, roses or shrubs. If you use only perennials, place spring-, summer- and fall-blooming plants in groups forming a set pattern of bloom through the border. Consider the horizontal and vertical relationship of the plants as well as the texture of the foliage. Remember the foliage will be there all season, while the blooms may not! If all-over bloom is your goal, consider a mixed border that includes annuals, biennials and flowering bulbs. In either design, be sure to include many perennials with long blooming periods for continuity.

Bloom Sequence

As perennials bloom for defined periods, timing the sequence of bloom in a perennial border is very important. When making your plant selection, choose perennials that are early-, mid- and late-season bloomers. Then use tracing paper to plan your sequence of bloom and color. Use a different sheet for each month and lay them on top of each other to see how one blends into the next. Don't be concerned if you don't get the results you want the first year. It's very hard to plan for the exact time of bloom until you see how the plants perform in your microclimate. And next season you can always move the plants; when you do get it right, the show is well worth the effort.

Mass Plantings

For maximum impact, group the plants together in masses of from three to a dozen. Remember, the smaller the plant, the more that are needed to make an impression. Smaller groups can look well in small gardens while larger gardens can support bold masses of color. Some bushy plants such as *Paeonia* (peony) or *Gypsophila paniculata* (baby's breath) can stand alone.

Plant Placement

The plant masses should mesh together from front to back and side to side. Form irregularly shaped masses of each perennial so the plant masses can be woven together. Position short masses in front and tall in back. But add some variety and surprises so the garden is not monotonous. Vary the height in the back row and pull some of the tall and medium-height plants forward into the shorter masses.

Spacing

Perennial plants look so small when you first plant them you can't believe they'll ever fill the recommended 12" or larger gap between plants. But believe me they do. As perennials send up new shoots every year, they'll fill in in no time, and you'll be digging up and dividing your plants sooner than you would like. See the spacing recommendations in "Best Bets For Your Garden" and follow them!

PLANNING AT A GLANCE:

The following elements are important to consider when making your plant list:

- Microclimate
- Soil
- Water
- Height and width
- Plant form and silhouette
- Flower texture and color
- Leaf texture and color
- Spacing
- Time and length of bloom
- Life cycle of the plants: growth, bloom and decline

BED PREPARATION

Perennials have the potential to grow in the same place for many years, even decades! The better the bed preparation, the happier the perennials, the longer the life. Prepare the beds in the fall to a depth of 12" (minimum) to 24" (ideal) by single or double digging (see "Digging the Bed," Chapter 2). If your planting plan includes shrubs or roses, I urge you to dig the full 24". Add soil amendments as required and let the beds settle over the winter before planting in the spring. If this is not possible, prepare them as soon as the soil is workable in the spring and water well to settle the soil before planting.

SEEDS OR PLANTS?

Although perennials reproduce by seed as well as by sending up new shoots, you are better off purchasing most of your perennials as plants. Perennials grown from seed take longer to reach flowering than annuals and often do not grow true in color and habit. Container-grown perennials are available from catalogs or your local nursery; bare-root plants are most often purchased by mail.

BUYING PERENNIALS

If you are buying your plants from a local nursery, you will have the opportunity to pick and choose.

To select a healthy plant, look for:

- Plants that are pest-free
- Plants that have healthy, new growth

and avoid:

- Plants with yellow leaves or dieback
- Potbound plants (Check to see if roots are growing out of the bottom of pot)
- Plants with underdeveloped root systems (Check to see if the plant is loose in the pot)
- Leggy plants

> *HINT: If you were unable to prepare the beds in advance, plant the perennials slightly deeper to accommodate for the settling of the soil.*

PLANTING

Now that you've prepared the bed, it's time to make your perennials feel at home. Make every effort to install your plants as soon as they arrive. If you're not ready to plant, be sure to keep them well watered and in the shade.

For Container-grown Plants:

1. Set the containers out on the bed according to your garden plan. Now, fine-tune your design. Water the containers, then begin to plant one at a time.
2. Dig a hole one-and-a-half times wider and deeper than the container.
3. Holding one hand over the top of the container, turn the container over and remove the plant. If the plant is potbound, you may need to loosen the plant by tapping the sides with a trowel. Do not pull the plant out by the stem; it may break! If the plant has an underdeveloped root system, and the root ball begins to crumble, retain as much soil around the root ball as possible.
4. Next, carefully scrape any weeds that may be growing from the top surface of the root ball, then gently loosen the roots along the sides and bottom to encourage their growth out into their new home.

5. Adjust the plant in the hole. Most perennials should be planted with their crowns at the same level as the surrounding soil.
6. Fill the hole with soil, gently firm the soil around the plant, then water thoroughly to settle the soil around the roots.

For Bare-root Plants:

Plant bare-root plants as soon as possible. The roots will be brittle, so remove any protective covering with great care, then rehydrate the roots by soaking them in a bucket of water with a couple of drops of liquid dish detergent for at least an hour. This will make the roots more pliable and less prone to damage.

1. Cut off any dead or damaged roots using sharp scissor pruners or a knife that has been cleaned with alcohol.
2. Dig a hole ample enough to avoid crowding the plant and form a mound of soil in the bottom.
3. Next, gently spread the roots over the mound so the base of the crown rests on the mound, yet is level with the surrounding soil. (The base of the crown is where the roots meet the stems.)
4. Fill the hole with soil. Be careful not to cover the crown!
5. Gently firm the soil and water in well.

FERTILIZING

If you have prepared your perennial beds well, there should be little need for much fertilizing. An annual top dressing of a balanced slow-release fertilizer and compost in the early spring should be enough. But established beds and beds with heavy feeders, such as *Paeonia* (peony) and *Phlox*, may need a little help. But don't apply fertilizer on top of your mulch. Remove the mulch, spread the fertilizer, then replace.

> *HINT: Do not add fertilizer to the planting hole. You risk burning the roots.*

Some Signs Of Nutrient Deficiency

You will see signs when your plants are suffering from nutrient deficiency:

- Small leaves
- Yellow leaves
- Yellow leaves with dark veins
- Plants are weak and wilted (although well watered)
- Lateral buds die before blooming
- Small blossoms

MULCH

Apply a light mulch, such as buckwheat hulls, ground-up leaf mold or spent hops, 2" thick. (Bark chips are too large and clumsy-looking in a flower bed.) Since some perennials are prone to crown rot, don't mound the mulch around the crowns of the plants. Reapply mulch as necessary.

PINCHING

"Pinching back" prevents the plants from becoming leggy and encourages them to develop into more compact, bushy plants. Pinching often delays flowering time, but produces more flowers, although they may be smaller in size. Perennials that benefit from a pinch here and there include: *Artemisia, Aster, Boltonia asteroides, Lobelia, Monarda*, and *Salvia. Helenium autumnale* (sneezeweed) and many species of *Chrysanthemum* actually require pinching to fill out and flourish.

To pinch back a plant, remove the tips of the stems. (See the Pinching Illustration on p.52.) The best time to start pinching back perennials is in the late spring or early summer just as they begin to grow. Two branches will grow from each pinched stem. Stop pinching when the flower buds are set.

HINT: Don't pinch back too late. In your cold climate you'll want to allow enough time for the plant to grow back and bloom prior to the cold weather.

STAKING

Whether or not to stake is just as personal a decision as the design of the garden and the plant selection. Some people feel that stakes detract from the beauty of the flowers; others accept them as a necessity. Some prefer a casual cottage garden look, others a formal garden. Whichever your view, there are some flowers that cannot stand alone. The first heavy rain or wind storm will flatten the tall spikes of *Delphinium* and the heavy flowers of double *Paeonia*. The type of staking you use should depend on the habit of the plant.

HINT: If staking is not to your liking, select lower-growing plants and plants with lighter flower heads.

For Tall Spike Flowers Such As Delphinium

Use a tall green bamboo cane long enough to go deep into the ground and rise to within 6" of the anticipated height of the flower stalk. Being careful not to disturb the plant's crown, push the stake in as close to the flower stalk as possible. Loop a piece of soft green twine around the stem, then loosely tie it to the stake and trim off the ends. Add more ties as the flower stalk grows.

For Medium Spike Flowers Such As Lilium

Stake as for tall spike flowers or use metal single-stem supports, which curl around the stalk.

For Bushy Plants Such As Paeonia

There are several approaches to bushy plants; choose from the following:

CIRCULAR METAL FRAMES Place above the plants in early spring to allow the stems to grow up through them. Some stems will need to be guided into the circle. The frames are conspicuous in the garden until hidden by the plants.

ZIGZAG SUPPORTS Available in different heights and lengths, these green metal supports are easily placed after plants, such as *Achillea*, have begun to grow. They lift plants up without totally restraining them.

LINKED STAKES Green metal stakes are installed around plants, such as *Monarda*, as they near maturity, but before they are at risk of flopping. The late installation will prevent your garden from looking like a sea of green metal early in the season.

BAMBOO STAKES Evenly space green bamboo stakes around clumps of perennials, such as chrysanthemums, and run dark green twine between them to support the flower stems. Bamboo stakes can be installed after the plants have filled out, but before they are top-heavy.

For Airy Plants Such As Achillea

BRUSH STAKES Stick a branch from a twiggy bush in the ground next to perennials such as *Gypsophila paniculata* (baby's breath) in the spring. The plant will grow up through the branch and eventually hide it. The only drawback — your garden will look like a mass of twigs in early summer until the perennials have filled out.

Some of the most picturesque plant supports can be found right in your garden. Look around. Perhaps you'll find a strong grapevine that curves in just the right direction or a birch stem that is just the right height.

HINT: Don't grow sun-loving plants in the shade — they will become leggy and require staking.

WEEDING

Keep an eye out for annual weeds. If you've prepared your beds well and applied your mulch, weeding should be minimal. But keep on top of it!

(From top left clockwise) Bamboo cane; circular metal frame; natural brush stakes, metal zigzag supports.

DISBUDDING

While you pinch back for a bushier plant, you disbud for a bigger flower. Locate the terminal bud on perennials such as *Paeonia* and *Dahlia*. Pinch out the smaller side buds growing at the base of its stem. The resulting blossom will be extra-large. Do not disbud perennials with spike blooms, such as *Delphinium*.

DEADHEADING

Behead your faded flowers! Use pruning clippers or your fingers to deadhead. For large masses of flowers with upward growing blossoms such as *Lavandula* (lavender), *Achillea* (yarrow), *Nepeta* x *faassenii* (catmint) and *Iberis sempervirens* (candytuft), use shears. Be sure to make a clean cut and don't tear the stems. On perennials such as *Hemerocallis* (daylily), which have several blooms per stem, only remove the individual spent bloom.

Deadhead after flowering to:
- Maintain the appearance of the flower bed
- Discourage disease
- Prevent seed formation and extend the bloom

If the foliage of your perennial is out of control, you can trim it back at the same time. But remember, perennials bloom for a limited time, and the foliage lingers to fill the gaps. Allow the spent flowerheads of showy *Sedum* and *Rudbeckia* (black-eyed Susan) to dry on the plants; they look wonderful all winter long.

CUT FLOWERS

Perennials can make lovely, long-lasting cut flowers. But remember, many perennials, unlike annuals, have one short blooming season. If you plan to cut your perennials, it is best to grow them in a separate cutting garden so your borders will look full and not ratty or moth-eaten.

When Picking Perennials

1. Cut flowers early in the morning when they are most turgid.
2. Cut stems at an angle using a sharp knife or Oriental shears.
3. Take as long a stem as possible without removing future flower buds.
4. Plunge freshly cut flowers immediately into a bucket of warm water you've carried into the garden.

Prolonging The Life Of Cut Perennials

- Cut flowers before fully open.
- Keep the vase filled with water!
- Change the water daily to prevent buildup of bacteria.
- Mist the flowers and foliage to prevent wilting.
- Keep the vase in a cool spot whenever possible.

Special Hints

FOR FLOWERS WITH SAP SUCH AS *PAPAVER* (POPPY) Cut stems to desired length then burn tips of stems in a flame or dip in boiling water for one minute. If stems are re-cut, repeat process.

FOR FLOWERS WITH HOLLOW STEMS SUCH AS *DELPHINIUM* Fill stems with water and plug up with cotton balls or Oasis.

FOR *CHRYSANTHEMUM* Crush or burn stems. Soak them up to their necks in a solution of eight drops of peppermint oil to two quarts of water.

FOR *PAEONIA* Cut when in bud. Crush stems four inches up and place in deep, cold water.

DIVIDING

Dividing perennials may sound like a lot of work, but it's well worth the effort. Not only can you rejuvenate older plants, but you will have many new plants for yourself or to give away to

Dividing (clockwise from left). For large clumps: Dig up the plant, lift and insert two digging forks back to back in the center of the clump and pry apart. For plants that become woody: Cut off the young side shoots with a spade and discard the woody parent plant. For plants with solid crowns or rhizomes: Divide with a sharp knife. For fibrous-rooted plants: Gently pull the plants apart.

friends. Divide your plants when they are overcrowded or when flower production is down.

FIBROUS-ROOTED PLANTS Dig up plants like *Asperula odorata* (sweet woodruff) and gently pull the plants apart.

PLANTS WITH SOLID CROWNS OR RHIZOMES Use a sharp knife to divide solid-crowned plants like *Paeonia* (peony) and *Astilbe* or rhizomes like bearded iris. Dust with fungicide.

PLANTS THAT BECOME WOODY As some perennials, such as *Aster*, age, the parent plants become woody and produce fewer blooms, but their side shoots show great potential. Dig all around the clump with a spade and lift up the whole colony. Cut off the young side shoots and replant them. Discard the parent plant.

LARGE CLUMPS Heavy-crowned plants like *Hemerocallis* (daylily) need a little more effort. Dig all around the clump with a spade, then lift the plant. Shake off excess soil so you can see the roots and set the clump to the side of the bed. Insert two digging forks back to back in the center of the clump. Pressing the handles together, pry the clump apart. Divide into as many smaller clumps as necessary and replant.

Time To Divide

Most perennials can be divided and transplanted in the fall when the foliage begins to die back. A general rule of thumb: If it blooms in the spring, divide in the fall. If it blooms in the fall, divide in the spring. More specifically, divide plants that bloom from midsummer to fall in the early spring and those that bloom in the spring and early summer in the fall prior to mid-October. *Papaver orientale* (poppy) should be divided in August when they have begun to produce new foliage.

TRANSPLANTING

Remember to prepare a planting bed for the newly divided plants prior to getting started, because you don't want any delays getting them back into the ground. (See "Bed Preparation" and "Planting" earlier in the chapter.) If you are incorporating new divisions into existing beds, amend the soil in the individual holes at planting time.

Before planting your new plants, cut back the foliage by one-half to ensure that most of their energy goes to the roots. (The foliage of spring-planted divisions is likely to be small and will probably not have to be reduced.) In newly prepared beds, plant the divisions deeper than their original level, as the soil is bound to settle. This will also protect the plants from drying out. New plantings may lose too much water from transpiring moisture through their leaves before new roots have formed. Thoroughly water all transplants.

WINTERIZING

Most plantings, but especially all first-year plantings, should be carefully winterized in Zones 3, 4 and 5. The first step to preparing for winter is a good fall cleanup. Look over the garden after the plants have died back. Save any plants that will add winter interest such as showy *Sedum spectabile* (showy stonecrop) or *Rudbeckia* (black-eyed Susan) and cut back all others to 4"-6". The remaining stems trap the snow, providing additional insulation.

When the ground is frozen, spread a 2" layer of compost and cover the garden with evergreen boughs, salt hay or straw, which will hold the snow for additional insulation. But do not rake leaves into the bed; they will flatten down and prevent water from penetrating the surface. Add them to your compost pile instead.

SPRING CLEANUP

When the weather starts to warm up and spring bulbs are in bloom, you know it is time to begin removing the winter mulch. If you leave the mulch on too late in the spring, it will slow down the growth of the young shoots. To give young shoots a chance to adjust to the sunlight, begin on a cloudy day. If you layered your mulch, remove it gradually. Begin by removing a few boughs or a little hay at a time. Then work the compost evenly over the bed.

Early spring is also the time to cut back all perennials left standing through the winter. Using scissor pruners, remove the stems down to the crown, taking care not to damage any young shoots.

Biennials

Digitalis

Biennials complete their life cycles within a two-year period. The first year, the plants produce leaves; the second, they bloom, set seed and die. Biennials sometimes self-sow, so some plants will be in bloom every year. However, biennials can't be counted on to return each year as perennials do, so gardeners often steer clear of them. But there are such beautiful flowers within their ranks, they deserve consideration. Much-loved biennials such as *Alcea rosea* (hollyhock) and *Campanula medium* (bellflower) are a wonderful addition to herbaceous borders and cottage gardens; *Digitalis* (foxglove) makes an impressive display naturalized in a woodland setting; *Myosotis* (forget-me-not) is an all-time favorite planted with spring-flowering bulbs.

Biennials have dual personalities. Plants raised from seed the first year winter over just like perennials. Yet in their second season they behave like annuals, leaving behind their seed to repeat the cycle the next year. Some gardeners treat biennials as annuals, while others treat them like perennials, reserving a special place for them in the garden. Since annual beds are tilled every year, biennials find a safer home in the perennial border.

Biennials are easily grown from seed. However, since they take two years to bloom from seed, many gardeners prefer to buy plants. To grow biennials from seed, follow instructions in the annuals section under "Sowing."

Biennials are readily available as container-grown plants from your local garden centers or through mail-order catalogs. Plant them as you would perennials. (See p.65.) For bloom every year, grow plants on alternate cycles.

Perennials

Best Bets For Your Garden

above left: Achillea 'Moonshine'

above right: Astilbe x *arendsii* 'Bridal Veil'

left: Aquilegia 'Red and White'

below: Aster novae-angliae 'Hella Lacy'

Botanical Name / Common Name	Color	Height / Spacing	Sun/ Shade
Achillea 'Moonshine' / Yarrow	Yellow	2' / 18"	○
Aconitum carmichaelii / Azure monkshood	Deep blue	3-4' / 2'	○ ◑
Alchemilla mollis / Lady's mantle	Yellow	1-2' / 18"	○ ◑
Anaphalis margaritacea / Common pearly everlasting	White	1-3' / 12"	○
Aquilegia spp. / Columbine	Various	18" / 8-12"	◑
Aruncus dioicus / Goatsbeard	White	4-7' / 3'	○ ◑
Asclepias tuberosa / Butterfly weed	Orange	18"-3' / 1-2'	○
Aster novae-angliae / New England aster	Pink, rose, crimson, purple, lavender	1-6' / 2'	○
Aster novi-belgi / New York aster	Pink, rose, crimson, purple, lavender	1-6' / 18-24"	○
Astilbe x *arendsii* / Astilbe	White, pink, red	18-36" / 18-24"	◑
Baptisia australis / False indigo	Blue	3-6' / 3'	○ ◑
Bergenia cordifolia / Bergenia cultivars	White, pink, red	18-24" / 2'	◑
Boltonia asteroides / Boltonia	White, pink, lilac	4-7' / 2'	○ ◑
Brunnera macrophylla / Siberian bugloss	Blue	18" / 2'	○ ◑

Microclimate	Planting Time / Bloom Time	Comments
Very hardy; tolerates hot sun, seashore, dry and humid climates	Spring or fall / *Summer*	Borders, cut flowers; well-drained soil; tolerates alkaline soil; attracts butterflies; try 'Coronation Gold'
Very hardy; prefers cool summer nights; low humidity	Spring or fall / *Early fall*	Borders, cut flowers; cool, rich, moist, well-drained soil; all parts poisonous
Hardy	Spring / *Late spring - early summer*	Borders, cut flowers, groundcover; most well-drained, moist soils; deer-resistant
Hardy; drought-tolerant	Spring / *Late summer - fall*	Borders, dried flowers; silvery foliage; prefers moist, well-drained soil
Hardy	Spring / *Mid-late spring, some later*	Well-drained, moist soil; tolerates alkaline soil; deer-resistant
Very hardy	Spring or fall / *Summer*	Borders; trouble-free; all moist, well-drained soils
Very hardy; heat-, humidity- and drought-tolerant	Spring / *Summer*	Borders, cut flowers; easily grown from seed; well-drained, sandy soil; tolerates clay soil; attracts butterflies; deer-resistant
Hardy to Zone 4; tolerates wet soils	Spring, late summer / *Fall*	Borders, cut flowers; rich soil; attracts butterflies; deer-resistant
Hardy to Zone 4; tolerates wet soils	Spring, late summer / *Fall*	Borders, cut flowers; moist, rich soil; attracts butterflies; deer-resistant
Hardy to Zone 4	Spring / *Summer*	Bedding, borders, woodland gardens; moist soil; tolerates clay soil; deer-resistant
Very hardy; drought-tolerant	Spring or fall / *Early summer*	Borders, cut flowers; well-drained, neutral to acid soil; deadhead for repeat bloom or enjoy the attractive seed pods
Hardy	Spring or fall / *Summer*	Rhizome; evergreen; borders, edging, bedding; tolerates many soils; deer-resistant
Hardy, humidity-tolerant	Spring or fall / *Late summer - fall*	Back of border, naturalizes; tolerates moist soils; cultivars are better behaved; does not require staking; deer-resistant; try 'Snowbank'
Very hardy	Spring or fall / *Early spring*	Borders, groundcover under trees; fertile, moist, soil; excellent with bulbs

Perennials

Best Bets For Your Garden

above left: Delphinium elatum

above right: Campanula persi-cifolia 'Telham Beauty'

left: Dianthus x *allwoodii* 'Doris'

below: Coreopsis verticillata 'Zagreb'

Botanical Name Common Name	Color	Height Spacing	Sun/ Shade
Campanula persicifolia Bellflower	White, blue	2-3' *12-18"*	○
Centaurea montana Mountain bluet	White, pink, blue	1-2" *2'*	○ ◑
Centranthus ruber Red valerian	Pink, red	18-36" *12-18"*	○ ◑
Chrysanthemum parthenium Feverfew	White with yellow centers	8-24" *12"*	○
Cimicifuga racemosa Snakeroot	White	3-8' *2'*	○ ◑
Coreopsis verticillata Threadleaf coreopsis	Yellow	1-3' *2'*	○
Delphinium elatum Delphinium hybrids	White, blue, lavender	3-8' *2-3'*	○
Dianthus x *allwoodii* Cottage pink	White, pink	12-18" *12"*	○
Dicentra spectabilis Bleeding heart	White, pink	2-3' *1-5'*	◑ ●
Echinacea purpurea Purple coneflower	White, purple	2-3' *18"*	○
Echinops humilis Globe thistle	Lavender	3-4' *2'*	○
Eupatorium purpureum Joe-Pye weed	Purple	4-6' *2-4'*	○ ◑
Filipendula rubra Queen-of-the-prairie	Pink	6-8' *4'*	○ ◑
Gaillardia x *grandiflora* Blanket flower	Red, orange, yellow	2-3' *18"*	○

Microclimate	Planting Time / Bloom Time	Comments
Hardy to Zone 4; light shade in hot climates	Spring or fall / *Spring - summer*	Borders, cut flowers; well-drained, rich, neutral to alkaline soil
Very hardy	Spring or fall / *Early summer - early fall*	Fillers in borders, cut flowers; very long blooming; easy to grow, may become invasive; well-drained soil
Hardy to Zone 4; drought-tolerant	Spring / *Summer*	Borders; cut flowers; fragrant; well-drained average soil; tolerates alkaline soil; cut back for second bloom; attracts butterflies; deer-resistant
Hardy to Zone 4; seashore-tolerant	Spring / *Summer - early fall*	Borders; light, sandy soil
Hardy; seashore-tolerant	Spring / *Summer*	Back of border, shrub border, woodland; rich, well-drained soil; low-maintenance; deer-resistant
Very hardy; drought-, seashore- and humidity-tolerant	Spring or fall / *Spring - summer*	Borders; cut flowers; average, well-drained soil; attracts butterflies; deer-resistant
Very hardy; heat-intolerant; will not flourish in hot summers; prefers cold winters	Spring / *Summer*	Borders, cut flowers; rich, well-drained soil; most require staking; requires more care
Hardy to Zone 4	Spring or fall / *Summer*	Borders, edging; fragrant; neutral, rich, well-drained soil; tolerates alkaline soil; deer-resistant
Hardy	Early spring / *Spring*	Borders, cottage gardens; rich, well-drained soil; tolerates alkaline soil; dies back in summer
Very hardy; seashore- and humidity-tolerant	Spring / *Summer*	Borders; cut flowers; rich, moist soil; tolerates clay and alkaline soil; attracts butterflies; deer-resistant
Very hardy; drought- and seashore-tolerant	Spring / *Midsummer - fall*	Borders, cut flowers; light, well-drained soil; attracts butterflies
Very hardy; tolerates cold, damp locations	Spring / *Summer - early fall*	Back of border, naturalizes well at water's edge; rich, moist soil
Very hardy; tolerates cool, damp locations	Spring or fall / *Summer*	Back of border, natural plantings, cut flowers; moist, rich soil
Very hardy; heat-, drought- and seashore-tolerant	Spring / *Summer - fall*	Borders, cut flowers; light, well-drained soils; short-lived

Perennials

Best Bets For Your Garden

above: Iris x germanica 'Edith Wolford'

right: Liatris spicata 'Kobold'

below left: Limonium latifolium

below right: Gypsophila paniculata 'Pink Fairy'

Botanical Name Common Name	Color	Height Spacing	Sun/ Shade
Geranium spp. Cranesbill	Pink, rose, blue, purple	18-24" *18-24"*	○ ◐
Gypsophila paniculata Baby's breath	White, pink	18-48" *4'*	○
Helenium autumnale Sneezeweed	Yellow	4-5' *18"*	○
Heliopsis helianthoides False sunflower	Orange, yellow	5' *2'*	○
Hemerocallis Daylily	Shades of pink, red, orange, yellow	2-3' *18"*	○ ◐
Hesperis matronalis Sweet rocket	Purple	1-3' *18"*	○ ◐
Heuchera x *brizoides* Coralbells	White, pink, red	12-30" *12-18"*	Morning sun only
Hibiscus moscheutos Rose mallow	White, pink, red	4-6' *30-36"*	○ ◐
Hosta spp. Plantain lily	White, blue, lavender	16-24" *1-4'*	●
Iris x *germanica* Bearded iris	Many	10-36" *12"*	○
Iris pseudacorus Yellow flag	Yellow	3-4' *15"*	○ ◐
Iris sibirica Siberian iris	White, blue, purple	2-4' *2'*	○
Liatris spicata Gayfeather	White, purple	3-4' *12"*	○
Limonium latifolium Sea lavender	Bluish white	2' *18"*	○

Microclimate	Planting Time / Bloom Time	Comments
Hardy; part shade in the heat	Spring or fall / *Late spring - summer*	Borders, rock gardens; all well-drained soils; deadhead for rebloom; deer-resistant
Hardy; seashore-tolerant	Spring / *Summer*	Borders, cut flowers, drying; rich, moist, well-drained neutral to alkaline soils; select smaller cultivars to avoid staking
Very hardy; heat-tolerant	Spring / *Summer - early fall*	Informal plantings; moist soil; tolerates alkaline soil; deadhead for more blooms; attracts butterflies; deer-resistant
Hardy to Zone 4; drought- and seashore-tolerant	Spring or fall / *Summer*	Back of border; any well-drained soil; deadhead to extend bloom
Very hardy; humidity- and seashore-tolerant	Spring or fall / *Spring - fall*	Borders, bedding; any soil; water regularly when blooming; long bloom period
Hardy; protect from strong sun	Spring / *Summer*	Borders; fragrant; self-seeds; well-drained moist soil; tolerates poor soil; deadhead to force second bloom; attracts butterflies
Hardy; seashore-tolerant	Early spring or fall / *Spring*	Edging; borders; moist, rich, well-drained soil; tolerates alkaline soil
Hardy to Zone 4; seashore- and humidity-tolerant; wind protection	Spring / *Summer*	Borders; moist soil; fertilize regularly; deer-resistant
Hardy	Spring / *Summer*	Mass plantings; borders; moist, rich soil; some tolerate clay soil; good drainage in winter; apply super phosphate in late summer
Hardy; some resent heat, others thrive; seashore-tolerant	Early fall / *Spring*	Rhizome; many hybrids; alkaline, well-drained soil; plant high to prevent crown rot; divide every 3-4 years; cut seed pods as they form; deer-resistant
Hardy to Zone 4; thrives in shallow water	Spring or fall / *Midspring*	Rhizome; moist, acid soil; deer-resistant
Hardy to Zone 4; seashore-tolerant	Spring / *Early summer*	Rhizome; prefers moist boggy soil; deer-resistant
Very hardy; drought- and humidity-tolerant	Spring / *Summer*	Borders; cut flowers; well-drained, moist soil; attracts butterflies
Very hardy; heat- and seashore-tolerant	Spring / *Summer - fall*	Borders, cut and dried flowers; well-drained soil

Perennials
Best Bets For Your Garden

above left: Monarda didyma 'Raspberry Wine'

above right: Phlox paniculata 'Fairest One'

left: Paeonia lactiflora 'Dinner Plate'

below left: Rudbeckia sullivantii 'Goldstrum'

below right: Lupinus 'Popsicle Mix'

Botanical Name / Common Name	Color	Height / Spacing	Sun/ Shade	
Lobelia cardinalis / Cardinal flower	Red	3-4' / 12"	○ ●	
Lobelia siphilitica / Great blue lobelia	Blue	2-3' / 12"	○ ◑	
Lupinus 'Russell hybrids' / Russell hybrid lupines	White, cream, pink, red, orange, yellow, blue, purple	3-4' / 18-24"	○ ◑	
Macleaya cordata / Plume poppy	White	6-8' / 2-3'	○ ◑	
Malva moschata / Musk mallow	White, pink	2-3' / 2'	○	
Monarda didyma / Bee balm	White, pink, red, lavender	30-40" / 18"	○ ◑	
Nepeta x *faassenii* / Catmint	Lavender	1-2' / 18"	○	
Paeonia lactiflora / Peony	White, pink, red	24-42" / 2-3'	○	
Papaver orientale / Oriental poppy	Red	2-4' / 2-3'	○	
Phlox paniculata / Border phlox	White, pink, red	2-4' / 12"	○ ◑	
Physotegia virginiana / False dragonhead	White, lavender	2-5' / 18"	○ ◑	
Platycodon grandiflorus / Balloon flower	White, pink, blue	18-30" / 12"	○ ◑	
Rudbeckia spp. / Black-eyed Susan	Yellow, gold, mahogany	2-3' / 18"	○	
Salvia spp. / Perennial salvia	Blue	2-3' / 1-2'	○	

Microclimate	Planting Time / Bloom Time	Comments
Very hardy	Spring or fall *Late summer - early fall*	Borders, naturalized beside streams or ponds; moist, rich soil; shallow-rooted, replant if soil heaves in winter
Hardy to Zone 4	Spring or fall *Late summer - early fall*	Borders, water's edge; tolerates moist, heavy soils
Hardy to Zone 4; intolerant of hot summers; water in dry weather; protect in areas with very cold winters	Spring or fall *Late spring - early summer*	Borders; naturalizes well; rich, well-drained soil, neutral to slightly acid; deadhead to encourage rebloom; stake tall plants
Hardy to Zone 4	Spring *Summer*	Back of border; average soil; deer-resistant
Hardy; seashore-tolerant	Spring *Summer - fall*	Borders; easy to grow; blooms over long season
Hardy to Zone 4	Spring *Summer*	Borders; fragrant foliage; moist soil; tolerates clay soil; attracts butterflies; deer-resistant
Very hardy; seashore- and drought-tolerant	Spring *Early summer*	Borders, edging; herb gardens; fragrant; well-drained soil; shear for second bloom
Very hardy; prefers long, cold winters	Fall *Spring*	Borders; fragrant; deep soil, enriched with compost and lime; deer-resistant
Very hardy; prefers cool summers	Fall *Early summer*	Borders; foliage dies down in summer; plant with leafy late bloomers such as *Gypsophila*; rich, well-drained soil
Very hardy	Spring *Summer*	Borders; fragrant; well-drained soil; attracts butterflies; deer-resistant
Very hardy	Spring *Late summer - fall*	Borders, cut flowers; sandy soil; invasive in moist, light soil; attracts butterflies
Hardy; seashore-tolerant	Spring or fall *Summer*	Borders, cut flowers; easy to grow; tolerant of most soils
Very hardy; drought-, seashore- and humidity-tolerant	Spring or fall *Summer - fall*	Borders, cut flowers; any type of well-drained soil; cut to encourage bloom; attracts butterflies; deer-resistant
Hardy to Zone 4; drought- and humidity-tolerant	Spring *Midspring - fall*	Borders, mass plantings, cut flowers; any type of well-drained soil; deer-resistant

Perennials

Best Bets For Your Garden

above: *Sedum spectabile* 'Meteor'

left: *Stachys byzantina*

below left: *Digitalis purpurea*
'Excelsior hybrids'

below right: *Alcea rosea*

Botanical Name Common Name	Color	Height Spacing	Sun/ Shade	
Scabiosa caucasica Scabiosa	White, lavender	18-30" *1-2'*	○	
Sedum spectabile Showy stonecrop	Pink, red	18-24" *18-24"*	○ ◐	
Solidago hybrids Goldenrod hybrids	Light to deep yellow	18-36" *12-18"*	○ ◐	
Stachys byzantina Lamb's-ears	Lavender	12-18" *12"*	○	
Veronica spicata Speedwell	White, pink, blue	12-18" *12"*	○ ◐	
Yucca filamentosa Adam's needle	White	4-6' *2-3'*	○	
BIENNIALS				
Alcea rosea Hollyhock	White, pink, red, yellow, purple	5-9' *3'*	○	
Campanula medium Canterbury bells	White, pink, blue, lilac	2' *12"*	○	
Daucus carota Queen Anne's lace	White	3-4' *12"*	○	
Dianthus barbatus Sweet William	Pink, rose, red, salmon	8-18" *9"*	○	
Digitalis purpurea Foxglove	Varied	1-2' *12"*	○ ◐	
Myosotis 'Blue Ball' Forget-me-not	Blue	8" *6"*	◐	
Papaver nudicaule Iceland poppy	White, red, yellow	8-12" *8"*	○	

Microclimate	Planting Time / Bloom Time	Comments
Hardy to Zone 4	Spring *Summer*	Borders, cut flowers; rich, moist, well-drained, alkaline soil; attracts butterflies
Hardy to Zone 4; drought-tolerant	Spring *Late summer - early fall*	Borders, rock gardens; average soil; attracts butterflies; deer-resistant
Very hardy; drought- and seashore-tolerant	Spring *Late summer - fall*	Borders, cut flowers; all well-drained soils; attracts butterflies; deer-resistant
Hardy to Zone 4; intolerant of damaging rains	Spring *Summer*	Edging; velvety gray foliage; rich soils
Hardy; seashore-tolerant	Spring *Summer*	Borders; edging; well-drained soil; tolerates alkaline soil; long-blooming; deer-resistant
Hardy to Zone 4; drought-, heat-, seashore-tolerant	Spring *Summer*	Evergreen; fast-draining soil; plants may not bloom annually
Hardy	Spring *Summer - fall*	Perennial treated as biennial; borders, cottage gardens; moist, well-drained soil; remove unattractive leaves to increase air circulation; for rebloom in fall cut back flower stem to just above ground
Hardy; needs winter protection	Spring or fall *Early summer*	Borders; any rich, well-drained soil; can be transplanted in full flower and removed after bloom
Hardy; seashore-tolerant	Plant or sow in fall *Summer*	Cut flowers; will reseed; may be invasive in Midwest
Hardy; seashore-tolerant	Sow in early summer *Spring*	Borders, cut flowers, containers; fragrant; well-drained, slightly alkaline soil
Hardy; seashore-tolerant	Fall *Summer*	Borders; reseeds; moist soil; tolerates clay soil
Hardy	Sow in fall *Spring*	Woodland and spring gardens; lovely with bulbs; rich, well-drained soil; tolerates moist soils
Hardy	Sow in fall *Spring*	Borders; colorful dainty blossoms; moist, well-drained soil

Peter C. Jones

ROSES

Rosa 'Queen Elizabeth,' grandiflora

Roses are among the most loved and beautiful plants in the garden. Yet many gardeners are afraid to include them for fear they won't grow. But roses have survived many centuries in all climates including the Arctic, so there's bound to be one that's just right for your garden.

Gardeners everywhere are discovering that roses are among the most elegant, yet versatile plants in the garden. In colors from white to deep burgundy, yellow and orange, roses come in all shapes and sizes. Some climb while others crawl; some grow stiff and upright while others sprawl. Roses can be single or double, have blossoms 4" across or as tiny as a thimble. Some grow alone on straight stems while others grow in full, showy clusters. There are hardy roses, roses that tolerate shade, and roses that bloom all summer long. For years of immeasurable pleasure, select the right rose for your garden.

flat · rounded

cupped · rosette

pointed · quartered

urn-shaped · pompom

Rose flower shapes: Rose blossoms are either single with four to seven petals; semidouble with eight to fourteen petals; double with fifteen to thirty petals or fully double with over thirty petals. While single roses may be either flat or cupped; the many-petaled roses come in a variety of shapes.

Plant a rose beside a walk, around a terrace or beneath a window where its lovely fragrance will ride the wind, delighting everyone in its path. Grow roses as standards (tree roses) to bring the fragrance up to nose level or give height to the garden. Train climbing roses up pillars and along chains, over arbors and trellises; let them soften the hard lines of a fence or sprawl over a wall. Add a touch of romance to an orchard by encouraging a rose to climb up into the gnarled branches of an old apple tree. Use groundcover roses in mass plantings and to cover a slope. Plant shrub roses close together to form an impenetrable hedge. Plan a formal rose garden or find a spot for them with your perennials. Everyone loves a bouquet of roses, and as potpourri, rose petals are hard to beat.

Grow Roses:

- In formal beds and borders
- In informal mass plantings
- To climb over walls, fences and arbors
- To edge a path
- As flowering hedges
- As flowering groundcovers
- As accents in the perennial or shrub border
- In your cutting garden
- In pots and planters

ROSE ROUNDUP
Roses are categorized into three basic groups: Species, Old and Modern. Climbers span all three.

Species Roses
The original roses, found in the wild, are the hardiest roses, tolerant of poor soil and shade; some are resistant to salt spray, pollution and disease. Species roses require very little care and can grow like wildfire.

SPECIES ROSES Found growing naturally, these spring bloom-ing roses have fragrant, simple flowers that look like apple blossoms. They require little care to succeed. *Rosa blanda*, commonly known as the Labrador Rose, survives harsh winters without any protection provided by man. A midpink single rose, it flowers early, prospers in poor soils and shade. If you have a wooded setting, this rose is for you! The foliage of *Rosa eglanteria* (hardy to Zone 4) has a lovely apple-and-spice fra-grance. *Rosa canina* is fragrant with blue-green foliage and is tolerant of alkaline soils. *(Up to 6' high)*

RUGOSA ROSES Indisputably the hardiest (most to Zone 3) and most successful in cold, difficult conditions. Grown on their own roots, these large, dense, fragrant shrubs with handsome crinkled foliage withstand the abuses of wind and salt beautiful-ly. Ranging in color from white to red and pink, with large hips and colorful fall color, rugosas put on a show over a long peri-od. *Rosa rugosa*, with its mauve pink blossoms, is one of the few species roses with repeat bloom. *Rosa rugosa* 'Alba' has showy orange hips, crinkled foliage and fragrant white blossoms.

Today there are many notable hybrid rugosas. 'Hansa,' with fragrant, double magenta blooms is a very hardy and vigorous favorite. 'Henry Hudson,' a semidouble white Explorer Rose, is a fine free-flowering low shrub hardy to Zone 3. 'Blanc Double de Coubert,' a vigorous, double white is disease resis-tant, also hardy to Zone 3, but definitely does not like wet feet. *(Up to 8' high)*

HINT: If you have very sandy soil, try rugosa roses.

Old Roses

Defined as roses in existence prior to the 1867 recognition of hybrid tea roses. Often very fragrant, these decorative roses may bring back memories of your grandmother's garden. Look for a full burst of bloom in the late spring.

ALBA ROSES Not all albas are white! Hardy to Zone 4, they have healthy blue-green foliage and pink to white nonrecurrent blooms, usually opening in July in Zones 4 and 5. Albas range from the full cabbage type to almost single. In damp climates, the double blossoms of 'Maiden's Blush' can rot on the bush. *Rosa* x *alba semi-plena* with its semidouble blooms, long arch-ing canes and red hips is wonderfully fragrant. 'Konigin von Danemark' with its quartered blooms is darker pink than most albas. *(Up to 5' high)*

HINT: Do not deadhead albas or rugosas; most set red hips.

DAMASK ROSES Very old garden roses with extraordinary fra-grance. Most are strong growers with double blooms in colors from crimson to white. Blossoms are loose and open, born in bunches, but usually nonrecurrent. Although some catalogs list them as hardy to Zone 4, in my experience they won't thrive below Zone 5. The many-petaled 'Madame Hardy' is an exquis-ite white with a distinctive, green eye. 'Leda' has crimson-edged, double white blossoms on a neat, small bush. *(Up to 4' high)*

GALLICA ROSES The oldest of the cultivated roses, most have an old-fashioned, many-petaled bloom. Gallicas are winter hardy to Zone 4, very fragrant and available in a palette of crimsons, lavender, mauve and purple. They tolerate poor and sandy soils and form a bushy, compact shrub. Most are one-time bloomers. The many-petaled varieties such as 'Belle de Crecy' prefer drier weather to open properly. Rich violet pink, 'Alexandre Laquemont' has a remarkable, old rose scent. 'Charles de Mills,' one of the most vigorous gallicas, flourishes in Zone 5. Its large, double and quartered blooms are a won-derful mix of deep crimson, purple and mauve. *(Up to 4' high)*

HINT: Old roses are more tolerant of alkaline soil.

Modern Roses

The fascination with modern roses began in 1867 with the introduction of 'La France,' which is accepted as the first hybrid tea. It was the first rose to combine the large flowers of hybrid perpetuals with the long stems, fragrance and everblooming habit of the tea rose. Elegant in the formal garden and excellent as a cut flower, it was a hybridizer's dream come true and marked the beginning of the craze for new roses. However, modern roses in general, and hybrid tea roses in particular, do require more care than most other roses.

HYBRID TEA ROSES   The excellent cut flowers we're all familiar with from the florist's, they generally have one bloom per long stem and come in a wide range of colors. Narrow and upright in habit, hybrid tea roses are repeat flowering, but most have little fragrance. Not recommended in Zone 3, most are hardy to Zone 4 when given careful winter protection. 'Olympiad,' a vigorous growing red, is disease resistant while the ivory 'Elina' is one of the more hardy. Coral red 'Fragrant Cloud' is very fragrant and easy to grow. *(Up to 4' high)*

GRANDIFLORAS   Grandifloras have blooms similar to hybrid teas, but in clusters. The buds open quickly and bloom repeatedly, making them a good choice for mass plantings. 'Aquarius' produces an abundance of light pink blossoms and is disease resistant. 'Queen Elizabeth,' a delicate pink, deserves a place in any rose garden. 'Sonia,' with its coral pink, fragrant blooms and long stems, is excellent for cutting. Grandifloras are hardy to Zone 4 with careful winter protection. *(Up to 6' high)*

FLORIBUNDAS   Hardy to Zone 4, floribundas come in shades from white and yellow to pink and carmine. Free-flowering with multiple blooms per stem, a mass of floribundas adds a big splash of color to the garden. The pink, gold and apricot 'Little Darling' is a vigorous, spreading rose with a spicy fragrance. 'Europeana' is an excellent ruby red. The white-blossomed 'Iceberg' is very hardy and tolerates cool summers. Floribundas need winter protection in Zones 4 and 5. *(Up to 4' high)*

POLYANTHAS   Hardy to Zone 4 and low-growing, polyanthas produce profuse clusters of small flowers. Many bloom continuously! 'The Fairy,' a hardy pink polyantha, is resistant to blackspot and excellent for bedding and low hedges. 'Marie Pavie' is a stunning yet very hardy white polyantha with pale pink centers and yellow stamens. *(Up to 2' high)*

MINIATURE ROSES   Hardy to Zone 5 with protection, miniature roses are like hybrid teas and floribundas in every way but size! Growing only 10" to 24" high, there are shrub types as well as climbers, trailers and cascading miniatures. They are perfect for planting in containers and as low hedges in the garden. 'Beauty Secret,' a medium red, is disease resistant and tolerates cool summers. 'Childs Play' produces a continuous display of white sprays. Plant 'Red Cascade' in a hanging basket for a steady stream of crimson flowers. *(Up to 18" high)*

Shrub Roses

Modern shrub roses are easily grown tall shrubs and groundcovers developed for hardiness, disease resistance and low maintenance. Many do exceptionally well in Zones 4 and 5, often blooming until Halloween. Unlike hybrid tea roses, which are grown primarily for the flower, modern shrub roses are grown for the masses of continuous color and overall beauty of the bush. They are often referred to as landscape roses.

SHRUB ROSES   Growing naturally broad and high, shrub roses create a dramatic effect in the landscape, and are a welcome addition to the mixed border. The very popular David Austin English Roses, known for their old-fashioned shapes and lovely fragrances, are generally more successful in warmer climates, but the light yellow 'Windrush' is hardy to Zone 4. 'Morden Centennial,' a Canadian rose with lightly fragrant, rose-pink blooms, will survive cold winters even when it dies back to the

ground. The bright red 'Prairie Fire' was raised in Minnesota and is easy to grow. 'Stanwell Perpetual' (hardy to Zone 3) is a sprawling, vigorous shrub growing 5' x 4'. With it's long season of fragrant, soft-pink, double blossoms, tolerance of poor soils and shade, it makes a perfect hedge in an informal setting. *(Up to 6' high)*

GROUNDCOVER ROSES Groundcover roses expand wide and low. They are an excellent choice for adding low masses of color to the garden. In Zones 4 and 5, Meilland's 'Alba Meidiland' blooms profusely, is weed smothering and self-cleaning (does not need deadheading!). 'Red Meidiland' has a mounding habit and is perfect on slopes. *(Up to 2 1/2' high)*

Climbing Roses

Climbing roses don't truly climb! Having no tendrils, they need our help to train them up walls and over supports. These long caned roses are categorized as either climbing or rambling, depending on the flexibility of their canes.

CLIMBING ROSES Climbing roses are long, stiff caned roses of various parentage. Both single and clustered, most climbers bloom more than once a season. The best climbers for Zones 3, 4 and 5 are two Explorer Roses: 'William Baffin' (hardy to Zone 2), a clear pink that blooms into November, and 'John Cabot,' a rich red double with a strong initial bloom followed by sporadic blossoms. The very hardy 'Henry Kelsey' produces clusters of deep red blooms with yellow stamens. *(Up to 15' high)*

RAMBLING ROSES Most often one-time bloomers, ramblers are commonly distinguished from climbers by their flexible canes, which are ideal for training horizontally on ropes and chains. Ramblers produce smaller leaves than climbers, and the blossoms are usually borne in clusters. 'Seven Sisters,' an old, soft pink rambler, hardy to Zone 4, tolerates poor soils and partial sun, yet blooms late in the summer. Hardy to

Zones 4 and 5, 'Veilchenblau' produces clusters of small, violet blooms. *(Up to 15' high)*

HINT: Don't use wood preservatives near roses.

ROSES IN YOUR MICROCLIMATE

Roses grown in ideal conditions will bring the gardener years of joy, while roses in less favorable conditions will require much more time and energy to succeed. An understanding of roses in your microclimate will help reduce the amount of maintenance required for a beautiful display.

TEMPERATURE

The climate in Zones 3, 4 and 5 affects the success of roses in two ways: temperatures plummeting as low as -40° Fahrenheit can cause winterkill during dormancy, and late frosts after the start of early growth can cause severe dieback. In addition, the growing season can be as short as 165 days. But the cold climate has at least one advantage: cool temperatures allow the rose's perfume to develop fully.

When selecting roses for a successful cold zone garden, look for the following:

- Cold-hardiness to withstand the harsh winters.
- Resistance to mildew to make up for the lack of drying, sunny days.
- Strong growth to compensate for the short growing season.

Some of the early-blooming, old roses often do very well in cold zones. Unfortunately, however, in the coldest areas you must avoid the beautiful, very full roses with closely rolled petals because they require warm, dry weather to open properly. But you can take advantage of single roses that open too quickly in warm zones; they open perfectly in cooler weather. All roses in Zones 3, 4 and 5 must be carefully

winterized to protect them from freezing soils and winter winds. (See "Winterizing" in this chapter.)

Most roses prefer warm weather, as warm temperatures encourage blooming. With hybrid tea roses, the warmer the climate, the bigger the blooms. In all zones, intense heat can stress your roses. Water your roses well during dry spells.

SUN/SHADE

For roses, the type of sunlight is just as important as the amount. Most roses require at least six hours of sunlight a day to produce healthy plants with good blooms, although there are a few that tolerate some shade, including the floribunda 'Gruss an Aachen.' Roses flourish in the morning sun; it is cooler and dries the nighttime dew off the leaves, discouraging pests and disease.

WATER

Roses have deep roots. Water thoroughly so water penetrates down through the soil to the entire root system. Give roses at least 1" of water per week. If you use overhead sprinklers, early morning watering is best; it gives the leaves time to dry off before nightfall. Soaker hoses and water breakers can be used to water the soil but not the foliage. For large rose gardens consider installing an irrigation system. Drip systems are best because they keep the leaves dry. If you prefer spray heads, install the heads at a low level.

Don't be surprised if growth and blooming slow down in a drought; the rose is just reserving its supplies. Continue to water your roses until the ground freezes.

HUMIDITY

Careful consideration of the humidity in your microclimate can make or break your rose garden. High levels of humidity can lead to disease and the rotting of buds. If your garden receives damp ocean winds or coastal fog, put rugosa roses, which open quickly and are resistant to blackspot and mildew, at the top of your list. In all microclimates be sure your rose garden has good air circulation so moisture won't settle on the leaves.

SOIL

Roses can grow in most soils, but the ideal soil for roses is a moist, well-balanced garden loam rich in organic matter. Organic matter is critical to the success of your roses. If you have heavy clay or sandy soils, amend the soil well with lots of compost and well-rotted manure. Although roses aren't particular about pH, they do prefer slightly acid soils with a pH of 6.0 to 6.6. And although they prefer moist soil, it must be well-drained. They cannot tolerate waterlogged soils.

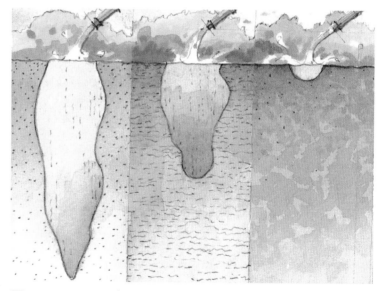

Water penetrates soil at varying rates depending on its composition. Water drains quickly through sandy soil; loam retains water for roots to absorb at their leisure; heavy clay soil is so dense that only a drenching rain will fully penetrate to deep roots.

Recipe For Ideal Soil In The Rose Garden

60 percent sandy topsoil
30 percent leaf mold
10 percent peat moss

Rose-sick Soil

A rose bed suffers from "rose sickness" when young plants added to it grow less vigorously than those previously growing in the same place. Many believe the cause to be soil depletion and possibly disease. Others think the soil structure breaks down over time. If your home has an existing rose garden, replace the soil in the planting holes prior to adding new roses. But if you are planting a lot of new rose bushes, it might be best to change the location of the bed altogether.

PLANNING THE ROSE GARDEN

When planning the rose garden match the natural habit of the rose to the type of garden. Hybrid teas, floribundas, polyanthas and climbing roses, for instance, fit wonderfully into a formal setting. Large, sprawling roses like species roses are best reserved for informal shrub plantings.

Form the enclosure with a low fence, trellis or posts with chains on which to grow climbing roses. Lay the beds out in a formal, geometric design. Beds that are 5' wide accommodate four rows of hybrid teas set 18" apart with easy access for maintenance. Add accents of evergreen topiary, rose standards or arches to give the garden height.

Spacing

Each type of rose has its own natural growth habits, which determine the spacing between plants. In microclimates with high humidity, space the bushes 6" further apart to allow for better air circulation, which will reduce the incidence of mildew. But in general, space as follows:

Hybrid teas, Floribundas, Grandifloras: 18"-24" apart
Large shrubs: 4'-6' apart
Climbing roses: 6' apart
Miniature Roses: 1' apart
Hedges: Large shrub roses: 3'-4' apart in a line; modern bush roses: 18"-24" on center, in two staggered rows.

Rose Companions

Some of my favorite companions in the rose garden include:

Artemisia	*Campanula* (bellflower)
Digitalis (foxglove)	*Gypsophila* (baby's breath)
Iris	*Lavandula* (lavender)
Nepeta x *faassenii* (catmint)	*Paeonia* (peony)

PLANNING AT A GLANCE

Consider the following when you select your roses:

- Microclimate
- Soil
- Water supply
- Disease resistance
- Natural habit of roses: compact, upright, sprawling or climbing
- Height and width
- Period of bloom: one-time, repeat or everblooming
- Color of blooms and leaves
- Significance of rose hips
- Roses that hold their foliage
- Roses that tolerate late spring frosts
- In areas with cool summers, fast-opening single roses with fewer, loosely rolled petals
- In damp microclimates, quick-opening roses with fewer petals, and roses resistant to blackspot and mildew
- Amount of maintenance required
- Companion plants

BED PREPARATION

Good drainage and deep, rich soil are essential in the rose garden. Prepare the beds to a depth of 2' by single or double digging (see "Digging the Bed," p.33). If the soil is waterlogged, install the necessary drainage beneath the bed or find another sunny site.

BUYING ROSES

Your goal when buying roses is to buy strong, healthy plants, appropriate for your climate. Roses are grown either on their own roots or are grafted onto a different root stock (the joint is known as a bud union). They are sold either bare-root (dormant, with no soil around the roots) or planted in containers.

Bare-root Roses

Mail-order catalogs provide a large selection of bare-root roses, both old and new. Buy from a reputable supplier known to ship well-packed roses with at least three canes and roots that are in proportion to the top growth. See "Sources" for a list of suppliers and remember to place your order early as supplies are limited. Bare-root roses are usually shipped at the appropriate planting time for your area, and should be planted immediately. If this isn't possible, never leave them in the package; heel them into the garden or store them in a cool, dark place.

Don't be concerned if the roses are coming from another part of the country, such as Maine. If the rose you have selected is compatible with your conditions, it will settle right in, often more quickly than container-grown plants.

Container Roses

Your local nursery may have a good selection of roses in containers. Nurseries get a head start by potting up bare-root roses in midwinter for sale in the spring. Container-grown roses are graded as follows:

NUMBER 1 The best quality with sound roots and three or four vigorous canes.
NUMBER 1-1/2 Fewer canes and intermediate quality.
NUMBER 2 The least developed, will need more care to establish.

For plants with the best root development, buy roses growing in at least a two-gallon, or preferably a five-gallon, container. Don't be surprised if your container-grown roses take longer to become established in your garden. Their roots have been confined and may not spread out into the surrounding soil as quickly as bare-root plants. Container-grown roses can be planted any time the ground isn't frozen.

When buying container-grown roses, look for:
- "All American Rose Selections."
- Number 1 container-grown plants.
- Healthy, vigorous plants with three to five canes.
- Roses that are pest free.
- Climbers with vigorous canes at least 1' high.
- Plants with developed root systems in two- or preferably five-gallon containers; the bigger, the better!

and avoid:
- Plants with yellow leaves or blackspot.
- Plants that are potbound. (Check to see if roots are growing out of the bottom of the pot.)

PLANTING

Planting your roses with care will give them the strength they need to survive in your climate. The best times to plant in Zones 3, 4 and 5 are April and May. Spring planting allows roses to develop a strong root structure over the summer months. Cloudy days are ideal for planting; the sun will not have an opportunity to dry out the exposed roots.

Prior To Planting

For bare-root roses, soak the roots in a bucket of muddy water for a few hours to make them less brittle and more pliable. The mud will adhere to the roots and protect them from drying out. Prune off any damaged or broken roots or canes.

> *HINT: Never plant a dried-out rose bush. Bury the entire bush, canes and all, for several days to resuscitate the canes before planting.*

The Planting Hole

Dig each hole 18"-24" deep and 18" wide. If you have a drainage problem, dig up to 6" deeper to accommodate gravel and perforated pipe. Mix a spade of compost and a spade of well-rotted manure into the hole and add the soil you've set aside.

For bare-root roses, make a mound with your soil mix in the bottom of the hole. Gently fan the roots over it in a natural pattern.

For container roses, first prune off any blooms or buds to channel all the plant's energy into establishing new roots, then gently remove the plant, retaining as much of the soil around the roots as possible and place in the hole without delay.

> *HINT: Some gardeners assure me that placing a medium-size fish head in the bottom of the hole and covering it with an inch of soil will give a rose an extra boost!*

The Depth

Roses on their own roots should be planted at the depth that they were grown in the nursery or with the roots beginning 2" below the surface. The amount of freezing weather you can expect determines the depth of grafted roses. In Zones 3, 4, and 5, position the bud union 3"-4" below the surface to protect it from freeze-thaw cycles. Dig the hole deeper if necessary to accommodate the extra depth.

In your cold zone, plant budded roses with the bud union 4" deeper for extra winter protection. Plant roses grown on their own roots at the same depth as they were growing in the container.

The Coverup

Hold the rose in place and gradually fill the hole with soil mix. Work the soil around the roots and gently tamp it to eliminate any air pockets. Water the bush in thoroughly. If the soil has compacted further, add more of your soil mix until it's level with the surrounding grade. Mound mulch high around the canes to prevent them from drying out in the sun and spring winds (see "Winterizing"). Gradually break down the mound as new growth begins to appear.

MULCH

Use a light mulch that breaks down readily such as well-rotted manure, shredded leaf mold, or licorice root. Avoid bark chips, which cause water to splash onto the leaves, or buckwheat or other seed hulls, which decompose slowly.

FERTILIZING

Do not fertilize roses when you first plant them. Wait for the first blooming, then apply monthly. If you plant with well-aged manure, fertilize after the second flush. For established roses, apply granular 10-6-4 fertilizer when first growth begins in spring, after the first blooming period, then monthly until August. Stop fertilizing in August; roses need a chance to harden off before they face the winter.

Epsom salts contain magnesium, which promotes healthy foliage, roots and canes and should be used in addition to your regular fertilizer. Using a hand fork, work two tablespoons into the soil around the base of each plant after the first blooming and a month before your first frost date.

Foliar feeding is liquid fertilizer that is sprayed on the leaves; it gives roses an extra push, particularly roses in planters. Applied in addition to granular fertilizer, it is easily absorbed by the leaves, giving them good color and encouraging flowering. Use liquid seaweed or fish emulsion and spray it on your roses every ten days. If leaves look light with dark veins, your rose is most likely suffering from iron deficiency. Apply a foliar feeding of chelated iron.

HINT: Manure tea (one part manure to five parts water) is also an excellent fertilizer for roses.

TRAINING CLIMBING ROSES

Climbing roses are perfect for adorning bare walls and fences. Because climbers bloom on laterals, it is important to train the canes in a horizontal position to encourage the development of laterals. The more laterals, the more blooms. And on windy sites, it's a good idea to tie off leggy canes so they won't snap in the wind. Use jute or cotton string to attach climbers and ramblers to wires or structures.

Since roses do not have tendrils with which to grab hold, it is necessary to provide support on vertical surfaces with wires and masonry hooks. Space horizontal wires 15"-18" apart and 3" from the surface to allow for air circulation between the wall and the plant. If you are growing climbing roses against a painted fence or wall, attach galvanized wire mesh over the surface and train roses on mesh. When it comes time to repaint, just fold the wire down.

If you are training roses against a house, note the drip line of the eaves. Plant roses about 18" out to avoid the dry area beneath the eaves and the water draining off the eaves. Dig an extra wide hole for the rose, position it at a 45° angle leaning toward the wall with its roots aiming out toward the moist soil. Spread climbers out in a fan shape so the canes are horizontal.

As ramblers have more flexible canes than climbers, they are your best choice for training on arches, pillars or chains. At the beginning of the growing season, remove all but two or three healthy canes and wrap them around the structure. In this way you gain the maximum horizontal exposure.

DISBUDDING

Hybrid teas often produce two or more buds per stem. If you prefer one bloom at the end of the stem, the side buds should be removed. This is called "disbudding." Disbudding eliminates the competition, allowing the single bloom to flourish.

Disbud your roses when the secondary buds are large enough to hold between two fingers and break off. To disbud, grasp the bud and pull it down and sideways so it snaps off close to the stem. Do not use your finger nails as you will leave a stub behind. Be sure to disbud early! You want all the energy to go to the chosen bloom.

However, if color in the garden is your goal you may prefer not to disbud thus creating a longer season rich with blooms.

PRUNING

There's a great stigma surrounding the pruning of roses. Don't let it scare you. Pruning isn't a case of life or death for you or your roses. You are simply pruning them to improve their performance, appearance, longevity and hardiness.

Don't prune bushes back to the ground. This will waste all the nourishment stored in the canes, forcing the plants to draw on reserves in the roots to support new growth. The reserves in the roots are best used to sustain the canes until the leaves can take over.

Pruning Goals

- To remove dead and diseased wood. (Injured wood is dark colored.)
- To remove unproductive, weak and twiggy growth. Cut the oldest, least productive canes back to the base of the plant.
- To remove all crossing canes.
- To open up the center of the bush to improve air circulation. (Make sure all growth buds are facing away from the center.)
- To shape bush to give it a pleasing and symmetrical appearance.
- To encourage repeat bloom.
- To remove suckers, which may grow up at the base of grafted roses.

Pruning Tools

BYPASS PRUNERS For canes up to 1/2" in diameter.
LOPPERS For canes 1" to 2" in diameter.
SMALL HAND SAW For any canes over 2".

HINT: Even with daily pruning, a wide-growing rose will never look well in a small space.

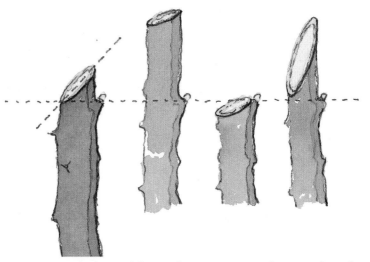

Pruning roses: (Left to right) A perfect cut, a cut too far away from the bud, a cut too close to the bud, too sharply angled a cut.

PRUNING BUSH ROSES
Where To Cut

Cut at a 45° angle 1/4" above a healthy, outward-facing growth bud (to direct new growth away from the center of the plant). Be sure not to cut too close to the bud, which could dry the bud out from exposure, or too far away, which would leave an expanse of dead wood above the bud.

When To Prune

Pruning begins in the spring, when the leaf buds have begun to swell but not grow. Some gardeners adhere to the rule of thumb: "Prune when the forsythia is in bloom," but this is not true of all roses. To determine when to prune, look for your roses in the following list:

SPECIES ROSES Most species roses flower on the second year's growth, so prune to remove dead and diseased wood, thin out crowded stems or to rejuvenate overgrown plants.

RUGOSA ROSES Don't prune for the first three years to allow the bush to establish a basic framework, then prune as for the species roses or to shape the plant.

GALLICAS, DAMASKS, ALBAS Give these roses a few years of unpruned growth to create a substantial, shapely plant. During these first years remove only dead, diseased or crowded canes. Once established, some canes may be removed after flowering, to be replaced by new growing canes. Deadhead after flowering. Once new canes reach mature length, shape them by trimming back if necessary.

MODERN SHRUB ROSES Prune as for rugosa roses. Keep deadheaded as many will rebloom if this is done.

HYBRID TEA ROSES, GRANDIFLORAS, FLORIBUNDAS, POLYANTHAS, MINIATURES Prune in early spring to remove dead, diseased or crossing canes and to shape the plant. First, remove all dead wood. After severe winters, this can be substantial, leaving only 4"-8" canes, but typically you can expect 12" canes after pruning, 6" on miniatures. During mild winters, very little damage may occur, allowing for taller plants if desired. Prune off discolored wood, twiggy growth and canes that rub against each other. Remember you want to keep the center of the rose bush open to allow better air circulation and sun penetration to help reduce disease and promote better growth. Floribundas, polyanthas and miniatures typically have twiggy growth that should only be removed if crowding the center.

PRUNING CLIMBING ROSES

Climbing roses bloom on laterals, which are small branches growing off the main canes. Prune climbing roses to promote development of the laterals, to increase bloom and to control growth.

Pruning climbers: Keep climbers vigorous by removing about one-third of the old canes, crossing, weak, dead or diseased canes. Shorten tips of the laterals by two-thirds.

What To Cut

Prevent climbing roses from becoming too dense by removing about one-third of the old canes. To encourage more bloom on repeat-blooming climbers, shorten the tips of the laterals by two-thirds after they have flowered. (Prune as on shrub roses at 45° angle 1/4" above the bud.) Cut back the laterals of ramblers and one-time bloomers after they bloom and only if they don't produce rose hips.

When To Prune

To rejuvenate climbers, prune them in the early spring at the beginning of the growing season, before the leaves hide the branching habit. Since climbers bloom on year-old wood, flowers will be sacrificed, but often this is necessary. Continue to cut back the laterals of everblooming climbers between

periods of bloom throughout the summer. Prune ramblers after they have bloomed.

CUT FLOWERS

Roses are among everyone's favorite cut flowers. Cut them early in the morning while the petals are still turgid and place them immediately in water. Remember that when you pick a rose, you are in fact pruning the bush.

Cut the stem 1/4" above an outward-facing leaf with five leaflets, leaving at least two leaf buds between the cut and where the branch joins the main cane.

Cutting Hybrid Teas

Conserve the foliage on your hybrid teas. Cut only as much stem as you will need and try not to cut too many long-stemmed flowers. You will leave the bush with too little foliage to sustain good growth. The fewer blooms cut the first year, the healthier the bush.

Prolonging The Life Of Cut Roses

Here are several methods from which to select:
- Hold the stems in boiling water for a minute, then plunge them in a deep container of cold water for several hours before arranging.
- Hammer the ends of the stems and place in warm water.
- Give freshly picked roses a clean cut. Burn the tip of the stem. Plunge the stem into a solution of one tablespoon of alum to one quart of water.
- To salvage drooping blooms, cut stems in deep warm water. This will force the air bubbles out of the stem.

DEADHEADING

"Deadheading" is the removal of flowers that have faded. On repeat bloomers, remove all faded roses before the petals have fallen. (See "Where To Cut.") This will channel all energy to pro-ducing new blossoms, not seed. Only let rose hips develop on one-time bloomers and on modern roses at the end of the season so that they will harden off — the slowing down of their metabolism to prepare them for the cold of fall and winter.

WINTERIZING

Protect your roses from low temperatures and damaging freeze-thaw cycles with good winterizing. Begin just before the surface soil starts to freeze after the first heavy frost in the fall. This will probably be around Halloween in Zones 3 and 4, Thanksgiving in Zone 5. Start by removing all the leaves that have fallen around your plants. Then form a mound of soil (from a source other than the rose bed) or compost with some aged manure mixed in or a mix of all three 10"-12" high around their crowns. Be sure you use more soil than organic matter, which holds moisture and could cause rot at the base of the canes. As the ground begins to freeze the soil mound will "knit" with the surface soil creating greater insulation. In Zone 3 also cover the beds with a layer of loose mulch that will not hold moisture such as salt hay, straw or evergreen boughs. Place the loose mulch around the canes of more tender roses to give them extra protection from winter winds and fluctuating temperatures.

In the extremely cold microclimates of North Dakota, Iowa and Minnesota, select only the hardiest roses and take extra precautions before winter. You may find it necessary to enclose your roses in well-vented boxes. Remember, no amount of winterizing will protect a weak rose; a healthy plant is the best defense against a cold winter.

Winterizing Climbing Roses

Climbing roses can be winterized just like hybrid tea roses or they can be swaddled in straw, filling your garden with straw men to stand guard over your garden on bleak winter days. But not all climbing roses must be protected from harsh winter conditions; look for naturally hardy roses such as 'William Baffin.'

Roses

Best Bets For Your Garden

above left: Rosa eglanteria

above right: Rosa 'Hansa,' hybrid rugosa

left: Rosa 'Henry Hudson,' hybrid rugosa

below left: Rosa 'Madame Hardy,' damask

below right: Rosa 'F. J. Grootendorst,' hybrid rugosa

Botanical Name/ Common Name	Color	Bloom	Size	
SPECIES				
Rosa blanda	Medium pink	Single	5 x 5'	
Rosa canina	Light pink	Single	8 x 8'	
Rosa eglanteria	Medium pink	Single	9 x 5'	
Rosa glauca	Medium pink	Single	6 x 5'	
RUGOSAS				
Rosa rugosa 'Alba'	White	Single	6 x 6'	
'Blanc Double de Coubert'	White	Semidouble	5 x 4'	
'Hansa'	Mauve	Large double	5 x 4'	
'Henry Hudson'	White	Double	3 x 4'	
'F. J. Grootendorst'	Red	Small double	6 x 5'	
'Magnifica'	Purple-crimson	Double	4 x 5'	
GALLICAS				
'Belle de Crecy'	Deep pink	Quartered double	4 x 3'	
'Charles de Mills'	Deep crimson, purple	Quartered double	5 x 4'	
Rosa mundi	Pale pink striped w/ crimson	Semidouble	3 x 3'	
DAMASKS				
'Ispanan'	Soft pink	Double	4 x 3'	
'Leda'	White edged w/ crimson	Double	3 x 3'	
'Madame Hardy'	White w/ green eye	Double	5 x 4'	
ALBAS				
x *alba semi-plena*	White	Single	6 x 5'	
'Celestial'	Clear pink	Double	6 x 4'	

Microclimate	Bloom Time	Comments
Very hardy; shade-tolerant	Late spring; no repeat	Informal screen; good choice for woodland sites; tolerates poor soils
Very hardy	Early summer; no repeat	Informal screen; blue-green foliage; excellent hips; fragrant; tolerates alkaline soil
Hardy to Zone 4	Early summer; no repeat	Informal screen; lovely apples-and-spice scented foliage; fragrant blossoms; long-lasting hips
Hardy to Zone 4	Early summer; no repeat	Informal screen; dark plum foliage and canes; elongated purple-red hips; excellent fall color
Very hardy; seashore-tolerant	Repeats	Hedge, screen, mass plantings; handsome crinkled foliage; fragrant; large orange hips
Hardy to Zone 4; seashore-tolerant	Repeats	Hedge, screen, mass plantings; heavy fragrance; dark green foliage
Hardy to Zone 4; seashore-tolerant	Early summer; fall repeat	Hedge, screen, mass plantings; very fragrant; large hips; vase-shaped habit
Very hardy; seashore-tolerant	Free-flowering	Hedge, screen, mass plantings; dark green foliage; dense shrub
Hardy to Zone 4; seashore-tolerant	Repeats	Hedge, screen, mass plantings; lightly fragrant; clusters of blooms
Very hardy; seashore-tolerant	Repeats	Borders, hedge, mass plantings; prominent stamens; spicy fragrance; good show in fall
Hardy to Zone 4; humidity-intolerant	June; no repeat	Hedge, mixed borders; tolerates poor soils, opens better in drier conditions
Hardy to Zone 4	June; no repeat	Hedge, mixed borders; loose but attractive habit; fragrant
Hardy to Zone 4	June; no repeat	Mixed borders; oldest-known striped rose; fragrant
Hardy	June; no repeat	Borders, cut flowers; longest-blooming damask
Hardy	June; September repeat	Borders; small and tidy
Hardy	June; no repeat	Borders, fences; light lemon fragrance; dark green foliage
Hardy	Early summer	Hedge, back of border; showy yellow stamens; very fragrant; grey-green foliage; good hips
Hardy; shade-tolerant	Early summer	Hedge, back of border; dark green foliage; sweet fragrance; tolerates poor soils

Roses

Best Bets For Your Garden

above left: Rosa 'Fragrant Cloud,' hybrid tea

above right: Rosa 'Tournament of Roses,' grandiflora

left: Rosa 'Iceberg,' floribunda

below left: Rosa 'Europeana,' floribunda

below right: Rosa 'The Fairy,' polyantha

Botanical Name/ Common Name	Color	Bloom	Size	
'Konigin von Danemark'	Rose pink	Quartered	5 x 4'	
'Maidens Blush'	Clear blush	Loosely double	5 x 4'	
HYBRID TEAS				
'Elina'	Ivory	Double	Medium	
'Fragrant Cloud'	Coral red	Large, double	Medium	
'Swarthmore'	Deep pink	Large	Tall	
GRANDIFLORAS				
'Aquarius'	Light pink	Small	Medium	
'Queen Elizabeth'	Clear pink	Large, flat	Medium	
'Sonia'	Coral pink	Medium, full	Medium	
'Tournament of Roses'	Pinky beige	Large	Low	
FLORIBUNDAS				
'Europeana'	Dark red	Medium, double	Low to medium	
'Iceberg'	White	Medium, double	Medium	
'Simplicity'	Midpink	Semidouble, flat	Medium	
POLYANTHAS				
'The Fairy'	Shell pink	Small, double	Low	
'Marie Pavie'	Pale white	Small	Low	
MINIATURES				
'Beauty Secret'	Medium red	Double	Low	
'Child's Play'	White w/ red edge	Semidouble	Low	
'White Mini-wonder'	White	Small	Compact	

Microclimate	Bloom Time	Comments
Hardy	Early summer	Back of border; wonderfully fragrant; darker pink
Hardy to Zones 4 (3*)	Early summer	Back of border; lovely bush; sweet fragrance; deep blue-green foliage; *with protection
Hardy to Zones 5 (4*)	Summer until frost	Cut flowers; upright; vigorous; dark green foliage; *with protection
Hardy to Zone 4	Summer until frost	Cut flowers; heavy tea fragrance; dark, glossy foliage; easy to grow; disease-resistant
Hardy to Zone 5	Summer until frost	Cut flowers; vigorous; dark leathery foliage; always in bloom
Hardy to Zone 4	Summer until frost	Cut flowers; urn shape; prolific; large sprays; light fragrance; thick foliage; disease-resistant
Hardy to Zone 4; tolerates cool summers	Summer until frost	Cut flowers, mass plantings; broad; fragrant; long stems; dark green foliage; all-time favorite; disease-resistant
Hardy to Zone 4	Summer until frost	Cut flowers, mass plantings; upright; light fragrance; long stems; long-lasting blooms
Hardy to Zone 4; tolerates cool summers	Summer until frost	Cut flowers, mass plantings; clusters of blooms; light fragrance; glossy dark green foliage; disease-resistant
Hardy to Zone 4; tolerates cool summers	Summer - fall	Mass plantings, hedges; spreading; light fragrance; clusters of blooms; disease-resistant
Hardy to Zone 4; tolerates cool summers	Summer - fall	Mass plantings, hedges; bushy; fragrant; vigorous and floriferous
Hardy to Zone 4; tolerates cool summers	Summer - fall	Cut flowers, hedges; dense and upright; produces sprays of blooms; floriferous
Hardy to Zone 4	Summer until frost	Borders; mass plantings; spreading; easy to grow; glossy foliage; prolific and continuous bloom; disease-resistant
Hardy to Zone 4	Summer until frost	Hedges, mass plantings; fragrant pink centers with golden stamens; thornless dark foliage
Protected Zone 5; tolerates cool summers	Summer until frost	Edging, mixed borders, containers; bushy and upright; semiglossy foliage; disease-resistant
Protected Zone 5	Summer until frost	Edging, mixed borders, containers; continuous bloom; sprays; dark green foliage; disease-resistant
Protected Zone 5	Summer until frost	Edging, mixed borders, containers; excellent white; bushy; dark foliage

Roses

Best Bets For Your Garden

above left: Rosa 'Bonica,' shrub

above right: Rosa 'Carefree Wonder,' shrub

left: Rosa 'Red Meidiland,' groundcover

below left: Rosa 'William Baffin,' climber

below right: Rosa 'Henry Kelsey,' climber

Botanical Name/ Common Name	Color	Bloom	Size
SHRUB ROSES			
'Bonica'	Light pink	Double	5 x 5'
'Carefree Beauty'	Coral pink	Semidouble	6 x 4'
'Carefree Wonder'	Pink/cream reverse	Semidouble	4 x 3'
'Elveshorn'	Coral pink	Double	3 x 3'
'Morden Centennial'	Rose pink	Large	3.5 x 3.5'
'Prairie Fire'	Bright red	Semidouble	5 x 4'
'Windrush'	Light yellow	Single	3.5 x 3.5'
GROUNDCOVERS			
'Alba Meidiland'	White	Small	2.5 x 6'
'Fuchsia Meidiland'	Mauve pink	Medium, double	2 x 4.5'
'Morden Amorette'	Deep Pink	Double	2 x 2'
'Red Meidiland'	Red	Medium, single	1.5 x 5'
CLIMBERS			
'John Cabot'	Red	Medium, double	Up to 8'
'William Baffin'	Clear pink	Semidouble	Up to 8'
'Henry Kelsey'	Deep red	Semidouble	Up to 8'
'Alchymist'	Yellow w/ peach	Large	10 x 6'
RAMBLERS			
'Seagull'	White	Small	12 x 5'
'Seven Sisters'	Deep to soft pink	Double	8'
'Veilchenblau'	Violet	Small, semidouble	12 x 4'

Microclimate	Bloom Time	Comments
Hardy	Late spring until frost	Borders, screen, mass plantings; clusters; floriferous; showy hips; easy care; disease-resistant
Hardy to Zone 4	Summer until frost	Borders, hedges; fragrant; good hips; easy care; disease-resistant
Hardy to Zone 4	Late spring until frost	Borders, hedges, screen, mass plantings; compact; floriferous; medium-green foliage; orange hips; easy care; disease-resistant
Very hardy	Summer until hard frost	Borders, small gardens; compact; sprays; light fragrance
Very hardy, crown hardy	Summer until frost	Borders, hedges; dark, glossy foliage; will survive cold winter when dies back to ground
Hardy to Zone 4; frost-resistant	Repeats summer until hard frost	Borders, screens, mass plantings; vigorous; disease-resistant; easy care; raised in Minnesota
Hardy to Zone 4	Summer repeats	Borders, screens; English rose; light fragrance
Hardy to Zone 4	Late spring until frost	Mass plantings; mounding; graceful; clusters; light fragrance; easy care; disease-resistant
Hardy to Zone 4; heat-tolerant	Summer until frost	Mass plantings; spreading; large clusters; lush foliage; disease-resistant
Very hardy	Summer until frost	Mass plantings, borders; low and bushy; clusters
Hardy to Zone 4	Summer until frost	Mass plantings; mounding; vigorous; graceful
Very hardy; shade-tolerant	Long bloom early summer; some repeat	Vigorous; fragrant; yellow-green foliage; disease-resistant
Very hardy (Zone 2)	Repeats until late fall	Yellow stamens; bright green foliage; disease-resistant
Very hardy	Consistent repeat	Clusters of blooms; yellow stamens; spicy fragrance; glossy foliage
Hardy to Zone 5	Spring until frost	Screen, cut flowers; fragrant; continuous bloom; glossy foliage; very thorny; tolerates poor soils
Hardy to Zones 5 (4*)	Midsummer	Vigorous; prominent yellow stamens; *with protection
Hardy to Zone 4; tolerates part shade	Late summer; no repeat	Old rambler; large clusters; tolerates poor soil
Hardy to Zones 5 (4*)	Late season; no repeat	Vigorous; clusters of small blooms; *with protection

BULBS, ETC.

Hyacinthus orientalis

When the first snowdrops poke their little heads out of the snow, you have reason to be optimistic. Spring is definitely on the way. Bulbous plants are fleeting beauties that make a short and often spectacular appearance before going dormant for the balance of the year. Given good conditions, spring-flowering bulbs such as *Galanthus nivalis* (snowdrop) and *Narcissus* spp. will multiply quickly, forming impressive sweeps of color. For some gardeners, planting additional spring-flowering bulbs each fall has become a family ritual.

Bulbous plants aren't for springtime alone. There are bulbous plants for every season and nearly every location in the garden. They make a wonderful show in herbaceous borders, en masse in formal beds, naturalized under shrubs and trees or as drifts in the lawn. Create an early spring garden in a warm spot near the house or have a container of bulbs to add a bright splash of color to the porch or terrace. For a cheerful display indoors, force bulbs in the middle of winter.

Bulb cycle: (From left to right) 1) In dormancy the flower bud is surrounded by stored food; 2) roots form and absorb water, which stimulates leaf growth; 3) the flower blooms while through photosynthesis the leaves replenish food supplies in the bulb; 4) after the flower fades, the leaves continue to store food; 5) after the leaves die back, new bulbets form.

WHAT ARE BULBOUS PLANTS?

Bulbous plants gather food from their leaves and store the nutrients in their swollen bases for future plant growth. There are five different categories of bulbous plants:

BULBS (*Tulipa* and *Narcissus*) have an underground stem made up of fleshy scale-like leaves tightly packed around a bud at the center of the bulb. The bulb is attached to a basal plate and has a growing point at its apex, wrapped in a papery covering called a tunic.

CORMS (*Crocus* and *Gladiolus*) are formed from the swollen bases of stems, often covered with fibrous tunics. Unlike bulbs, they have distinct nodes and internodes.

TUBERS (*Caladium* and *Ranunculus)* are swollen stems that function as storage organs.

TUBEROUS ROOTS (*Dahlia*) have thickened horizontal underground roots.

RHIZOMES (*Bergenia cordifolia* and some *Iris*) are tuber-like stems that store food and produce roots along their length.

TEMPERATURE

Temperature is critical to the success of many bulbous plants. Some plants, such as *Narcissus* and *Tulipa*, require a cold period to bloom, while tender plants, such as *Dahlia* and *Gladiolus*, must be protected from freezing temperatures. However, there is a large selection of plants winter hardy to Zones 3, 4 and 5 including *Narcissus*, *Tulipa*, *Galanthus nivalis* (snowdrop), *Crocus*, *Muscari armeni-*

acum (grape hyacinth), and many species of *Lilium*. For additional recommendations for your microclimate, see "Best Bets For Your Garden," p.110.

> *HINT: To outwit early frosts, select only early-blooming varieties of* Dahlia *and* Gladiolus. *Your local garden center should have recommendations.*

SUN/SHADE

Most bulbs prefer full sun to light shade. This isn't a problem for spring-flowering bulbs since they generally bloom and begin to go dormant before the trees have fully leafed out. Plant summer-flowering *Dahlia* and *Gladiolus* in sunny flower beds. Bulbs that grow naturally in the woods, such as *Galanthus nivalis* (snowdrop), *Scilla* spp. and certain kinds of *Lilium* (lily), are perfect for shade locations.

> *HINT: To extend your spring bulb blooming season, use your microclimates! Plant bulbs in protected sun pockets for early bloom.*

SOIL

Well-drained soil is the key to success for all bulbous plants. A bulb planted in a low, overly moist site will most likely rot. If your soil is soggy, try planting your bulbs in raised beds. In clay soil add organic matter, such as compost, to improve drainage. However, in sandy soil, add organic matter to help retain moisture.

Spring- and fall-flowering bulbs can grow in most types of soil. Summer-flowering bulbs are more particular, requiring moderately fertile planting beds with a pH of between 6.0 and 7.2.

WATER

Bulbous plants require regular and deep watering during the growing season up until the leaves die back. However, when bulbs enter dormancy, hold back on the water. (Spring- and fall-flowering bulbs are dormant during the summer; summer-flowering bulbs are dormant in the winter.)

PLANNING AT A GLANCE

When planning your garden, consider the following:
- Microclimate
- Soil
- Water
- Time of bloom
- Color
- Height
- How to disguise the yellowing leaves

BUYING BULBS, ETC.

Bulbs are usually sold dry, but occasionally some, such as *Lilium* (lily), *Dahlia* and *Caladium*, are sold in moistened wood shavings or peat moss. They can be sold individually or prepackaged in mesh through mail-order catalogs and from local nurseries and hardware stores.

Mail order bulbs should come from a reputable bulb importer (see "Sources"). If you're going to pick them up from a local garden center, you will be able to pick and choose. Some tips for selecting healthy bulbs follow:

When buying dry bulbs, look for:
- The largest bulbs: "double-nosed," "top size," "jumbo."
- Bulbs that are firm and dry. As in buying a head of garlic, look for bulbs that feel heavy, not light and dried out.
- Strong growing points.
- Solid basal plates.
- Tunics that are intact.

and avoid:
- Moldy or rotten bulbs.
- Bulbs with signs of disease, insects or mildew.

When buying other bulbous plants, look for:
- Firm, plump tubers.
- Woodland bulbs should be in moist peat or packing materials.
- Stong growing points on corms.

Mail-order bulbs usually arrive at the correct planting time for your zone. But if you're buying bulbs locally, buy them when you are ready to plant. If you do need to store them temporarily, keep them in a cool, dark, dry place.

TIME TO PLANT

Spring-flowering bulbs use the fall to prepare for their early spring performance. They set their roots in the fall opening up the flow of nutrients, which will ensure a spectacular show. To be their best, many spring-flowering bulbs, like *Narcissus* and *Tulipa*, must be exposed to a long period of cold.

Ideally, the soil temperature 6" below the soil should be 60° Fahrenheit before you plant, but it is possible to plant any time before the soil freezes. Pot-grown bulbs can be planted any time during the season.

Spring Bulbs

Plant spring bulbs in September in Zone 3; September to early October in Zones 4 and 5.

Summer Bulbs, Corms And Tubers

DAHLIA Tubers and clumps can be planted one to two weeks before the last frost date. Container plants in leaf should be planted after threat of frost.

GLADIOLUS AND TENDER SUMMER-FLOWERING BULBS Plant *Gladiolus* corms and tender bulbs after all threat of frost.

Fall Bulbs

Plant in late summer to early fall as they become available.

PLANTING DEPTH

The size of the bulb determines its planting depth: the bigger the bulb, the deeper it is planted. A general rule of thumb is to plant at a depth three to five times the height of the bulb. Plant spring-flowering bulbs a little deeper to avoid damage from heaving or the cold. For more specific requirements, see the Bulb Depth Illustration as well as "Best Bets For Your Garden" on p.110.

HINT: For more years of flowers, plant Tulipa 12" deep; for better support, plant tall varieties of Gladiolus a little deeper than the specified 4".

SPACING

Spacing should be two to three times the width of the bulb. See "Best Bets For Your Garden" for specific requirements.

PLANTING BULBS AND CORMS

Bulbs and corms are fleshy and damage easily. Take great care not to bruise them when planting. Use a trowel or garden fork for planting small bulbs; a spade, bulb planter or bulb drill for larger bulbs.

Planting Single Bulbs In Beds

Using a trowel, dig a hole to the required depth that is several times wider than the bulb. Place the bulb growing point up in the hole, cover with soil and gently tamp with your hands.

HINT: For a natural look, avoid planting in rows.

Planting Many Bulbs Together In Beds

In well-prepared beds, dig a hole to the required depth large enough to accommodate the number of bulbs. Smooth the bottom of the hole. Place bulbs right side up and carefully cover with soil. Using the flat end of a rake, gently tamp soil, but do not stamp on them with your feet.

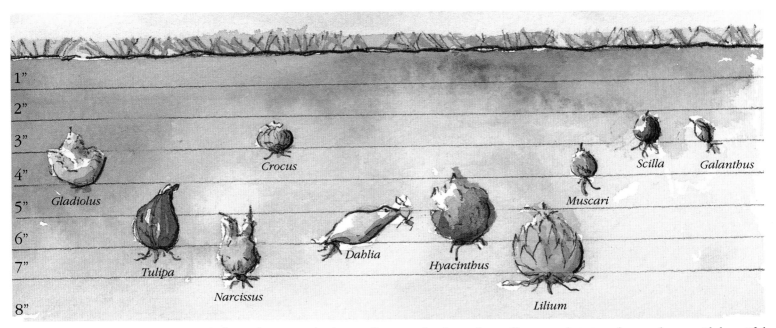

1"
2"
3"
4"
5"
6"
7"
8"

Crocus
Scilla
Galanthus
Muscari
Gladiolus
Tulipa
Narcissus
Dahlia
Hyacinthus
Lilium

Bulb Planting Depth: Planting your bulbs at the correct depth in well-prepared soil gets them off to a good start and rewards you with beautiful blooms at the right time.

Planting Single Large Bulbs In A Grassy Area

Consider using a bulb planter or bulb drill for larger bulbs such as *Narcissus* spp. However, in very rocky soil, try a spade. For one or two bulbs, simply insert the spade at a 90° angle as deep as required for the bulb, then push the handle away from you, opening up the soil. Toss in a little bulb fertilizer, place the bulbs, then release the soil and gently tamp down.

HINT: If you can't tell which side of the bulb is up, plant it sideways. Bulbs will naturally right themselves.

Planting Many Small Bulbs In A Grassy Area

Use an edger to outline the area, then cut a line down the middle. Using a spade, undercut the sod and gently fold back both sides as if you are opening shutters. Work the exposed soil with a hand fork to the required depth, mix in bulb fertilizer, then gently press the bulbs into the loose soil. Score the back of the sod with a hand fork to loosen the roots, then carefully fold it back into place, working the edges together. Tamp to ensure good root contact.

For very small bulbs, use a garden fork to puncture the sod, pour a little bulb fertilizer in the holes and place a bulb in each hole. Fill the holes with soil.

Planting Bulbs In Layers

Dig the hole to the depth required for the largest bulb, place the largest bulb in the hole and cover to the depth for the next bulb. Continue for the desired number of layers.

HINT: If naturalizing bulbs, try to avoid areas with lots of roots, which might compete for water and nutrients.

PLANTING TUBERS

Dig a hole that provides for the required planting depth plus room for the roots. The hole should be wide enough for the roots to comfortably spread out. Fill the hole with soil and gently tamp down.

PLANTING TUBEROUS ROOTS

Dig a hole 6" to 8" deep and a good 9" wide. Plant tuberous roots, such as *Dahlia*, horizontally. Cover with soil. Insert a stake for later support.

PLANTING RHIZOMES

Rhizomes are propagated by division and are planted in the same way as most perennials. To help prevent crown rot, plant new divisions or container plants at a slightly higher depth then they were growing. Be sure to spread out the roots of new divisions. Fill the hole with soil, water well and let settle. Add more soil to the top if needed.

FERTILIZING

Add a covering of compost, manure or 10-10-10 fertilizer in the spring when the leaf tips first appear and again after blooming. Spraying leaves with foliar fertilizer every ten days during the growing season can encourage newly developed offset bulbs to grow to flowering size more quickly.

If your perennial bulbs such as *Narcissus* spp. have stopped blooming or produce more leaves than flowers, they are in need of fertilizer, preferably a bulb fertilizer. If you still can't get them to bloom, dig them up and divide them.

DISBUDDING DAHLIA

Dahlia respond beautifully to disbudding. If your goal is one large, glorious flower for arranging, locate the terminal bud and pinch out the buds to the side. This will channel all the energy to developing a larger terminal blossom. Do not disbud if you prefer a full, colorful display in the garden.

CUT FLOWERS

Use sharp scissors to cut the flowers right down to the base of the stems. Place in water immediately.

Special Hints

NARCISSUS Daffodils or jonquils last longer when "broken," not cut. Grasp the stem at its base where it emerges from the ground and snap it off. In this way the hollow stem is not exposed; the solid stem lasts longer in water. You may find this inconvenient for flowering arranging, as all the stems will be of similar lengths. Arrange in low containers; never place in deep water.

DAHLIA Place stem ends in boiling water, then arrange in tall vase with a little sugar and an aspirin in the water.

GLADIOLUS Place in solution of one tablespoon alcohol to one quart water.

HYACINTHUS Squeeze slippery substance out of stem, then plunge immediately into cold water.

IRIS Burn tip of stem and immediately plunge in cold water.

DEADHEADING

Deadhead flowering bulbs to prevent seed production. This will direct all the plant's energy into food storage instead of the production of seed.

CUTTING BACK THE FOLIAGE

Allow the foliage to turn yellow prior to removing it. The longer it remains, the more nutrients it can direct to the bulbs. If you hate the way it looks, plant quick growing annuals around your bulbs to disguise their fading leaves.

When the foliage has turned yellow, it can be cut off using hand clippers or scissors. Be careful not to damage the bulbs when removing the leaves.

HINT: Never tie or braid the leaves. While it may look neat and stylish, it reduces the surface area thereby reducing the amount of food they produce.

DIVIDING BULBS

Small bulbs can be left to multiply indefinitely, but large bulbs such as *Narcissus*, which have not been naturalized, should be divided every five years or so. Lift them after the leaves have yellowed in the late spring. Shake off the soil and pull clumps apart, discarding any that show signs of rot. Replant the remaining bulbs, leaving the leaves to nourish the newly divided bulbs.

Look for the large cup varieties of *Narcissus*, which naturalize readily in your zones. *Tulipa* and *Hyacinthus* tend not to multiply in your climate; for continued bloom, they must be replaced every few years.

WINTERIZING

Be sure to dig up tender bulbs before freezing temperatures arrive. For hardy bulbs, apply mulch to the planting beds.

Lifting And Storing Tender Bulbs

While tender bulbs are more work, they are often worth it. *Gladiolus* and *Dahlia* make excellent cut flowers, while *Caladium* and *Zantedeschia* (calla lily) add an exotic touch to containers and herbaceous borders. In the garden, after frost, cut the foliage of tender bulbs to ground level. Lift and clean the clumps and discard any bulbs with signs of disease or rot. Dust the remaining bulbs with fungicide and store them indoors in a cool (45° to 50° Fahrenheit), dark location in mesh bags or wire-bottomed trays. And don't forget to label them with name and color!

If you have tender bulbs in pots or containers dig them up or, if you have enough space, bring them indoors before the first frost.

Storing Dahlia And Gladiolus

DAHLIA Let the soil dry on the tubers. If you have the space, store them as is; if not, gently knock off the soil, treat with fungicide and place the tubers in perlite or vermiculite in plastic bags with holes in them. Keep an eye on the tubers. If they begin to wither, sprinkle them with water. In the spring, inspect the tubers carefully, discard any that are withered, then cut the clumps into pieces allowing one eye per piece.

GLADIOLUS Remove all the foliage and gently shake off all the soil. Separate and discard the old corm. Hang the new corms in a mesh bag in a dry area with good air circulation.

HINT: Do not store bulbs in air tight plastic bags. Moisture can collect and cause the bulbs to rot.

Bulbs, Etc.

Best Bets For Your Garden

above: Tulipa 'Apricot Beauty,' single early

left: Scilla siberica 'Spring Beauty'

below: Narcissus 'Unsurpassable,' trumpet

Botanical Name Common Name	Color	Height	Spacing	Depth	
Allium moly Lily leek	Yellow	14"	4-5"	4"	
Chionodoxa luciliae Glory-of-the-snow	Blue	6-8"	3"	2"	
Crocus spp. Crocus	White, yellow, purple	2-6"	2-3"	2-3"	
Galanthus nivalis Snowdrop	White	3-8"	3"	3"	
Gladiolus spp. Gladiolus	Many colors except blue; bicolors; blends	To 3'	6-8"	3-6"	
Hyacinthus orientalis Dutch hyacinth	White, pink, blue, purple	8-15"	6-8"	4-6"	
Leucojum aestivum Snowflake	White	18-30"	4-5"	4-5"	
Lilium hybrids Lily hybrids	Many colors except blue	3'-4'	8-12"	6-8"	
Lilium auratum Gold-band lily	White with gold band	4-6'	8-12"	6-8"	
Lilium candidum Madonna lily	White	3-4'	8-12"	1" below soil	
Lilium speciosum 'Album,' 'Rubrum'	White, pale pink w/ crimson spots	4-6'	8-12"	6-8"	
Muscari armeniacum Grape hyacinth	White, blue	6-12"	3-4"	3-4"	
Narcissus spp. Daffodil	Orange, yellow, white or tricolor	8-20"	3-6"	7"	
Scilla siberica Siberian squill	Dark blue	4-6"	6"	3-4"	
Tulipa spp. Tulip	All colors, except blue	6-30"	6"	6"	

Sun	Microclimate	Planting Time / Bloom Time	Comments
○	Hardy to Zone 4; seashore-tolerant	Fall / *Late spring*	Borders; repels rodents when planted among other bulbs; well-drained soil; attracts butterflies; deer-resistant
○ ◐	Hardy; seashore-tolerant	Fall / *Midspring*	Naturalizes well in woodlands, rock gardens; well-drained soil; deer-resistant
○	Hardy; seashore-tolerant	Fall / *Midspring*	Corm; mass plantings, naturalizes well; well-drained soil; deer-resistant
○ ◐	Very hardy; seashore-tolerant	Fall / *Early spring*	Naturalizes well; well-drained soil; deer-resistant
○	Frost to half-hardy; lift annually in the fall	Spring / *Summer until frost*	Corm; cut flowers; rich, moist, well-drained soil; to extend the blooming season, plant at 10-day intervals
○	Hardy to Zone 5; prefers cold winters	Fall / *Spring*	Bedding, containers; fragrant; well-drained soil
◐	Hardy to Zone 4	Fall / *Late spring*	Borders, rock gardens, under shrubs; rich, sandy, well-drained soil; tolerates alkaline soil; deer-resistant
○ ●	Very hardy	Fall or early spring / *Spring - summer*	Borders, cut flowers; fragrant; deep, loamy, well-drained soil; deep mulch; divide in fall only when bulbs become overcrowded; fertilize in spring; attracts butterflies
◐	Hardy to Zone 5	Fall / *Summer*	Borders, cut flowers; acid to neutral, well-drained soil; attracts butterflies
○	Hardy to Zone 4	Late summer / *Summer*	Borders; fragrant; lime-rich, well-drained soil; tolerates alkaline soil; attracts butterflies
◐	Hardy; cool roots; shade from hot afternoon sun in Zone 5	Fall / *Late summer*	Borders, cut flowers; fragrant; rich, well-drained, neutral to acid soil; attracts butterflies
○ ◐	Hardy to Zone 4; seashore-tolerant	Fall / *Spring*	Naturalizes well; plant in large numbers for best effect; well-drained soil; deer-resistant
○ ◐	Hardy; seashore-tolerant	Fall / *Late spring*	Mass plantings, cut flowers; fragrant; naturalizes well; well-drained soil; tolerates alkaline soil; deer-resistant
○ ◐	Very hardy; seashore-tolerant	Fall / *Mid - late spring*	Mass plantings; naturalizes well; well-drained soil; mulch in fall; deer-resistant
○ ◐	Hardy; seashore-tolerant	Winter / *Early - midspring*	Borders, beds, cut flowers; rich, sandy soil; plant 12" deep for more years of good blooms

All plants on this list are bulbs unless otherwise noted. For additional bulbous plants, refer to the Annual and Perennial plant lists.

Erik Simmons

IV
GREENSCAPES

Vines
Ornamental Grasses
Groundcovers
Shrubs

Peter C. Jones

VINES

Hedera helix 'Baltica'

Vines are the "garnish" of the garden. They are excellent for softening the hard lines of fences or posts, house corners and entrances, and are often perfect for hiding an architect's mistakes! With their often lush foliage, showy fruit and fragrant flowers, vines add a touch of romance to the garden and, in nonblooming trees, vines add a splash of color. A wisteria-covered pergola is a refreshing destination on hot summer days. As vines take up little planting space, only 6", they are also a small garden's best ally.

Whatever the requirements of your garden, there's a vine for you. Some are annuals, others perennials or evergreen; some are herbaceous, others are woody; some are blooming, others are not; some have large, exotic leaves, others have small leaflets. What all vines do have in common is that although they like to climb, they do require support to continue their upward growth.

Vines climb by different means: (Clockwise from top left) Twining stems wrap around their supports; tendrils spiral around anything they touch; disks and rootlets hold fast to stone and wood vertical surfaces.

HOW VINES CLIMB

Vines are categorized by the means by which they climb: twining, tendrils, or clinging rootlets. Twining vines, such as *Akebia quinata* (five-leaf akebia), *Polygonum aubertii* (silver lace vine) and *Wisteria*, climb by stems that twine around their supports. Others, such as *Parthenocissus quinquefolia* (Virginia creeper), have tendrils that twist around supports to climb. Clinging vines have two kinds of rootlets that attach to surfaces: hairlike and disks. *Hedera helix* (English ivy), *Euonymus fortunei radicans* (wintercreeper) and *Campsis* (trumpet vine) are aerial root climbers with hairlike rootlets. *Parthenocissus tricuspidata* (Boston ivy) and *Hydrangea anomala petiolaris* (climbing hydrangea) cling to surfaces by means of adhesive disks.

Use twining vines on fence posts, pillars, or anything with a small diameter that is strong enough to support the vine.

Train tendril climbing vines on wire, lattice or shrubs. Vines with rootlets are best used for covering masonry walls.

Grow Vines:
- To provide vertical interest in your garden
- To soften hard lines of fences and garden walls
- To obscure chainlink fences or other unattractive structures
- To provide temporary shade in the summer
- To add interest to blank building walls
- To frame an entranceway
- To add colorful height to small gardens
- To bring fragrance up to nose level
- On fences, pillars, posts, pergolas and arbors
- In trees

SUN/SHADE

Most flowering vines prefer sun, although some, like *Lonicera japonica* 'Halliana' (Hall's honeysuckle) and *Polygonum aubertii* (silver lace vine) can withstand partial shade, although the flowering may not be as prolific. Most of the vines that thrive in shade are nonflowering, such as *Parthenocissus tricuspidata* (Boston ivy), *Hedera helix* (English ivy), *Euonymus fortunei radicans* (wintercreeper) and *Parthenocissus quinquefolia* (Virginia creeper), with the exception of *Akebia quinata* (five-leaf akebia). *Akebia quinata* is a good choice for east- or north-facing locations.

TEMPERATURE

Vines are sensitive to heat and cold. The warmer the temperature, the longer the growing season, the more a vine will grow. This is an important consideration when determining how many plants are needed to cover a surface quickly. Temperature can also influence whether a vine is deciduous or evergreen. *Lonicera japonica* 'Halliana' (Hall's honeysuckle) is semievergreen in Zone 5, but may be deciduous in colder zones.

HUMIDITY

Good air circulation is critical in areas with high humidity. If you live in a humid area select vines that flourish in that environment, such as *Campsis* (trumpet vine).

SOIL

Since some vines can grow up to 50' long in one season, they need vigorous root systems to provide them with nonstop nourishment. Rich, deep, well-drained soil will help your vines flourish. Most vines are pH adaptable, but some, such as *Campsis* (trumpet vine), are especially tolerant of alkaline soils.

> *HINT:* Actinidia kolomitka (*Arctic beauty kiwi) has less variegation in its leaves in acid soil.*

WATER

All vines require ample water until they are established and most prefer regular water to thrive. A few, such as *Parthenocissus quinquefolia* (Virginia creeper), *Parthenocissus tricuspidata* (Boston ivy) and *Polygonum aubertii* (silver lace vine), tolerate drought conditions. Vines grown against western walls, which receive hot afternoon sun, will require additional water.

PLANNING FOR VINES

Leaf texture, flower, fragrance, season of bloom, growth rate and whether a vine is deciduous or evergreen are all primary considerations when selecting vines. Vines chosen incorrectly can be disappointing or get out of hand, becoming more of a nuisance than a pleasure.

When selecting vines for your garden first ask yourself what the vine's purpose will be. This will help you select the one that best suits your needs. As rampant growers, such as *Lonicera* (honeysuckle) and *Polygonum aubertii* (silver lace vine), have a tendency to take over, they are not the best choice for small gardens. *Clematis* would be a better choice. The delicate foliage of *Akebia quinata* works well on small arbors, while the large leaves of *Wisteria* look good against large structures. Beware of training tendril climbers such as *Parthenocissus quinquefolia* (Virginia creeper) on shingle siding as they tend to creep under shingles and hold on voraciously. Ivies, such as *Parthenocissus quinquefolia* 'Saint-Paulii' (Virginia creeper) and *Parthenocissus tricuspidata* 'Veitchii' (Boston ivy) are equipped with strong gripping disks and grow extremely well on stone surfaces.

SPACING

Most vines should be planted 3' to 5' apart. Vigorous growers, such as *Wisteria* and *Campsis* (trumpet vine), should be planted 6' to 10' apart. In Zone 3, where vines grow less in each season, you may wish to plant vines closer for faster coverage.

PLANNING AT A GLANCE

- Microclimate
- Sun/shade
- Soil
- Water
- Use of vine
- Evergreen or deciduous
- Ultimate size
- Growth rate
- Spacing
- Means of attachment
- Foliage size and texture
- Flower color and time of bloom
- Fruit color and season

BED PREPARATIONS

Dig a hole 2' deep and 1-1/2' to 2' wide and amend the soil as necessary. (See "Soil," p.18.)

BUYING VINES

Most vines are sold in containers, although some deciduous vines are also available as bare-root plants. To select a healthy plant, see "Buying Perennials," p.64.

PLANTING

Spring is the best time to plant woody perennial vines as it allows enough time for them to establish a strong root system prior to the onset of winter. See "Planting" in "Perennials," p.65.

TRAINING VINES

How you train a vine is determined by how it grows. Vines with aerial roots and adhesive discs need just a bit of encouragement to climb on their own, while scramblers require tying. As long as there are supports nearby, twining and tendril climbing vines need only be pointed in the right direction.

Twining vines naturally twine in either a clockwise or counterclockwise direction. If you are training a twining vine in a set direction, be sure to determine which way it naturally twines before planting it.

Use soft twine, green plastic ribbon or plastic clips to attach vines to their supports, taking care not to constrict the stems. If you plan to leave a tie on for more than one growing season, be sure it is loose enough to accommodate future growth. To train vines on brick walls, glue on masonry hooks that have wires to bend around the stems.

FERTILIZING

You can use fertilizer like a gas pedal to control the growth of vines. If you feed a vine regularly, it will grow more quickly; if you hold off on the fertilizer, plant growth will slow down. Vines that are grown for foliage and flowers are generally fertilized in early spring and again in early summer. Fertilize flowering and fruiting vines with a balanced fertilizer such as 12-12-12. Spring-flowering vines will also benefit from a high-phosphorus fertilizer such as 10-20-10 in early fall. Foliage vines prefer a high nitrogen fertilizer such as 16-4-8 or 15-5-10. Always thoroughly water after fertilizing.

Fertilizing Wisteria

Wisteria has a habit of slowing down flower production, sometimes coming to a complete halt. If your *Wisteria* is producing lush foliage but few blooms, withhold nitrogen fertilizers for a summer to channel the plant's energy from producing leafy growth to the formation of flower buds.

MULCH

Vines, like other perennials, benefit from a 2" layer of light mulch. Some, such as *Clematis*, actually require mulch to keep their roots moist during the summer. Renew the mulch in the fall to moderate the soil's temperature during the cold winter months and to prevent frost heaving.

PRUNING

How you prune a vine is determined by both your pruning goals and the vine's flowering habit. To train most vines, flowering or nonflowering, you will want to prune them in late winter or early spring and then again in the late fall. To increase flower production, prune vines that bloom on the previous year's growth after they have flowered; prune vines that bloom on the current season's growth in the early spring.

While tip pruning (the removal of the ends of the branches) will provide temporary shaping for moderate growers, vigorous vines require regular removal of entire stems to avoid the inevitable tangled mess. If the stems are intricately entwined, cut the stem you wish to remove in several places to untangle it. And remember, pruning encourages new growth. Avoid stimulating new, tender growth by pruning

heavily in the early fall when plants should be slowing down in preparation for the winter.

If you have young plants you may have to wait two to three years for them to grow enough to establish a framework. Just a light pruning may be all that's necessary to shape and direct their growth.

AT INSTALLATION AND TO ENCOURAGE DENSE BRANCHING AT GROUND Locate the two or three healthiest stems and cut them back by one-half.

BLOOMERS ON THE CURRENT SEASON'S GROWTH To maintain an established vine, determine the framework for the vine's growth and cut it back to this framework each winter.

BLOOMERS ON THE PREVIOUS SEASON'S GROWTH To maintain an established vine, after flowering in the spring, remove all shoots that have flowered. Cut back other shoots to just above start of new growth. As new shoots grow, thin them, retaining just enough to fill the framework.

FOR REJUVENATION Locate two or three easily traceable stems and prune out all other growth. Cut back the laterals, leaving two or three buds on each.

Pruning Goals:
- To train
- To control a vigorous grower
- To renew shape
- To increase flower production
- To encourage dense branching close to the ground
- To rejuvenate a plant

Pruning Clematis
SPRING BLOOMERS Minimal or selective pruning in February or March to remove dead wood and oldest growth as they flower on old wood, which must be preserved and maintained.

SUMMER AND FALL BLOOMERS In early spring (February or March) cut stems back to a pair of strong buds; remove dead growth.

REJUVENATION PRUNING Every three to five years in early spring (February or March) prune stems to 1' from ground. This encourages new growth from the base and prevents unattractive bare stems.

Pruning Wisteria
Wisteria can grow to be so large it is best to begin training it immediately. Remember that *Wisteria sinensis* (Chinese wisteria) grows clockwise, while *Wisteria floribunda* (Japanese wisteria) grows counterclockwise. First determine the framework for growth, then decide whether the vine should be single or multistemmed. Plan ahead for the size and weight of wisteria trunks. A well-established, healthy trunk can be the size of a tree trunk!

TO TRAIN A NEW MULTISTEMMED *WISTERIA* Select as many vigorous stems as needed to fill your framework. Prune out all other stems. Pinch back side stems and streamers.

ANNUAL PRUNING *Wisteria* responds enthusiastically to severe annual pruning. Reduce the main stems by one-half each summer and side stems to three or four flower buds in late winter. Remove any suckers that may grow up at the base of the vine.

> HINT: To train a new single-stemmed Wisteria, *remove all buds along the single stem and keep streamers pruned during the growing season.*

WINTERIZING
When selected carefully for climate and location, hardy vines need little care in the winter. Simply renew the mulch when putting the rest of the garden to bed and securely tie any wayward stems.

Vines

Best Bets For Your Garden

above: Hydrangea anomala petiolaris

left: Clematis paniculata

below: Wisteria sinensis

Botanical Name / Common Name	Key	Bloom Color	Height	Sun/ Shade
Actinidia kolomitka (Male) / Arctic beauty kiwi	D	White	15-20'	○
Akebia quinata / Five-leaf akebia	D	Purple	30-40'	○ ●
Campsis x *tagliabuana* 'Madame Galen' / Trumpet vine	D	Orange and scarlet	40'	○ ◐
Clematis x *jackmanii* / Jackman clematis	D	Purple	10'	○
Clematis paniculata / Sweet autumn clematis	D	White	30'	○
Euonymus fortunei radicans 'Coloratus' / Wintercreeper	E	Inconspicuous green	15'	○ ●
Hedera helix 'Baltica' / English ivy	E	Foliage	30-50'	◐ ●
Hydrangea anomala petiolaris / Climbing hydrangea	D	White	50-75'	○ ◐
Lonicera japonica 'Halliana' / Hall's honeysuckle	SE or E	White	30'	○ ◐
Parthenocissus quinquefolia / Virginia creeper	D	Foliage	50'	○ ●
Parthenocissus tricuspidata 'Veitchii' / Boston ivy	D	Foliage	60'	○ ●
Polygonum aubertii / Silver lace vine	D	White	20-40'	○ ●
Wisteria floribunda / Japanese wisteria	D	Lilac, white	25'	○
Wisteria sinensis / Chinese wisteria	D	Lilac	25'	○

KEY: Deciduous (D); Evergreen (E); Semievergreen (SE)

Microclimate	Bloom Time	Comments
Hardy to Zone 4	Early summer	Vigorous, twining climber; foliage pink and white variegated, more so on male; less pronounced variegation in acid soil; small, cup-shaped flowers; moist, well-drained soil; tolerates alkaline soils
Hardy to Zone 4	Late spring through early summer	Vigorous, twining climber; dark blue-green foliage; small, vanilla-scented flowers; sausage-shaped fruit; well-drained soil; tolerates east- or north-facing location; tolerates alkaline soils; deer-resistant
Hardy to Zone 5; seashore-tolerant	Summer	Climbs by aerial roots; trumpet-shaped blossoms in clusters; rich, moist, well-drained soil; tolerates alkaline soil; prune in early spring to encourage flowering; may be invasive
Hardy to Zone 4; seashore-tolerant	Summer	Cultivars; twining climber; velvety, single, 3-4" blossoms; rich, well-drained soil; shade roots from hot sun; can prune in early spring as flowers on current growth; deer-resistant; hardy cultivars available
Hardy to Zone 4; seashore-tolerant	Late summer	Vigorous, twining climber; profusion of small blossoms; dense, glossy foliage; rich, well-drained soil; shade roots from hot sun; prune out old wood annually; blooms on new wood; deer-resistant
Hardy to Zones 4 and 5; drought-tolerant	Summer	Under trees, slopes; creeper and prostrate or climbing by aerial roots; dark green, glossy leaves turn reddish-purple in winter; inconspicuous flowers; intolerant of wet soil
Hardy to Zone 5; hardy; moderately drought-tolerant	NA	Fast-growing, aerial root climber; dull, dark green leaves; not as tolerant of sun; moist, well-drained alkaline soil; variegated varieties prefer more light; will grow on north wall; deer-resistant
Hardy to Zone 4; seashore-tolerant	Early summer	Clinging, root climber; lateral branches up to 3'; glossy, dark green foliage, gold in fall; fragrant, large, flat flower clusters; rich, moist, well-drained soil; tolerates alkaline soils
Hardy to Zone 4; seashore-tolerant	Summer	Woody, twining climber; dark green foliage; fragrant, trumpet-shaped blossoms; black fruit; any rich, well-drained soil; deer-resistant
Hardy to Zone 4; drought- and seashore-tolerant	NA	Vigorous, woody, tendril climber; five-toothed, dull green leaflets; crimson fall color; blue-black berries; well-drained soil; deer-resistant
Hardy to Zone 4; drought- and seashore-tolerant	NA	Vigorous, woody, tendril climber with adhesive disks; glossy, dark green maple-like foliage; crimson fall color; blue-black berries; well-drained soil; one of best for clinging to stone; deer-resistant
Hardy to Zone 5; drought- and seashore-tolerant	Late spring through fall	Vigorous, twining climber; heart-shaped leaves; frothy, fragrant, flowers; pinkish fruits; most well-drained soils; may freeze to ground in winter, but rebounds in spring; deer-resistant
Hardy to Zone 5; seashore-tolerant	Early summer	Woody, twining climber; fragrant, pea-like flowers in long clusters after leaves appear; rich, well-drained soil; buy only cutting-grown, grafted or budded *Wisteria*; deer-resistant
Hardy to Zone 4; seashore-tolerant	Early summer	Woody, twining climber; fragrant, pea-like flowers in 1' long clusters before leaves appear; rich, well-drained soil; tolerates alkaline soils; buy only cutting-grown, grafted or budded *Wisteria*; deer-resistant

Peter C. Jones

ORNAMENTAL GRASSES

Deschampsia caespitosa 'Schottland'

Ornamental grasses are the great showmen in the landscape, putting on a continuous performance as they progress through their life cycles, developing and producing showy flower heads and seed. They change color through the season, sway in the wind and add a gentle rustling sound to the garden. When bathed in sunlight, the foliage sparkles; when backlit, some glow. The flamboyant plumes and seedheads challenge the imaginations of the best costume designers. And during the winter they add color, structure and drama to the sleeping garden.

Ornamental grasses comprise a wonderfully diverse group of low-maintenance plants that grow everywhere and at almost every elevation. Short and compact like a pincushion, open and spreading like a waterfall or tall and columnar, they range in color from blue-green to yellow-green, red or variegated. Some are rampant spreaders while others are clump forming and better controlled. Graceful and beautiful, ornamental grasses can add a sense of mystery, magic or even a wild feeling to the home landscape.

Ornamental grasses are grown for their fine foliage as well as their dramatic inflorescences (flowerheads). Combine them with annuals and perennials or use them as softening contrasts with shrubs in the border for year-round interest. As solitary, sculptural elements, large grasses can stand majestically in the lawn. Low-growing, running grasses make quick-spreading groundcovers that can control dust and erosion. Tall grasses make excellent hedges and screens. Plant ornamental grasses near the seashore where their plumes will move with the wind or in an intimate garden to obscure irritating ambient sounds. With their contrasting life cycles, grasses and bulbs are excellent companions. Grasses begin to grow just as bulbs are coming into bloom; as grasses expand, their blades conceal the dying bulb foliage. Grasses are always marvelous additions to fresh and dried flower arrangements.

Grow Ornamental Grasses:
- In herbaceous borders
- In mixed perennial and shrub borders
- In mass plantings
- In seashore gardens
- As specimens and accents
- As groundcovers
- As edging
- As screens and hedges
- As background plantings
- As bulb companions
- In dried arrangements
- To control dust and erosion
- To add a touch of the wild, fun or mystery to the garden
- For dramatic inflorescences
- For color and texture
- For the rustling sound

HOW ORNAMENTAL GRASSES GROW
Ornamental grasses are classified by how they grow:

CLUMPING GRASSES grow as individual tufts that gradually get fatter and fatter. *Calamagrostis acutiflora* 'Stricta' (feather reed grass) is a tall, erect clumper; *Carex morrowii* (Japanese sedge) short and turf-like.

SPREADING (OR RUNNING) GRASSES spread by rhizomes (underground stems), such as *Elymus arenarius* 'Glaucus' (blue lyme grass), or by stolons (above-ground stems). Because of their spreading habit, running grasses can cover an area very quickly. But watch out, they can be invasive!

TEMPERATURE
As most ornamental grasses are either annuals or perennials, temperature is an important factor in their life cycles. Warm weather signals the beginning of an annual's cycle; cold weather, the end. Perennials go into dormancy with the arrival of cold weather, but return year after year. But all perennial grasses have their own tolerance to cold, so be sure to select those that are hardy to your zone.

SUN/SHADE
Most grasses prefer full sun; however, others, such as *Calamagrostis acutiflora* 'Stricta' (feather reed grass), *Carex morrowii* 'Variegata' (variegated Japanese sedge), *Chasmanthium latifolium* (inland sea oats) and *Miscanthus sinensis* 'Variegatus' (Japanese silver grass) can tolerate partial shade.

SOIL
Ornamental grasses tolerate most moderately fertile, well-drained soils with an average pH. If you have clay soil, amend it to improve drainage. See "Soil," p.18.

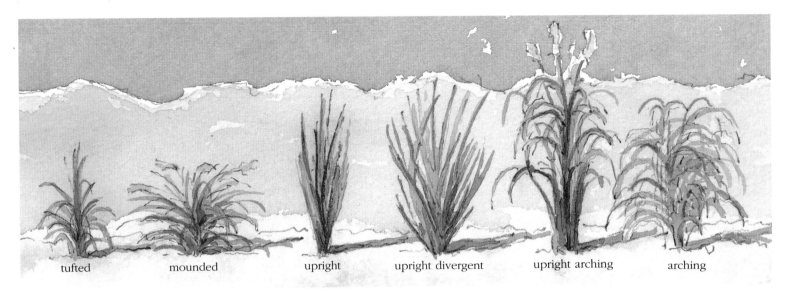

tufted   mounded   upright   upright divergent   upright arching   arching

Ornamental grasses come in many shapes and sizes, so there's bound to be one that's just right for your garden.

WATER

All grasses respond well to water, especially when newly planted, but in moderation. Too much water or sitting water will rot their roots. This is particularly true of blue grasses, such as *Elymus arenarius* 'Glaucus' (blue lyme grass), which are coated with a protective blue-gray wax to reduce water loss.

In hot summer climates, water regulates plant growth. The less grasses are watered, the less they grow. Some, such as *Pennisetum alopecuroides* (rose fountain grass), require water to keep them green.

PLANNING FOR ORNAMENTAL GRASSES

Ornamental grasses offer the gardener lots of shapes and sizes from which to choose. Their foliage can be tufted, like *Carex morrowii* (Japanese sedge); mounded, upright, upright divergent,

upright arching, *Calamagrostis acutiflora* 'Stricta' (feather reed grass); or arching, like *Miscanthus sinensis* (Japanese silver grass).

If sound is your goal, plant tall grasses such as *Miscanthus sinensis* and *Calamagrostis acutiflora* 'Stricta' where they will catch the breeze. For strong winds, use low, narrow-leafed grasses that won't bend with the force of the wind. For a shimmering effect, plant *Miscanthus* where sunlight will reflect off its leaves; to capture the full drama of showy inflorescences, such as those of *Miscanthus sinensis* 'Gracillimus' (maiden grass), plant them against a dark background such as a fence, wall or hedge. When planting grasses with perennials, do not use vigorous runners or aggressive seeders; they would soon disrupt the balance. Rampant runners are best reserved for stabilizing steep slopes or covering large areas.

Ornamental Grass Companions
- *Aster*
- *Narcissus*
- *Eupatorium*
- *Rudbeckia*
- *Sedum*

Ornamental Grasses For Strong Winds
- *Calamagrostis acutiflora* 'Stricta' (feather reed grass)
- *Panicum virgatum* (switch grass)
- *Schizachyrium scoparium* (little bluestem)

SPACING
How an ornamental grass grows is integral to its use in the garden. Clumping grasses spaced far apart will give a hummocky look; those planted close together will soon meld into a solid mass. A good rule of thumb is to plant them as far apart as their ultimate height. If you want a massed effect or would like to see faster results, space plants closer together.

PLANNING AT A GLANCE
- Microclimate
- Warm or cool season
- Sun/shade
- Soil
- Water
- Evergreen or deciduous
- Plant size and shape
- Foliage color and texture
- Plant inflorescence or seedhead color
- Time of display
- Seasonal appearance
- Year-round interest
- Plant spacing
- Grass's growth and spreading habits

BED PREPARATION
Ornamental grasses are prone to root rot so good drainage is the goal when preparing the bed. Dig beds a minimum of 12".

For larger grasses, such as *Miscanthus*, dig the bed 24". If you have clay soils, dig the beds deeper and amend the soil to improve drainage.

BUYING GRASSES
Although ornamental grasses reproduce by seed as well as runners, most are purchased as plants. Container-grown grasses are available from catalogs or your local nursery; bare-root plants are most often purchased by mail. Many grasses don't bloom until the second year, so buy the largest plant possible. For guidelines for selecting a healthy plant, see "Buying Perennials" on p.64.

Bare-root Plants
Bare-root plants are shipped dormant. Be forewarned, dormant grasses are not an appealing bunch. Although they show no signs of their future glory, they should respond enthusiastically to careful planting and regular water when purchased from a reputable source. But remember, roots dry quickly, so plant them as soon as possible.

PLANTING
In the coldest areas, spring is always the preferred time to plant ornamental grasses. To plant container-grown and bare-root plants, see "Planting" in "Perennials," p.65. Remember, water is critical for the success of newly planted grasses. To reduce transpiration, keep plants cut back by one-third until they are well established. If scorching should occur, simply cut back the plants. With water, new growth should quickly appear.

DIVIDING AND TRANSPLANTING
Divide and multiply! Not only does dividing rejuvenate your older, overcrowded plants but it also provides you with many young, new plants to spread around your garden. When you see your older plants begin to take over the garden or flop over, you know the time has come to brace yourself and bring out the heavy artillery: an axe, saw and spade. Divide orna-

mental grasses just as new growth begins to show in late winter or early spring; fall-divided grasses rarely winter well.

Begin by cutting back the existing foliage by about one-third to reduce the loss of moisture through transpiration during dividing and transplanting. Dig all around the clump with a spade, then lift the plant. If your grasses are very large, ask a friend to help you. Next, using the appropriate tool for the size of your grass, cut the plant into substantial chunks. For stoloniferous or rhizomateous plants, cut off the runners, keeping as much soil on the roots as soon as possible, and replant right away. If plants must be out of the ground for a while, keep them moist and out of direct sunlight.

FERTILIZING

Grasses grow in direct relation to soil fertility. Grasses given a diet of very fertile soil and regular water will take off; those that are starved will stand still.

Most grasses excel with an application of slow-release, low-nitrogen fertilizer in spring. Too much nitrogen weakens them — particularly important on exposed sites where the wind threatens to bend the foliage.

HINT: If your grasses are flopping over, they may be suffering from over fertilization, too much nitrogen, or insufficient light.

MULCH

Keep them mulched! Apply 2" to 3" at the time of installation and renew regularly. If an ornamental grass is questionably hardy, winter mulch will help it through, especially if there is little snow cover. See "Mulch," p.36.

WEEDING

Once grasses are established as groundcovers, weeding is over because most grasses outgrow the weeds! However, beware of planting invasive runners or self-sowing grasses in perennial beds; you will have a continual battle weeding your garden.

STAKING

Staking should not be necessary for healthy grasses. If the need does arise, see "Staking" in "Perennials," p.66. Brush stakes often work well for smaller grasses.

CUTTING BACK

Once a year, cut back ornamental grasses to remove thick, old or dried-out leaves. To avoid damaging new shoots, the best time to cut plants back is in late winter just before growth begins. Those who like to enjoy the winter foliage and feathery plumes to their fullest can hold off pruning until the new green shoots begin to appear in the spring. But spring pruning does have its consequences. Grasses become very brittle as they dry over the winter and may break up into thousands of little pieces when cut. Before pruning surround the grasses with a tarp to easily collect the clippings. Some ornamental grasses, such as *Elymus arenarius* 'Glaucus' (blue lyme grass), benefit from an additional shearing in midseason to force new, blue foliage.

Hand pruners will do the job for most ornamental grasses, but to save time, use weed trimmers on mass plantings of tall perennial grasses.

DEADHEADING

The plumes of ornamental grasses are so attractive you may want to leave them as long as possible. However, if they get broken or no longer look attractive, cut their stems back to below the foliage.

WINTERIZING

Leave any ornamental grasses that are elegant or sculptural for winter interest in the garden; cut back those that are less attractive (see above). Protect your tender ornamental grasses with 2" to 3" of mulch, taking special care of those growing on the cusp of their hardiness zone. In late winter, before any signs of new growth, cut back all grasses that were left standing.

Ornamental Grasses

Best Bets For Your Garden

above: Miscanthus sinensis 'Morning Light'

right: Calamagrostis acutiflora 'Stricta'

below: Carex morrowii 'Variegata'

Botanical Name Common Name	Height	Spacing	Sun/ Shade	
Calamagrostis acutiflora 'Stricta' Feather reed grass	4 1/2 -7'	24"	○ ◑	
Calamagrostis arundinacea brachytricha Silver spike grass	24-30"	18-24"	○ ◑	
Carex morrowii 'Variegata' Variegated Japanese sedge	12"	8"	◑	
Chasmanthium latifolium Inland sea oats	3'	2'	○ ◑	
Deschampsia caespitosa Tufted hairgrass	1-3'	2-3'	◑	
Elymus arenarius 'Glaucus' Blue lyme grass	3-4'	3-4'	○	
Miscanthus sinensis Japanese silver grass	5-6'	3-4'	○	
Miscanthus sinensis 'Morning Light' Silver-variegated maiden grass	4-5'	3-4'	○	
Molinia caerulea subsp. *arundinacea* 'Windspiel' Windplay tall moor grass	6-7'	3'-4'	○ ◑	
Panicum virgatum 'Strictum' Tall switch grass	5'-6'	4'	○	
Panicum virgatum 'Haense Herms' Red switch grass	3-4'	2-3'	○	
Phalaris arundinacea 'Picta' Ribbon grass	18-30"	12-18"	◑	
Schizachyrium scoparium Little bluestem	3'	12"	○	
Sesleria autumnalis Autumn moor grass	12-18"	18"	○ ◑	

Microclimate	Planting Time	Comments
Hardy to Zone 4; drought-tolerant	Spring or fall	Deciduous; background, mass plantings; course, narrowly erect; upright panicles in early summer, persists through winter; growth begins early in spring
Hardy to Zone 5	Spring or fall	Mass plantings, accent; clumper; purple-rose inflorescence in early fall; winter-persistent; prefers alkaline, well-drained soil
Hardy to Zone 5; drought-tolerant	Spring	Semievergreen; groundcover or accent; green leaves with white margins; very tolerant but prefers cool, moist soil
Hardy to Zone 5; seashore-tolerant	Spring	Accent, mass plantings; clumper; bamboo-like; dangling seed heads from summer to fall; most soils; protect from wind
Very hardy; moderately drought-tolerant	Spring or fall	Semievergreen; specimen, mass plantings, groundcover; flowers in airy panicles 2-3' above foliage; moist, rich soil; tolerates moist sites; intolerant of hot, dry sites; rabbit food; many cultivars
Hardy to Zones 4 and 5	Spring or fall	Accent, groundcover; runner; blue-grey foliage; very aggressive
Hardy to Zones 4 and 5; warm-season	Spring	Accent; screen; clumper; all *Miscanthus sinensis* have white midribs; broad blades and medium texture; magenta plumes; outstanding winter color
Hardy to Zones 4 and 5	Spring	Fine-textured foliage; elegant; bronze-red inflorescence turning silver
Hardy to Zones 4 and 5; warm-season	Spring	Accent; clumper; fine blue-green foliage; elegant, transparent flower stalks sway in the wind; moist, acid, well-drained soil
Very hardy; seashore-tolerant	Spring or fall	Accent, groundcover; runner; fine blue-green foliage; most soils
Very hardy; drought-tolerant	Spring or fall	Foliage turns reddish in fall; airy reddish inflorescence
Hardy to Zones 4 and 5	Spring or fall	Groundcover, accent, borders, slopes, at water's edge; spreading; white variegated foliage turns white with frost; showy white flower above foliage; moist, fertile soil; tolerates rocky or sandy soil
Very hardy; drought-tolerant	Spring or fall	Groundcover, massing, accent in low groundcover, erosion control; clumper; erect; light green, narrow foliage; fluffy plumes in late summer; bronze to orange in fall; any well-drained soil
Hardy to Zone 4; extremely drought-tolerant	Spring or fall	Accent, groundcover, rock gardens; clumper; yellow-green foliage; yellow fall color; silvery panicles; alkaline, well-drained soil

Peter C. Jones

GROUNDCOVERS

Sedum kamtschaticum

Groundcovers are the carpets of the garden. Although usually selected for their foliage, many flowering plants also make great groundcovers, so you have an array to choose from including low growing shrubs, roses, perennials, succulents or vines. The only prerequisite — that they cover the ground quickly and thoroughly.

For the best effect, groundcovers should be perennial, low maintenance, long lasting and provide year-round visual interest. The best choices for areas with little snow cover are hardy evergreens, which bring a little color and texture to an otherwise monotone winter landscape. In Zones 3 and 4, select very hardy groundcovers that stand up to the weight of deep snow, ice, strong winds, cool summers and a short growing season.

Groundcovers usually spread by means of trailing branches, underground roots or above-ground runners. There is a happy medium however, between plants that are vigorous spreaders and those that are invasive. Avoid invasive vines, such as *Celastrus scandens* (bittersweet), no matter how tempting they may be. You will be pulling shoots out of your garden for years on end.

Use groundcovers as the transition between your lawn areas and taller shrubs or in places where grass refuses to grow. Plant groundcovers to reduce weeding or even mowing! Fill in between the stones of a path or plant them along the edge. For the best erosion control on slopes too steep to mow, select vigorous growers that have deep roots to hold the soil. If you use vines as groundcovers, remember that almost all vines like to climb. To avoid unnecessary maintenance in shrubs and trees, choose groundcovers that prefer to hug the ground.

Grow Groundcovers:
- To carpet the floor of the garden
- To control dust
- To reduce weeding
- To keep the soil cool and reduce evaporation
- To reduce lawn area
- To visually unify planting areas
- To edge a path
- To fill in between stones in a path
- To edge lawn areas with color and texture
- As a transition between the lawn and taller shrubs
- To obscure fading bulb foliage
- To prevent erosion from wind and rain
- On slopes too steep to mow
- As fire retardants

SUN/SHADE
Most groundcovers require at least four to six hours of sunlight daily, preferably in the morning. Fortunately, there are groundcovers that grow in difficult areas in the landscape. In deep shade, try *Osmunda cinnamomea* (cinnamon fern), *Convallaria majalis* (lily-of-the-valley), *Galium odoratum* (sweet woodruff) or *Epimedium grandiflorum* (bishop's hats); in sunny spots try *Ajuga reptans* (bugleweed), *Euonymus fortunei radicans* (wintercreeper), or *Cerastium tomentosum* (snow-in-summer).

TEMPERATURE
There is a good selection of groundcovers that flourish in your cold climate, but some may take more effort to establish. The short growing season, cool temperatures and constant, seed-bearing (and thus weed-bearing) winds may provide a challenge to some groundcovers. To cover large areas, select only the most competitive groundcovers, such as *Vinca minor* (periwinkle), *Epimedium grandiflorum*; (bishop's hats) or *Phalaris arundinacea* (ribbon grass), and mulch well. If your Zone 3 garden is chilled by stormy blasts from the north, select only the hardiest plants. In areas of the Midwest that regularly experience snowless weeks in midwinter, select evergreen groundcovers, such as *Juniperus* spp., that look well year-round, yet survive without protection from the snow. Flowering and fragrant groundcovers, such as *Hemerocallis* (daylily) and *Convallaria majalis* (lily-of-the-valley) thrive in areas with hot summers and cold winters.

HUMIDITY
Humidity can be a problem for groundcovers, especially in coastal areas. They grow close to the ground where low light levels, high humidity and poor air circulation provide the perfect conditions for mold and mildew. In humid areas look for

plants more tolerant of humidity, such as ferns and daylilies, and increase air circulation in and around the garden.

SOIL

Groundcovers spread by underground rhizomes, rapid multiplication or by sending out stems that root wherever they touch down, so good preparation of the soil is essential to their quick growth. Most groundcovers prefer loose, rich, well-drained soil with an average pH. However, some, such as *Adiantum pedatum* (maidenhair fern), do well in alkaline soils; *Arctostaphylos uva-ursi* (bearberry) does well in acid soils. Groundcovers must thrive to solidly cover an area, so be sure the groundcover you select is compatible with your soil's pH.

> *HINT: Once groundcovers are established, it's practically impossible to work the soil, so the soil must be well prepared before you plant.*

WATER

Although most groundcovers prefer humus-rich soil and regular water, they generally do not like wet feet. In areas with low rainfall and water restrictions, there are many drought-tolerant plants to chose from including many succulents, *Cerastium tomentosum* (snow-in-summer) and *Ajuga*. But even drought-tolerant plants need water until they are established. If water supplies permit, drip irrigation is very helpful in establishing groundcovers, especially on slopes. Be sure to install it prior to planting.

WIND

Cold winds lower the temperature and dehydrate plant stems. In Zones 3 and 4, cold winds combined with cold temperatures can be tough on some commonly grown hardy groundcovers, such as *Pachysandra*, *Hedera* (ivy) and *Cotoneaster*. Select hardy groundcovers such as *Ajuga*, *Vinca* (periwinkle) and low-growing *Juniperus* that stand up well to cold winds.

SPACING

Buying enough plants is always a concern when it comes to groundcovers. The quantities are so large, you always think you've gone overboard only to find you haven't bought enough. To make an accurate count, measure your planting area carefully, then calculate the number of square feet. The recommended spacing between plants will determine how many will be necessary to cover the area. Use the chart below to help you.

Space Between Plants	Area 64 Plants Will Cover	Area 100 Plants Will Cover
4"	7 Sq. Feet	11 Sq. Feet
6	16	25
8	28	44
10	45	70
12	64	100
15	100	156
18	144	225
24	256	400

PLANNING AT A GLANCE

- Microclimate
- Sun/shade
- Soil
- Water
- Cold hardiness
- Evergreen or deciduous
- Plant form and texture
- Flower color and time of bloom
- Fruit color and season
- Plant spread and spacing

BED PREPARATION

When planting large areas of groundcovers, weeds can be a nightmare. Once the plants have covered the area, it's very difficult to reach the base of a weed to properly pull it out, roots and all. Your best defense is to eradicate weeds and grasses, especially perennial quack grass, several weeks prior to installation. (See "Removing Sod," p.33). Prepare the beds to a depth of 10"-12" by single digging (see "Digging The Bed," p.33) and adding amendments as necessary. If you can, allow the soil to settle for a few weeks, then rake the bed smooth.

HINT: Although groundcovers are the "carpet" of the garden, they do not appreciate being walked on. Provide a path or stepping stones if you think people will be tempted to tiptoe through your groundcovers.

BUYING GROUNDCOVERS

Groundcovers can be succulents, vines, shrubs, perennials or grasses, so you will find them available in many different types of containers, ranging from flats of seedlings to 2" pots and gallon containers. Vines, such as *Vinca* (periwinkle) and *Hedera* (ivy), can be purchased as bare-root plants, usually through mail-order catalogs.

To select a healthy plant, look for:
- Plants that are vigorous (those that fill the pot or flat).
- Plants that are pest free.
- Plants that have several healthy stems.

and avoid:
- Plants with smaller new growth.
- Plants with yellow leaves or dieback.
- Plants that are potbound. (Check to see if roots are growing out of the bottom of the pot.)

- Plants with broken stems or twigs.
- Plants with underdeveloped root systems. (Check to see if plant is loose in the pot.)
- Plants in containers with low soil levels or hard-packed soil.

HINT: When purchasing groundcovers, buy the largest size possible. Larger plants are more vigorous and will rapidly cover an area, quickly restricting the ability of weeds to take hold.

TIME TO PLANT

The winter's freeze/thaw cycles have a tendency to heave young plants out of the ground. Plant most groundcovers in the spring to give them an entire growing season to establish their root systems prior to the onset of winter's cold.

PLANTING

Plant your groundcovers in either straight or staggered rows. If you are planting on a slope, staggered rows will help prevent soil erosion. For specific planting recommendations, see "Planting" in the appropriate chapter.

HINT: To maintain a clean edge between the lawn area and your groundcovers, install a metal, plastic, brick or wood garden edge that is deep enough to thwart the progress of spreading underground roots.

Planting On Steep Slopes

When planting groundcovers on steep slopes in areas with below-average rainfall, create flat terraces for each plant. "Terracing" interrupts the flow of water down the slope, thereby increasing the amount of water that goes to the plant's roots. It will also raise the plant up to help prevent it from being buried by soil washing down the slope.

Planting on a slope: (Left) On gentle slopes, use the guidelines for planting perennials, vines or shrubs. (Right) On steep slopes, plant groundcovers on individual terraces, which interrupt and capture water for the plants, but be sure the root balls are not exposed.

To plant on a terrace, dig a hole in the middle of the terrace that is about two-thirds as deep as the container. Place the plant in the hole and mound soil over it. The crown of the plant will be high, forming a basin between it and the slope. Water will collect in the basin and percolate down into the soil instead of running down the slope.

HINT: In cold climates with heavy rainfall, do not plant in terraces. Pockets formed by terraces could collect ice and kill the plants.

FERTILIZING

Fertilize your new transplants with a balanced fertilizer two to three weeks after installation. For more specific fertilizing recommendations, see "Fertilizing" in the appropriate chapter.

MULCH

Mulch is critical on sites with constant winds. In the summer it prevents weed seeds carried by the wind from germinating; in the winter it moderates soil temperatures and is a good defense against the damaging freeze/thaw cycles that can heave plants out of the ground. Year-round, mulch will help your soil retain moisture.

It will take time for newly planted groundcovers to cover the given area, so remember to mulch them well right from the start. Some gardeners prefer spreading the mulch before planting. This prevents damage to the seedlings and ensures a solid defense against invading weeds.

DEADHEADING/SHEARING

As groundcovers often span very large areas, it is best to select plants that are self-cleaning and require little pruning. But do prune out stray branches that have turned brown. If you want a formal look or want to revitalize the plants, you may wish to shear groundcovers such as *Euonymus fortunei radicans* (wintercreeper) and *Iberis sempervirens* (candytuft).

WINTERIZING

For specific winterizing recommendations, see "Mulch" in the appropriate chapter.

Groundcovers

Best Bets For Your Garden

above left: Ajuga reptans

above right: Arctostaphylos uva-ursi

left: Epimedium grandiflorum

below left: Dennstaedtia punc-tilobula

Botanical Name Common Name	Key	Bloom Color	Height	Spacing	
Adiantum pedatum Maidenhair fern	D	Foliage	18"	12-18"	
Ajuga reptans Bugleweed	E	Purple	2"	8-12"	
Arctostaphylos uva-ursi Bearberry	E	White	2-3"	3-4'	
Athyrium filix-femina Lady fern	D	Foliage	2-4'	1-3'	
Cerastium tomentosum Snow-in-summer	D	White	6-12"	2'	
Convallaria majalis Lily-of-the-valley	D	White	8"	12"	
Dennstaedtia punctilobula Hay-scented fern	D	Foliage	12"	12"	
Epimedium grandiflorum Bishop's hats	D	Rose pink, white	12-18"	12"	
Epimedium x *versicolor* 'Sulphureum'	D	Yellow	12"	12"	
Euonymus fortunei radicans 'Coloratus' Wintercreeper	E	Inconspicuous green	4-6"	18-24"	
Galium odoratum Sweet woodruff	E	White	3-4"	6"	
Hedera helix 'Baltica' Baltic ivy	E	Foliage	30-50'	12-18"	

KEY: Deciduous (D); Evergreen (E)

Sun	Microclimate	Bloom Time	Comments
◑	Hardy	NA	Under trees, borders, woodlands; dainty, divided, medium-green fronds; dark brown stems; moist, neutral to alkaline soil; excellent in Northeast; may be difficult to grow in Midwest
○ ●	Hardy; drought- and salt-intolerant	Early summer	Under trees, on slopes, edging; dark green foliage; spike bloom; spreads rapidly; any well-drained soil; nematode-sensitive; deer-resistant; bronze foliage
○	Very hardy; drought- and seashore-tolerant	Summer	Groundcover, slopes; trailing; small, bright green foliage red in winter; small, urn-shaped flowers; bright red fruit; prefers acid soils; tolerant of poor soils and sand. May be difficult to grow in Midwest
●	Hardy to Zones 4 and 5	NA	Under trees, borders, woodlands; delicate, lance-shaped, divided, arching, pale green fronds; humus-rich, moist soil; remove fading fronds regularly
○	Hardy; drought- and seashore-tolerant	Spring through early summer	Slopes, rock gardens, walls, borders, edging, between stepping stones; prostrate; silvery foliage; clusters of star-shaped flowers; aggressive; must have well-drained soil; tolerates pure sand; good for mountains, coast, or desert; deer-resistant
◑ ●	Hardy	Spring	Rhizomes; under trees; vigorous roots allow little else to grow near it; very fragrant, bell-shaped flowers; pairs of leaves wrap around stems; leaves turn brown in late summer; humus-rich soil; divide when crowded; deer-resistant
●	Very hardy	NA	Under trees, borders, woodlands; oval to triangular, much-divided, lacelike, green fronds; humus-rich, moist soil
◑ ●	Hardy to Zone 4	Spring	Under trees, borders; clump forming; dainty flowers in clusters on wiry stems; heart-shaped leaves, pink when first appears; slow but steady spreader; deer-resistant
◑ ●	Hardy to Zone 5	Spring	Rhizome, under trees, borders; dainty flowers in clusters on wiry stems; heart-shaped leaves; more rapid spreader than *Epimedium grandiflorum*; cut back old foliage in late winter; deer-resistant; good fall color
○ ●	Hardy to Zones 4 and 5; seashore-tolerant	Summer	Under trees, slopes; creeper and prostrate or climbing by aerial roots; dark green, glossy leaves turn reddish-purple in winter; inconspicuous flowers; intolerant of wet soil
●	Hardy to Zones 4 and 5; drought-intolerant	Late spring	Under trees, edging; hay-scented foliage when dried; moist, acid soil; self-sows freely; divide in spring or fall; deer-resistant
◑ ●	Hardy to Zone 5; moderately drought-tolerant	NA	Fast-growing, aerial root climber; dull, dark green leaves; not as tolerant of sun; moist, well-drained alkaline soil; variegated varieties prefer more light; will grow on north wall; deer-resistant

Groundcovers

Best Bets For Your Garden

above left: Lamium maculatum 'Pink Pewter'

above right: Phlox stolonifera 'Bruce's White'

left: Pachysandra terminalis

below: Hosta 'Great Expectations'

below right: Vinca minor

Botanical Name Common Name	Key	Bloom Color	Height	Spacing
Hemerocallis Daylily	D or E	Shades of orange, pink, red, yellow	18-36"	18-30"
Hosta spp. Plantain lily	D	White, blue, lavender	16-24"	1-2' or more
Iberis sempervirens Candytuft	SE or E	White	6-9"	12"
Juniperus spp. Juniper	E	Inconspicuous	Varies	Varies
Lamium maculatum Dead nettle	D	White	12-18"	12"
Lamium maculatum 'White Nancy'	D	White	6-8"	12"
Osmunda cinnamomea Cinnamon fern	D	Foliage	3'	18"
Pachysandra terminalis Japanese pachysandra	E	White	4"	5"
Phalaris arundinacea 'Picta' Ribbon grass	D or E	White	18-30"	2-3'
Phlox stolonifera Creeping phlox 'Bruce's White'	E	Pale blue, white	6-12"	6"
Polystichum acrostichoides Christmas fern	E	Foliage	2'	18"
Sedum kamtschaticum Sedum	E	Yellow	3"	6"
Vinca minor Common periwinkle	E	Purple, light blue, white	5-8"	8-12"

KEY: Deciduous (D); Evergreen (E); Semievergreen (SE)

Sun	Microclimate	Bloom Time	Comments
○ ◐	Most hardy to Zone 4; humidity, drought- and seashore-tolerant	Spring through fall	Slopes, borders; any soil; water regularly when blooming
●	Hardy to Zone 4	Summer	Under trees, borders; moist, rich soil; good drainage in winter; apply super phosphate in late summer; keep a lookout for slugs
○	Hardy; prefers cool nights; humidity-tolerant	Early spring	Cut flowers; rock gardens; well-drained soil; deer-resistant
○	Very hardy; drought-, heat- and seashore-tolerant	NA	Groundcovers, slopes, mass plantings; needles of varying colors; cones; tolerates some alkalinity; deer-resistant; many cultivars
◐ ●	Hardy; heat-tolerant	Spring through late summer	Evergreen in Zones 6 and 7; blunt leaves with white stripe up midrib; small flowers; tolerates most soils; easy to grow; spreads vigorously; shear in midsummer for compact growth; deer-resistant; green-edged silver leaves; tolerates sun given moist soil
◐ ●	Hardy; heat-tolerant	Spring through late summer	Evergreen in Zones 6 and 7; blunt leaves with white stripe up midrib; small flowers; tolerates most soils; easy to grow; spreads vigorously; shear in midsummer for compact growth; deer-resistant; green-edged silver leaves; tolerates sun given moist soil
●	Hardy to Zones 4 and 5	NA	Under trees, borders, woodlands; lance-shaped, divided, pale green, sterile fronds surrounding cinnamon brown, fertile fronds; best in humus-rich, wet soil; remove dead fronds regularly
◐ ●	Hardy to Zones 4 and 5	Early summer	Under trees, slopes, edging; small spike flower; leathery leaves clustered at stem tips; all moist soils; deer-resistant
○	Hardy to Zones 4 and 5	Early summer	Groundcover, accent, borders, slopes, at water's edge; spreading; white variegated foliage turns white with frost; showy white flower above foliage; moist, fertile soil; tolerates rocky or sandy soil
○ ◐	Hardy to Zone 4	Early summer	Under trees, border; flowers in loose clusters; oblong to oval leaves; moist, acid, peaty soil; may be difficult to grow in Midwest
◐	Hardy	NA	Under trees, borders; slender, lance-shaped dark green fronds; rich, moist, well-drained soil
○	Hardy to Zone 4; drought-tolerant	Early fall	Open areas, between stones; star-like flowers; small, fleshy, light green leaves; any well-drained soil; easy to grow; deer-resistant
○ ●	Hardy to Zones 4 and 5	Spring - early summer	Under trees, slopes; glossy, dark green leaves; any soil but prefers rich, moist soil; deer-resistant

Peter C. Jones

SHRUBS

Picea glauca 'Conica'

Shrubs are a gardener's best friend. Human in scale, they are the multiple stemmed woody plants that help make the transition between tall trees and groundcovers in the landscape. Evergreen or deciduous, large or small, spreading, rounded, upright or vase-shaped, shrubs are the workhorses of the garden. Not only can you fill a space faster with shrubs than any other type of plant, but you can use them to create the structure or "backbone" of the garden.

Use mass plantings of shrubs to divide the lawn into smaller garden spaces, or plant a single flowering shrub, such as *Philadelphus* (mock orange) or *Syringa* (lilac), to make an impressive accent in a bed of low growing groundcovers. Fragrant shrubs surround a terrace or deck with their sweet perfume, while flowering shrubs add variety to your perennial border. Use shrubs as hedges or screens to increase your privacy or obscure a view. A thorny hedge will provide protection from unwanted visitors; evergreen shrubs will hide an unattractive foundation.

Juniperus is among the most versatile evergreen shrubs, growing naturally in many different shapes and hues of green.

In Borders

With their height, leaf color and texture, shrubs add a bold accent to mixed perennial and shrub borders. On a large scale, shrub borders can give shape to a lawn by defining the edges; on a smaller scale they can elegantly enclose a terrace. Evergreen and topiary shrubs, such as *Juniperus* spp. (junipers), *Taxus cuspidata* (Japanese yew) and *Picea glauca* 'Conica' (dwarf Alberta spruce), planted at regular intervals within the perennial border impart rhythm and order to the design. With their height, shrubs such as lilacs bring the color and fragrance of the border up to nose level. But, remember, shrubs grow vigorously, so place them where they will enhance, not overwhelm, the neighboring perennials.

At The Front Entrance

Shrubs can create a welcoming approach to your front door, frame the entrance and link the house with the surrounding landscape. To have your front entry look inviting year-round, select shrubs such as *Rhododendron, Ilex* spp. (holly) and *Mahonia aquifolium* (Oregon grape holly) for flower, fragrance and winter color. Use shrubs in a foundation planting to obscure unattractive concrete.

> *HINT: Consider the scale of your house and the ultimate size of the shrubs when making your selection. Your shrub planting should frame, not hide, your front door.*

Hedges

Hedges are one of the most popular uses for shrubs and an excellent way to organize your garden spaces. Formal or informal, hedges are comprised of shrubs planted closely together to create a solid line in the landscape. Evergreen shrubs provide year-round interest and are an excellent choice. Their leaves can be broad and leathery like *Ilex glabra* 'Nordic' (inkberry) or narrow, scale-like or needled like some *Juniperus, Taxus* spp. (yew) and *Thuja* spp. (arborvitae).

Select shrubs such as *Ligustrum* spp. (privet) and *Ilex* x *meserveae* (meserve hybrid holly) for their glossy leaves, *Spiraea* spp. for its showy flowers, *Cotoneaster* spp. for its fruit. To create a protective barrier, use thorny shrubs such as *Berberis thungbergii* (barberry); to frame flower beds and herb gardens, use low *Buxus sempervirens* 'Suffructicosa' (true dwarf boxwood) or *Santolina*. To build a private garden room, select shrubs that respond well to pruning, such as privet and arborvitae. Hedges hide unattractive pool or tennis court fencing with ease and are a friendly way to enclose a child's play area. A tall evergreen hedge makes the perfect backdrop for a perennial border.

HINT: For privacy, select shrubs that will grow as a solid mass to above eye level.

Screens

Shrubs massed together create a soft, friendly visual block, or a screen that can hide almost anything. For the best effect, use evergreen and deciduous shrubs of varying heights and combine them with flowering shrubs, such as *Rhododendron*, *Viburnum* and *Syringa* (lilac). Remember, to block noise, a screen planting must be solid and deep.

Windbreaks

To provide a windbreak, plant shrubs in conjunction with trees to the north and west of your home. Planted close together they form a green mass that allows at least 50 percent of the wind to pass through its branches. The branches not only reduce the force of the damaging winds, but also act as a filter, trapping airborne particulate matter causing it to fall harmlessly to the ground. (See the Windbreak Illustration on p.17.)

On A Hillside

If your home is on a steep hillside, erosion control is of primary importance. Use deep-rooted shrubs such as *Cotoneaster* spp., *Mahonia aquifolium* (Oregon holly grape) and *Rhus* spp. (sumac). For variety in height, plant them with groundcovers, such as *Hedera* spp. (ivy) and *Euonymus fortunei radicans* (wintercreeper).

Grow Shrubs:

- For their form, color, foliage, flower and fruit
- For fragrance
- To provide structure in the garden
- As hedges or screens
- As a thorny, protective hedge
- As windbreaks
- To reduce erosion
- As low edging around perennial, herb or rose gardens
- In borders to shape your garden spaces
- In foundation plantings
- In mixed perennial and shrub borders
- In mass plantings
- To frame an entrance

SUN/SHADE

There are shrubs for all levels of light. Understory shrubs, such as *Clethra alnifolia* (sweet pepper bush), thrive in the shade. *Taxus cuspidata* (Japanese yew) prefer partial shade, and others, such as *Rhus* spp. (sumac), *Buddleia davidii* (butterfly bush) and *Syringa* (lilac) prefer direct sunlight. There are some versatile shrubs, like *Spiraea vanhouttei* (Vanhoutte spirea) and *Calycanthus floridus* (sweetshrub), that thrive in sun or shade.

On cold, windy sites protect broadleafed evergreens such as *Rhododendron* and *Ilex* (holly) from the drying effects of late winter and early spring sun by planting them in a north- or east-facing location. Intense southern or western sun combined with strong winds can cause "winter injury," the burning (or browning) of the foliage. In your very cold climate you may wish to wrap your shrubs to protect them against winter sun and winds. See "Winterizing" on p.154.

TEMPERATURE

Cold hardiness, wind and long winters are the most important considerations when selecting shrubs for your cold climate. When cold weather arrives, deciduous shrubs drop their leaves; and in bitter cold the leaves of some broadleaf evergreens, such as *Rhododendron*, actually curl up for self-protection. Some shrubs, such as *Buddleia davidii* (butterfly bush) and *Hydrangea arborescens* 'Annabelle' (hydrangea), die back to the ground altogether in very cold climates. Cold temperatures combined with a short growing season influence the growth habits of shrubs as well. A shrub that may grow 3' tall in Zone 5 may not reach 18" in Zone 3!

As shrubs are the mainstay of the landscape, choose shrubs that are tough enough to survive very cold winters with strong winds. Be sure to consider the coldest expected winter temperature when selecting shrubs.

HUMIDITY

In humid areas, it is always a good practice to provide good air circulation in the garden. Overcrowding can lead to poor air circulation, which opens plants up to disease. Whenever possible select humidity-tolerant shrubs and avoid daily light watering, which can promote fungal growth.

SOIL

Most shrubs prefer well-drained soil and, although they are not as particular as perennials, most do develop better in a soil rich in nutrients. Many shrubs are pH adaptable. For example, *Potentilla* spp. (cinquefoil), *Cotoneaster* spp. and *Symphoricarpos* x *chenaultii* 'Hancock' (chenault coralberry) tolerate alkaline soils. Others, such as azaleas, *Fothergilla* spp. and *Clethra alnifolia* (sweet pepper bush) are less flexible and must have acid soil to thrive.

WATER

Most shrubs require regular water and well-drained soils. If you live in an area with high winds and little rainfall select drought-tolerant shrubs, such as *Hypericum patulum* (Saint John's-wort), *Potentilla fruticosa* (cinquefoil), *Caragana arborescens (*Siberian pea shrub) and *Hippophae rhamnoides* (seabuckthorn). But water all shrubs, including your drought-tolerant shrubs, thoroughly after planting and continue to provide regular water until they are established (two to three years). Then water thoroughly whenever the soil becomes dry, particularly during the growing season. Even drought-tolerant shrubs will look better with a little water, and well-watered plants, in general, can survive greater extremes of temperature.

SNOW AND ICE

A blanket of snow provides the garden with welcome insulation in winter. However, the weight of wet snow or ice can break the branches of woody plants. If wet snows are common in your area, avoid flat-topped hedges, which hold the snow, and select instead rounded or pointed tops with angled sides that allow the snow to slide off. If selecting arborvitae for a hedge, select a single leader variety such as *Thuja occidentalis* 'Wintergreen' (wintergreen arborvitae). Multiple leaders are prone to snow damage, as the snow tends to settle down into the shrubs, opening them up. Never allow snow to accumulate on your shrubs; brush it off as often as necessary. However, be careful of ice-covered branches; they are very brittle. Do not try to knock the ice off; the branches are likely to snap.

WINTER INJURY

Evergreens are prone to "winter injury," the burning (or browning) of evergreen foliage due to excessive moisture loss during the winter. Evergreens continue to transpire throughout the winter although the ground may be frozen and water unavailable from the soil. For survival, the shrub will resort to tapping living tissue to replace moisture. The drained living tissue will then turn brown, causing winter injury. Drought-stressed plants are most susceptible to winter injury, so water your evergreen shrubs regularly during dry falls to help prepare them for winter. And avoid planting evergreens in windy areas with intense southern or western exposure. Strong winds and intense sun are an especially lethal combination for susceptible evergreens as they increase transpiration.

HINT: As needle-leafed evergreens have a smaller amount of exposed surface, they transpire less and survive better on cold, windy sites than broadleaf evergreens.

PLANNING A SHRUB BORDER

Planning a shrub border can be as much fun as planning a perennial border and the results just as visually exciting. Select shrubs for the style of your garden, their leaf color and texture, flower and time of bloom as well as height and shape.

When planning the shrub border, first consider the theme or concept. Will it be a foliage border in varying textures and shades of green or a flowering border that blooms from spring to late fall? Will the flowers be all white or graduated shades of pink? Don't forget to consider the bloom time and color of your flowering trees. Select shrubs to contrast or to repeat the color of the trees.

For maximum impact, group shrubs in masses of three or more plants. The smaller the shrub, the more you will need to make an impact. Small groups of shrubs will be in scale with a small garden; large shrub masses make an impact in large landscapes.

Consider the horizontal and vertical lines of the border. Place the shrub masses in relation to vertical elements such as your existing trees. Use shorter shrubs, such as low-growing azaleas and *Ilex cornuta* 'Helleri' (Heller holly), in front of the border to create a visually smooth transition from lawn to shrubs to surrounding trees. Weave together irregularly shaped masses of different shrubs. Place shorter shrubs in front and taller in back, but don't be afraid to break the rules. Vary the height by bringing some taller shrubs into the medium height shrubs toward the front.

SPACING

Shrubs always look small in their containers, but with proper care, they will grow to their mature size faster than you think. Always consider the ultimate height, width and shape of the shrub before digging the hole. A general rule of thumb is to space small shrubs a minimum of 2' apart; larger shrubs 5' apart.

Hedge spacing is critical to the success of a formal hedge. For narrow hedges, plant in a single row; for wider hedges, plant in a double staggered row.

Spacing Hedges

For hedges, the general rule of thumb is to plant shrubs tip to tip. Space narrow plants, such as privet, 18" apart; larger plants, such as x *Cupressocyparis leylandii* (Leyland cypress), 24" to 36" apart. Hedges can be planted in single, straight rows or two staggered rows, which will provide a more solid block immediately. When staggering rows, the plants should be equidistant in both directions.

PLANNING AT A GLANCE
- Microclimate
- Sun/shade
- Soil
- Water
- Goal; i.e., privacy, wind block
- Evergreen or deciduous
- Spacing

- Ultimate size
- Growth rate
- Growth habit, form or shape
- Foliage size, color and texture
- Flower color, fragrance and time of bloom
- Fruit color, season, edibility, persistence
- Fall leaf color
- Winter interest: bark color, branching
- Garden style; i.e., natural, informal, formal

BED PREPARATION

Most shrubs will prosper in the same place for many years, so it's important to start them off right with good bed preparation, which stimulates new root growth, and encourages healthy, vigorous shrubs. Prepare the shrub beds to a depth of 12"-24", amending the soil as necessary. (See "Soil," p.18.) Water the beds well and allow them to settle for as long as possible. Fill in any sink holes and rake the bed smooth before planting.

BUYING SHRUBS

Shrubs can be purchased as container-grown, balled-and-burlapped or bare-root as follows:

Container-grown Shrubs

Most shrubs, but especially broadleaf evergreens, are grown in containers of varying sizes. The container size you select depends on your budget and your patience. If you want immediate satisfaction, buy the five-gallon size. If you are patient, a one-gallon size shrub will catch up to a five-gallon size plant in about three years.

> HINT: You can buy container-grown plants in bloom, taking the guesswork out of color selection.

Balled-and-burlapped Shrubs

Many deciduous shrubs, evergreen shrubs (such as *Rhododendron*), and conifers (cone-bearing plants such as *Juniperus*) are available as balled-and-burlapped (B-and-B) plants. They are grown in the field and will not tolerate bare-root transplanting. Instead, they are dug with a solid ball of soil to protect their roots. The root ball is then wrapped in burlap and tied with biodegradable twine to keep the ball intact. Once you have placed the shrub in its planting hole, remove the burlap and all nonbiodegradable materials from around the trunk and stems, leaving the burlap around the root ball.

B-and-B plants must be treated with great care to prevent the soil from loosening around the roots. While it is tempting to pick up B-and-B plants by their trunks or stems, never do so. Carry them with good support under the root ball and put them down gently. Dropping a B-and-B plant could shatter the root ball, damaging the roots.

When buying container-grown or B-and-B shrubs look for:
- Plants held in a partly shaded area.
- Healthy, vigorous plants.
- Well-shaped, densely branched plants.
- Dense foliage on evergreens.
- Plants that are in proportion to their containers.
- Firm, moist root balls if plants are B-and-B.
- Biodegradable twine around B-and-B plants.
- Wire baskets around B-and-B plants grown in sandy soil.

And avoid shrubs that:
- Are stressed from being held in the sun.
- Are weak or unhealthy.
- Are poorly formed.
- Have scarred or cracked branches or trunks.
- Have leaves of abnormal size.
- Have yellowing foliage.

- Are loose in the container (gently lift the shrub by its stem).
- Are potbound (examine the container for roots emerging from the bottom).
- Have "girdling" roots (roots wrapped around the trunk) if plants are in containers.
- Are tied with plastic twine (if plants are B-and-B).
- Have broken or cracked root balls (if plants are B-and-B).

HINT: If your shrub is in a straight-sided, metal can, ask the nursery to cut the sides to facilitate planting.

Bare-root Shrubs

Generally a good buy, bare-root shrubs are available in winter and late spring at local nurseries and through mail-order catalogs. See "Sources," p.219. Bringing no soil with them, bare-root shrubs grow in only one type of soil: yours. This allows them to adjust more quickly than container-grown or B-and-B shrubs. Buy bare-root plants with many healthy, thick, brown roots growing in different directions and be sure to keep them moist. Buy and plant them before they leaf out.

HINT: Use bare-root plants for the least expensive installation of a privet hedge.

TIME TO PLANT

The best time to plant most shrubs in Zones 3, 4 and 5 is when they are dormant in the early spring. This allows shrubs to establish good root systems prior to the onset of winter. However, fall planting can be successful if you select easily transplanted shrubs, such as needled evergreens, lilacs and viburnums, and complete the installation before October 15. To encourage new root growth before the ground freezes, be sure to water regularly and mulch them well. In parts of Zone 5 with stressful, hot summers, fall planting will give shrubs a better opportunity to become established prior to the onset of the next summer's heat and/or drought.

But how you purchase your shrubs will also determine the planting time. Bare-root shrubs are best planted while they are dormant in the spring to give them the many months they may need to become established before the cold of winter. Both balled-and-burlapped and container-grown shrubs can be planted as soon as the soil is workable in the early spring up until October 15. If you must plant during the heat of the summer, be sure you have an ample water supply and use it!

Plants lose moisture through transpiration and through their roots when they are out of the ground. To reduce stress, transplant your shrubs on cool, cloudy days whenever possible and install your plants as soon as possible after they arrive. If there are unforeseen delays, be sure to keep them well watered and in a cool, shady spot. Always water the shrubs in well, apply mulch, then water regularly during the growing season.

PLANTING
Transplanting Container-grown Shrubs

If you are planting more than one shrub, set your plants out on the bed according to your garden plan. Step back and take a good look. Fine-tune the design as necessary. Then begin to plant one by one.

1. Dig a hole twice as wide and 12" deeper than the root ball.
2. Carefully "knock" plants out of their containers.
3. Loosen the roots (which may be potbound) by spraying the soil off the outer edges of the root ball with water. Tease the roots loose with your hands, or make vertical cuts down the sides of the root ball with a sharp knife.
4. Return enough soil to the bottom of the hole for the top of

the root ball to be 1"-2" above the surrounding soil. Never plant lower than the surrounding soil.

5. Spread the roots at the bottom of the hole and gradually fill the hole with soil mix, watering midway to remove air pockets.
6. Form a soil rim above the existing grade to contain water around the plant.
7. Water thoroughly, but gently, so as not to break through the rim.
8. In two to three weeks break down the soil rim and mulch.

Transplanting Balled-and-burlapped Shrubs

B-and-B plants are generally grown in heavy or clay soils that hold together, forming sturdy root balls. If your soil is similar in texture, it will not be necessary to add amendments to change your soil's texture. If your soil is lighter than that of the root ball, the B-and-B plant won't be able to absorb water at the same rate as the surrounding soil and may have trouble adjusting to its new home. To prevent the root ball from drying out, equalize the soils by adding water-retentive, organic amendments to the backfill and carefully puncture the root ball with a narrow, pointed instrument such as a planting stake. The holes will allow additional water penetration and help prevent dehydration. (See "Soil," p.18.)

1. Prepare the hole as for container-grown plants
2. Set the shrub in the hole with the top of the root ball 1"- 2" above existing grade.
3. Untie the burlap, removing all synthetic twine, and fold it back to expose the top half of the root ball. (If burlap is synthetic, it should be removed entirely.)
4. Backfill to level of existing grade and firm soil.
5. Form a water moat as above.
6. In two to three weeks break down the soil rim and mulch.

(From the top) Plant bare-root shrubs while they are dormant. Container-grown shrubs can be planted whenever the soil is workable. Balled-and-burlapped shrubs should be planted soon after they are dug in the spring or fall.

Planting Bare-root Shrubs

Unlike container-grown plants that can be planted year-round, bare-root shrubs must be planted during their dormancy. If you can't plant them immediately upon their arrival, heel them in and keep them moist.

1. Prior to planting, soak the roots in a bucket of muddy water for a few hours. This will make them less brittle and more pliable. The mud will adhere to the roots during planting, protecting them from dryness.
2. Prune off any damaged or broken roots or branches.
3. Prepare the hole as for container-grown shrubs.
4. Make a mound with your soil mix in the bottom of the hole. Gently fan the roots over the mound in a natural pattern, keeping the shrub at the same depth or slightly higher than it was growing in the field.
5. Replace soil mix nearly to the top, and gently firm the soil with your hands so as not to damage roots.
6. Water thoroughly, allow soil to settle around roots, and then continue to fill to grade level.
7. When the shrub begins to grow, form a watering basin and water regularly.
8. Mulch during the summer to conserve moisture.

Like moving into a new neighborhood, it takes time for new shrubs to become established in the garden. They arrive packed full of stored nutrients that nourish them through the first year while they spread out their roots and get settled into their new soil. If you've planted the shrubs well, they will flourish the second year in their new community.

FERTILIZING

The type and amount of fertilizer required depends on both the shrub you are planting and the soil. A soil fertility test (see "Soil," p.18) will help you determine what nutrients are lacking in your soil. Or take a close look at your shrubs. If they have pale or small leaves, few flowers and/or spindly growth, they could benefit from fertilizing. Most shrubs planted in soils with average fertility will thrive with an application of liquid fertilizer or a light layer of well-rotted manure in the early spring and fall.

MULCH

Mulch your shrubs to moderate soil temperature extremes and fluctuations and to conserve moisture in all seasons. To keep the soil cool during the summer, apply 2"-3" of light mulch. Apply a heavier mulch in the fall, especially in areas with little snow cover and severe freeze/thaw cycles. The mulch will help protect your shrubs from the cold and reduce heaving, the result of the drastic temperature fluctuations during freeze/thaw cycles. For additional information, see "Mulch," p.36.

PRUNING

All shrubs have natural growth habits and structure, whether tall and leggy or short and round. Successful pruning works within these bounds to maintain shape, direct growth and increase fruit and flower production, as well as improve the health and longevity of both your evergreen and deciduous shrubs.

Pruning influences the growth and structure of the plant. Before you begin, carefully review the shrub, analyze what it can and cannot do, and then set a pruning goal. Maintain the natural character of the shrub while also improving its vigor. Use hand pruners, loppers, shears or pruning saws and make sure all pruning tools are sharp and clean to reduce the risk of disease in the open wounds.

Be selective. With every cut, you are directing plant growth. All plant growth eminates from the buds located along the branches. The terminal bud, located in the branch's tip, dominates a branch's growth and determines its length. When it is removed, the plant's energy is redirected to the buds grow-

ing along the stems, the side buds, which then expand, making a branch bushy. Where you cut controls which buds will grow and ultimately determines the shape of the shrub.

Pruning Goals:
- To maintain health
- To maintain or change shape
- To direct plant growth, as in espaliers
- To encourage flower and fruit production
- To eliminate limbs damaged by storm, insects or disease
- To create pathways and vistas

Pruning Tools
When heading out to prune your shrubs, be prepared to cut branches ranging from 1/4" twigs all the way to hefty main stems of 2" or more. Hand pruners are the perfect tool for getting the small twigs; loppers, the branches up to 1" thick. If you are rejuvenating a shrub, such as *Syringa* (lilac), a small saw may be necessary for removing thicker, old, nonproductive stems. When shaping a formal hedge, hedge shears with nice long blades will give you a clean, controlled cut. Use hand pruners for the selective pruning necessary to maintain an informal hedge.

Where To Cut
Always cut just above a bud to avoid stubs and ensure that the cut will be obscured by new growth. Prune branches with opposite buds using a straight cut just above a pair of buds. Prune branches with alternate buds just above a bud at a 45° angle with the bottom of the cut opposite the base of the bud and the top of the cut just above the tip of the bud.

When removing branches, position the shears with the blade on top of the branch, the hook beneath it. To avoid leaving unattractive stubs, the blades should be as close as possible to the branch collar, without cutting into it.

Prune shrubs with alternate buds (left) at a 45° angle just above the bud. Use a straight cut to prune shrubs with opposite buds (right).

Maintenance Pruning Of Deciduous Shrubs
For general maintenance, in late winter prune:
1. Crossing or crowded branches.
2. Diseased, dead or broken branches.
3. Weak branches.
4. Branches that detract from the shape of the bush.

HINT: When growing plants in masses, allow the plants to grow naturally together. Do not prune each plant individually, which would result in a "meatball" look.

Thinning Deciduous Shrubs

Thinning opens up the center of deciduous shrubs for better air circulation, allows sunlight to penetrate to the center and reduces its size.

To thin a shrub, in late winter prune:

1. For maintenance. (See "Maintenance Pruning.")
2. Lateral branches back to main stems or by about one-third their length.

Pruning For Shape

Pruning for shape is an art. It takes careful consideration as well as muscle power. Before you shape a shrub, step back and look at its natural form and branching structure. Always think twice before removing major branches; imagine what the shrub will look like without them.

To shape a shrub, prune:

1. For maintenance. (See "Maintenance Pruning.")
2. Shoots that may interfere with the shape.
3. To encourage growth in a chosen direction.

> HINT: *Prune to maintain the shape and density of a plant, not to control its size. A shrub growing in the right place should not require controlling.*

Pruning To Stimulate Flower Production

Pruning stimulates flower production by channeling the shrub's energy to selected buds. The most important consideration when pruning flowering shrubs is whether the shrub blooms on new growth or the previous year's growth. Spring- and early summer-flowering shrubs, such as *Deutzia, Forsythia*, and *Syringa* (lilac), bloom so soon after breaking dormancy they don't have time to produce new buds before flowering. Instead, they bloom on the previous year's growth. Prune them after they have bloomed. Deciduous shrubs that bloom during the summer, such as *Spiraea* and *Symphoricarpos* (coralberry), flower on the current season's growth and should be pruned in early spring.

For summer- and fall-flowering shrubs that flower on the current year's wood, in early spring prune:

1. For maintenance. (See "Maintenance Pruning.")
2. Several main stems down to the base to maintain open form.
3. Back stems of previous year's growth to two to four buds to stimulate flowering.

For spring- and early summer-flowering shrubs that flower on the previous year's wood, after flowering prune:

1. For maintenance. (See "Maintenance Pruning.")
2. Shoots that have flowered.
3. Several main stems down to the base.

Pruning For Rejuvenation

A well-maintained shrub should not need the drastic pruning called for below. However, if you are moving into a new house with a garden that has been let go, rejuvenation pruning may be necessary.

To rejuvenate a deciduous shrub:

1. Cut back all main stems close to the ground during dormancy.
2. Fertilize, water and mulch well.

Be patient; the shrub should flourish in the second year. Then prune selectively to establish a new framework for the shrub.

Pruning For Color

As young shoots are the most colorful, it is necessary to regularly prune shrubs, such as *Cornus alba* 'Siberica' (red-twig dogwood), to encourage colorful new growth. There are

two methods; the second is more drastic than the first. In the first you remove one-third of the older branches each year by cutting them back to the ground. In the second method you cut all the branches back to about 6" every three years. For either, the best time to prune is late winter or early spring, which allows you to enjoy the colorful branches all winter.

Pruning Evergreen Shrubs

Needled, narrow- and broad-leafed evergreen shrubs have varying growth habits. The type and amount of pruning you will need to do responds directly to their natural growth and the use of the shrub in your landscape. A *Taxus* spp. (yew) hedge can take shearing, while azaleas look best pruned with hand clippers. Keep the final shape of the shrub in mind at all times and always select the branches you remove with care. An elegantly branched shrub is a beautiful sight in the garden.

Needled evergreens, such as *Juniperus* spp., naturally grow in many shapes ranging from narrow columns to prostrate groundcovers. While columnar *Juniperus* spp. will require little more than the removal of dead or broken branches, prostrate *Juniperus* may require the pruning of branch tips to keep it within bounds.

Most narrow- and broad-leafed evergreens with open growth habits, such as *Pieris japonica* (andromeda), will benefit from "thinning out." (See "Thinning Deciduous Shrubs.") Those with columnar habits, such as some hollies, need only their side stems pruned for shape.

Pruning Hedges

Shrubs used for hedges tolerate severe pruning. Give your hedge a good start by carefully training it during the first few years. When planting a new hedge, the fear is that the hedge will thin out at the bottom. With careful pruning from the outset, this can be avoided.

To shear new hedges:

1. Remove one-third of the top and side growth with pruning shears at the time of installation.
2. Shape them narrower at the top to allow more sunlight to the bottom branches.
3. Cut back half the new growth several times during the first growing season.
4. Trim off 3" to 4" three times during the second growing season.

To maintain a hedge:

1. Prune in spring and late summer.
2. For straight sides and flat tops, use a straight edge or a string stretched taught with a level on it as a guide.
3. For shaped hedges, use a wood template as a guide.

DEADHEADING

Deadhead by removing the spent blossoms after they have faded to direct the plant's energy from seed production to leaf production. Always cut just above a bud. Shrubs that benefit from deadheading include azaleas and *Syringa* (lilac).

SHRUBS FOR FLOWER ARRANGEMENTS

Shrubs often produce lovely flowers, and their fruit, foliage and bare branches can be impressive in flower arrangements. Use the foliage of shrubs, such as *Ilex* (holly), to form the structure of flower arrangements or the delicate foliage of *Tamarix* as filler to offset flowers. Bare branches of *Cornus alba* 'Siberica' (red-twig dogwood) can make striking accents.

Forcing Branches

Get a head start on spring. Cut branches of *Forsythia*, *Cornus mas* (cornelian cherry), *Chaenomeles* spp. (flowering quince), *Cornus* (dogwood) or *Magnolia* with lots of flower buds and force them to flower indoors by placing the branches in a

vase of warm water on a sunny windowsill. They should bloom in two to four weeks. To speed up the process, some gardeners believe in soaking the branches overnight in a tub (or bathtub) of warm water.

Picking Flowers
Remember that cutting flowers is like pruning a bush. Step back and take a good look. Only remove branches from areas where they will not affect the overall shape. Ideally the removal of a branch should enhance the bush's appearance!

To Prolong The Life Of Cut Flowers:
1. Use sharp clippers to make a clean cut.
2. Cut flowers before they are fully open.
3. Remove all foliage that will be below the water line.
4. Keep vase filled with water!
5. Change water daily to prevent buildup of bacteria.

Special Hints
FOR AZALEAS Burn the ends of the stems over a gas flame then soak them in a solution of one tablespoon of alcohol per gallon of water. Or hammer the ends well and plunge in deep water.

FOR *CORNUS* (DOGWOOD) BRANCHES AND FLOWERS Hammer the ends well and place in deep, cold water for twelve hours prior to arranging.

FOR *COTONEASTER, HAMAMELIS* (WITCH HAZEL) Hammer the ends well and place in deep, cold water.

FOR *DAPHNE, HYDRANGEA, RHODODENDRON* Hammer the ends well or plunge them in 1' of boiling water, then soak in deep cold water.

WINTERIZING
Rake up all fallen leaves, add them to your compost pile, and renew the mulch in your shrub beds. Protect your tender shrubs from temperature extremes by applying a thicker layer of mulch, such as pine straw, composted leaves or other organic material (see "Mulch," p.36).

Tie together twiggy deciduous shrubs that might break apart in strong winds or snap under the weight of heavy snow. Lightly tie together the branches of upright evergreen shrubs such as *Thuja* spp. (arborvitae) and *Juniperus* spp. to prevent them from bending out of shape. On cold, windy sites, protect tender broadleaf evergreens, such as *Rhododendron* and *Ilex* (holly), by surrounding them with burlap supported by wood or metal stakes. For extra insulation fill the burlap enclosure with leaves. Use plywood A-frames to shelter foundation plantings from snow falling off the roof.

SPRING CLEANUP
Remove excess mulch from your tender shrubs and add it to your compost pile. Prune any branches that may have been damaged during the winter.

Azaleas and Rhododendrons

The genus *Rhododendron* comprises an enormous number of species and varieties of azaleas and rhododendrons. But, while all azaleas are *Rhododendron*, not all *Rhododendron* are azaleas! Both rhododendrons and azaleas have evergreen and deciduous varieties, although azaleas are primarily deciduous. Available in a wide range of sizes and colors, azaleas and rhododendrons are justly famous for their spectacular show each spring.

Although most prefer a moderate climate, there are several natives and hybrids that are hardy to Zone 4 and do well along the Atlantic coast. Although both rhododendrons and azaleas are difficult to grow in many areas of the central states because of their dislike of alkaline soils, the very hardy 'Northern Lights' and 'P.J.M.' rhododendrons have been quite successful. However, in the Rocky Mountains even the hardiest varieties cannot survive the low humidity and rainfall, intense sun and strong, drying winds.

PLANNING *Rhododendron* are available in a brilliant range of colors from white to yellow, magenta and orange. When making your selection, coordinate the bloom sequence to prevent an unsettling clash of colors. Mass them together to create drifts of color in your garden.

SUN/SHADE Most *Rhododendron* prefer part shade. Avoid dense shade as they may fail to bloom. Rhododendrons and azaleas do require some sunlight to set their buds. However, full sun can cause sunburn, or brown patches on the leaves. Summer sunburn appears as brown spots along leaf edges and tips; winter sunburn as long brown patches adjacent to the mid-vein. Although not life-threatening themselves, sunburn spots do open the plant up to fungal infections, which can weaken your shrubs.

In your cold zone, exposure is just as important as the amount of light. Northern exposures are usually preferable. Avoid planting your *Rhododendron* in eastern exposures where they will receive early morning sun. In the winter, direct early morning sun can damage early-flowering hybrids by thawing the leaves and buds too quickly. Western and southern exposures are generally too hot for *Rhododendron.*

TEMPERATURE *Rhododendron* are sensitive to both the heat and cold. Many evergreen rhododendrons, for example, thrive in southern New England but expire in extremely hot, dry summers. 'Scintillation' is unusual in that it is heat tolerant. If your summers are very hot, ask your local nurseryman for suggestions. And to avoid damage from alternating freeze/thaw cycles during mild winters with little snow cover, mulch your rhododendrons well.

FROST Late spring and early autumn frosts do the most damage to *Rhododendron.* Leaves may become misshapen and rough or be killed altogether.

WIND *Rhododendron* are sensitive to the drying effects of wind, especially during the winter when the soil is frozen. If new growth has brown edges, your shrub may be suffering from windburn. Move it to a more protected spot in your garden or protect it with burlap. See "Winterizing" on p.154.

SOIL *Rhododendron* thrive in moist, acid soils (pH 4.5 to 6.5) rich in organic matter. If you have dry or very alkaline soils, they may not be for you. *Rhododendron* will be happiest if you add up to 50 percent leaf mold, peat moss or other well-rotted organic matter to your planting bed. The organic matter will improve the soil structure and retain moisture but allow for good drainage. Azaleas are susceptible to root rot in poorly drained soils. Yellowing leaves, wilting or the total collapse of plants are indications of root rot.

PLANTING *Rhododendron* are shallow rooted and require excellent drainage. Plant azaleas with the root ball slightly above ground level. Do not bury stems with soil. Never cultivate around rhododendrons. They are surface rooters and cultivation could damage their roots.

> HINT: Pine trees are good companions for Rhododendron. *Their deep root systems don't interfere with the shrub plantings, they provide filtered light and their needles create an attractive acid mulch.*

FERTILIZING Fertilize with an acid fertilizer in the early spring when growth starts, just after they've bloomed, and monthly throughout the summer as necessary. If your plants are showing signs of weakness or yellowing leaves, give them a foliar feeding of an algae solution mixed with liquid fertilizer. Use organic fertilizers whenever possible as the salts from most synthetic fertilizers may damage the roots.

PRUNING All *Rhododendron* benefit from occasional pruning. *Rhododendron* bloom on the previous year's growth, so prune

them after they have bloomed to thin and to remove broken, diseased or dead branches.

MULCH *Rhododendron* prefer cool roots, so apply a 2" to 3" layer of well-rotted oak leaves, pine needles, sawdust or other acid-rich mulch during the spring and replenish it in the fall to moderate soil temperatures and retain moisture.

DISEASE *Rhododendron* are generally trouble free when provided with the proper growing conditions. Sucking insects may affect the leaves in hot weather and fungal infections may develop in leaves with winter injury.

AZALEAS
Native Or Species Azaleas
Most native azaleas, many of which are fragrant, are hardy to Zone 5, a few to Zone 3, including:
R. arborescens (Sweet azalea, Zone 4)
R. atlanticum (Coast azalea, Zone 5)
R. calendulaceum (Flame azalea, Zone 5)
R. periclymenoides (Pinxterbloom azalea, Zone 3)
R. vaseyi (Pinkshell azalea, Zone 4)
R. viscosum (Swamp azalea, Zone 3)

Evergreen Azaleas
GABLE HYBRIDS (Zone 5) grow to about 3'-4'.
GLEN DALE VARIETIES (Zones 5 to 8) vary in growth (generally to 4'-6') and leaf size.

Deciduous Azaleas
EXBURY AND KNAP HILL HYBRIDS (Zone 5) have the largest blossoms of all deciduous azaleas and grow up to 12'.
GHENT HYBRIDS (Zone 5) are very hardy, upright shrubs that grow to 4'-6'.
NORTHERN LIGHTS HYBRIDS (Zone 3) are very hardy and generally grow to 4'-5'.

RHODODENDRON
Native Rhododendon
Native *Rhododendron* that are evergreen and hardy include:
R. maximum, the hardiest (Zone 3).
R. catawbiense (Zone 4), the most common in the East.

Evergreen Rhododendron
CATAWBIENSE HYBRIDS include 'Catawbiense Album' (protected Zone 4), a vigorous, wide-spreading white and 'Roseum Elegans' (protected Zone 4), a very hardy lavender-pink with excellent heat tolerance.
CAUCASIAN HYBRIDS are early blooming and hardy, including 'Boule de Neige' (Zone 5), a dense, rounded, low-growing rhododendron with white blossoms.
DEXTER HYBRIDS have large leaves, generally grow to 6-8'and include 'Scintillation' (Zone 5), a favorite luminous pink that grows to 8' and is heat resistant.
'MEZITT' HYBRIDS (Zone 4) are small-leaved, very hardy, grow to 3'-4' and include 'Olga Mezitt,' a clear pink with leaves turning plum in winter.
'PJM' HYBRIDS (Zone 4) have small leaves which turn a rich mahogany in winter, are very hardy and grow up to 6'.

Deciduous Rhododendron
R. mucronulatum (Korean rhododendron, Zone 4) is the first to flower and grows to 6'.

Shrubs

Best Bets For Your Garden

above left: Deutzia gracilis

above right: Potentilla fruti-cosa 'Gold Star'

left: Spiraea x *bumalda* 'Mrs. Anthony Waterer'

below left: Buddleia davidii

below right: Clethra alnifolia 'Rosea'

Botanical Name Common Name	Bloom Color	Height Spacing	Sun/ Shade
DECIDUOUS SHRUBS			
SMALL			
Cotoneaster spp. Cotoneaster	Pinkish-white	Varies	○ ◑
Deutzia gracilis Slender deutzia	White	2-5' 3-4'	○ ◑
Potentilla fruticosa Cinquefoil	Red, orange, yellow	3' 3'	○
Rhus aromatica 'Gro-low' Fragrant sumac	Yellow	24-30" 4-6'	○ ◑
Spiraea x *bumalda* 'Goldflame' Goldflame spirea	Rose pink	3' 3'	○ ◑
Symphoricarpos x *chenaultii* 'Hancock' Chenault coralberry	Pink	2' 3-4'	○ ◑
MEDIUM			
Berberis thunbergii Barberry	Red-tinged yellow	4-6' 4-6'	○ ◑
Buddleia davidii Butterfly bush	White, purple, purple-red, pink	5-8' 4-6'	○
Chaenomeles speciosa Flowering quince	Pink, coral, red, orange, apricot	4-6' 4-6'	○ ◑
Clethra alnifolia Sweet pepper bush	White	3-8' 4-6'	○ ◑
Cornus alba 'Siberica' Red-twig dogwood	Cream white	7' 4-5'	○ ◑

Microclimate	Bloom Time	Comments
Hardy to Zone 4; seashore- and drought-tolerant	Late spring - early summer	Banks, groundcover, mass plantings; glossy dark green leaves, red in autumn; small flower; red fruit; tolerates most soils but not waterlogged soils; deer-resistant
Hardy to Zones 4 and 5	Spring until early summer	Low hedge, mass plantings, borders; upright or spreading; bright green foliage; rich, well-drained soil; five-petaled flowers in clusters on arching stems; prune after flowering; pest-resistant
Hardy; drought- and heat-tolerant	Early summer - fall	Dense, bushy; grey-green foliage; small, saucer-shaped flowers; well-drained soil; tolerates alkaline and poor soil; cut out older stems annually; many cultivars
Very hardy	Midspring	Groundcover, shrub border; irregular, mounding habit; suckering; glossy green foliage; tiny flowers; tolerant of many soils; pest-resistant
Hardy to Zone 4	Summer	Borders, foundations; upright, rounded; leaves open orange-red, turning yellow then pale green; clusters of small flowers; tolerant of all moist soils; prune in late winter
Hardy to Zones 4 and 5	Summer	Groundcover, borders; low-spreading, arching; blue-green foliage; small flowers on current season's growth; pink or white fruit; tolerant of any soil; native on limestone and clay; prune in early spring
Hardy; seashore- and drought-tolerant	Midspring	Hedges, barriers, borders; dense, arching; spiny branches; medium-green foliage; brilliant orange-red in fall; small flowers; bright red fruit; tolerates all but waterlogged soil; deer-resistant
Hardy to Zone 5; seashore-tolerant	Summer	Mixed borders; arching shrub; long, pointed, dull green leaves; fragrant plumes; rich, well-drained soil; tolerates alkaline soils; attracts butterflies; deer-resistant
Hardy to Zones 4 and 5; drought-tolerant	Late winter - early spring	Accent, mass plantings, borders; tangled mess of spiny branches; showy blossoms before foliage; edible fruit; most soils
Hardy; seashore-tolerant	Summer	Mass plantings, hedges; vertical branching; dark green foliage; tiny, fragrant flowers in spires; moist, acid soil; tolerates wet soil
Hardy	Late spring - early summer	Mass plantings, borders; multistemmed, vase-shaped; current year's growth is coral red in winter; dark green foliage; small flowers in flattened heads; round blue fruit; moist acid to neutral soil; cut out old stems to maintain good color

Shrubs

Best Bets For Your Garden

above left: Enkianthus campanulatus

above right: Fothergilla gardenii

left: Hydrangea quercifolia 'Snowflake'

below left: Ilex verticillata

below right: Kerria japonica 'Picta'

Botanical Name Common Name	Bloom Color	Height Spacing	Sun/ Shade
Enkianthus campanulatus Redvein enkianthus	White, creamy yellow, light orange, red	6-8' 6-8'	○ ◑
Forsythia ovata 'Northern Gold' Northern Gold forsythia	Yellow	4-6' 4-6'	○
Fothergilla spp. Fothergilla	White	Varies	○ ◑
Hydrangea arborescens 'Annabelle'	White	3-5' 3-5'	○ ◑
Hydrangea quercifolia Oakleaf hydrangea	White	6-8' 5-6'	○ ◑
Ilex verticillata Winterberry	White	6-9' 4-6'	○ ◑
Kerria japonica Japanese kerria	Yellow	4-6' 3-5'	○ ◑
Ligustrum obtusifolium regelianum Regal border privet	White	4-5' 2-3'	○ ◑
Philadelphus x *virginalis* 'Minnesota Snowflake' Mock orange	White	6-8' 5-6'	○ ◑
Physocarpus opulifolius Ninebark	White	4-6' 4-6'	○ ◑
Rhododendron spp. Azalea	White, pink, red, coral, yellow, purple	Varies	○ ◑
Shepherdia argentea Silver buffaloberry	Yellow	6-10' 4-5'	○

Microclimate	Bloom Time	Comments
Hardy to Zones 4 and 5	Late spring - early summer	Specimen, borders; narrow, upright, layered branching; medium-green foliage, bright yellow to orange-red in fall; moist, acid, well-drained soil; excellent with *Rhododendron*; many cultivars
Very hardy	Spring	Specimen, massing, borders; upright with grey-yellow branches; dense foliage; blooms well in cold climates; fertile, well-drained soil; thin out after flowering; deer-resistant
Hardy; drought-tolerant	Late spring	Borders, mass plantings, foundations; rounded; dark green to blue-green foliage, brilliant yellow, orange to red in fall; fragrant flowers in terminal spikes; acid, peaty, sandy, well-drained soil; many cultivars
Very hardy	Midsummer	Borders, massing; rounded; dark green foliage; very large, showy flower heads; rich, well-drained, moist soil; pH adaptable; flowers on new growth; prune to ground and lightly fertilize in late winter
Hardy to Zone 5	Summer	Mass plantings, shrub and mixed borders; upright, little branching; older stems exfoliate; oaklike leaves; large, cone-shaped flower clusters; rich, moist, well-drained soil; pest-resistant
Hardy to Zones 4 and 5	Spring	Borders, mass plantings; dark green foliage; small flowers; very showy red fruit; male needed for fruit; rich, moist, acid (pH 4.5 to 6.5) soil; tolerates light, heavy and wet soils; deer-resistant
Hardy to Zones 4 and 5	Spring	Specimen, borders; rounded with arching stems; bright green stems year-round; toothed, bright green leaves; buttercup-like flowers; moist, rich soil; pest-resistant
Very hardy	Midsummer	Hedge, screen, mass plantings; graceful, arching branches; glossy, dark green foliage; panicles of small, unpleasantly fragrant, tubular flowers; black fruit; all well-drained soils; pH adaptable; prune in early summer to prevent bloom; takes pruning well; any well-drained soil
Hardy to Zones 4 and 5	Early summer	Shrub and mixed borders; arching, vase-shaped; fragrant, very double flowers; rich, moist, well-drained soil; prune after flowering to control
Very hardy; tolerates dry, windy sites	Late spring - early summer	Borders, hedges, mass plantings, foundations; small flowers; red seed pods; extremely adaptable; tolerates acid and alkaline soils; renew by cutting to ground in late winter
Hardy	Early: January - March Mid: March - April Late: April - May	Borders, mass plantings, foundation plantings; rounded to upright; small to large leathery leaves; some blooms fragrant; constantly rich, moist, well-drained, acid soil; intolerant of soil salts; surface roots benefit from acid-rich mulches such as pine needles and oak leaves; do not cultivate soil
Very hardy	Late spring	Borders, mass plantings, screen; rounded; thorny; silvery foliage; flower not showy; edible red fruit in summer; very tolerant of poor, dry or alkaline soils

Shrubs

Best Bets For Your Garden

above left: Spiraea x *vanhouttei*

above right: Euonymus alatus
'Compacta'

left: Viburnum plicatum

below: Syringa vulgaris

Botanical Name / Common Name	Bloom Color	Height / Spacing	Sun/ Shade
Spiraea vanhouttei 'Renaissance' Vanhoutte spirea	White	5-7' 4-6'	○ ●
LARGE			
Caragana arborescens Siberian peashrub	Yellow	12-15' 6-8'	○
Buddleia alternifolia 'Argentea' Butterfly bush	Lilac-purple	10-20' 5-8'	○
Euonymus alatus 'Compacta' Burning bush	Inconspicuous	8-10' 5-6'	○ ●
Hippophae rhamnoides Common seabuckthorn	Yellowish	8-12' 4-6'	○
Myrica pensylvanica Bayberry	Yellowish-green	5-10' 5-8'	○ ◑
Rhus typhina 'Laciniata' Laceleaf staghorn sumac	Greenish white	10-20' 5-8'	○
Syringa vulgaris Lilac	White, pink, rose, purple	8-15' 5-6'	○
Viburnum spp. Viburnum	White	Varies	○ ◑
EVERGREEN SHRUBS			
SMALL			
Arctostaphylos uva-ursi Bearberry	White	2-3" 3-4'	○
Buxus microphylla 'Koreana' Wintergreen boxwood	Inconspicuous	24-30" 2-3'	○

Microclimate	Bloom Time	Comments
Hardy to Zones 4 and 5; seashore-tolerant	Early summer	Mass plantings, mixed and shrub borders; compact with arching shoots; dark green foliage; covered with small, dense clusters of flowers; rich, well-drained soil; disease-resistant foliage
Very hardy; drought- and wind-tolerant	Late spring - early summer	Hedges, screen, windbreak; upright; bright green foliage yellow-green in fall; flowers on previous year's wood; seed pods; tolerates poor, alkaline, and salty soils; nitrogen fixing; withstands heavy pruning
Hardy to Zone 5; seashore- and drought-tolerant	Summer	Mixed borders; arching shrub; long, pointed, dull dark green leaves; fragrant plumes; loose, loamy soil; tolerates alkaline soils; attracts butterflies; recommended for the high desert; deer-resistant
Hardy to Zones 4 and 5	Spring	Mass plantings, shrub border, hedge, screen; broad, spreading; dark green foliage, brilliant red in fall; well-drained soils; pH adaptable; water and mulch in dry areas; withstands heavy pruning
Very hardy; drought- and seashore-tolerant	Early spring	Mass plantings, shrub borders, stabilizing sand; spreading, irregularly rounded; silver-green foliage; small flowers; one male bush required for every six females for bloom; sandy, infertile soil
Very hardy; seashore-tolerant	Spring	Borders, mass planting; semievergreen; upright, rounded; dark green, leathery foliage; gray fruit; poor, sandy soil as well as clay; lower-growing by coast; select plants grown in your region
Hardy; drought-tolerant	Summer	Borders; spreading, open; suckering; velvety branches like deer's antlers; dark green foliage, brilliant orange-red in fall; well-drained soil; tolerant of poor soils
Hardy	Spring	Specimen, borders; upright, open; dark green to blue-green foliage; fragrant clusters of flowers; rich, moist, neutral soil; deadhead after flowering; select disease-resistant cultivars; deer-resistant; many cultivars
Hardy to very hardy	Spring - early summer	Borders, specimen, mass plantings; upright, rounded to broad rounded; medium to dark green, glossy to leathery foliage; showy flowers; often showy fruit; moist, well-drained soils
Very hardy; drought- and seashore-tolerant	Summer	Groundcover, slopes; trailing; small, bright green foliage red in winter; small, urn-shaped flowers; bright red fruit; prefers acid soils; tolerant of poor soils and sand. May be difficult to grow in Midwest.
Hardy to Zones 4 and 5	Late spring	Excellent for low edging; slow-growing dwarf, dense; bright green leaves turn yellow-brown in winter; takes shearing well; tolerates all but waterlogged soils; best for colder zones; deer-resistant

Shrubs

Best Bets For Your Garden

above: Thuja occidentalis

right: Buxus sempervirens 'Variegata'

below: Kalmia latifolia 'Raspberry Glow'

Botanical Name Common Name	Bloom Color	Height Spacing	Sun/ Shade
Buxus sempervirens 'Suffructicosa' True dwarf boxwood	Inconspicuous	2-3' *1-3'*	◯
Juniperus spp. Juniper	NA	Varies	◯
Pinus mugo Mugo pine	NA	Varies	◯ ◑
MEDIUM			
Ilex glabra 'Nordic' Inkberry	Inconspicuous	6-8' *4-6'*	◯ ●
Kalmia latifolia Mountain laurel	White, pink, red	Varies	◯ ●
Mahonia aquifolium Oregon holly grape	Yellow	3-6' *3-5'*	●
Rhododendron spp. Rhododendron	White, pink, red, coral, yellow, purple	Varies	◯ ◑
Taxus cuspidata Japanese yew	Inconspicuous	Varies	◯ ●
LARGE			
Ilex x *meserveae* Meserve hybrid hollies	Inconspicuous	10-12' *3-4'*	◯ ◑
Picea glauca 'Conica' Dwarf Alberta spruce	NA	10-12'	◯ ◑
Thuja occidentalis 'Wintergreen' Wintergreen arborvitae	NA	20-30' *3-6'*	◯

Microclimate	Bloom Time	Comments
Hardy to Zone 5; heat-tolerant	Late spring	Excellent for low edging; slow-growing dwarf, dense; bright green leaves; can be clipped and maintained at as low as 6"; tolerates all but waterlogged soils; susceptible to nematodes; deer-resistant
Very hardy; drought-, heat- and seashore-tolerant	NA	Groundcovers, slopes, mass plantings; needles of varying colors; cones; tolerates some alkalinity; deer-resistant; many cultivars.
Very hardy	NA	Borders, mass plantings, foundations; prostrate or rounded; dark green, two-needled; deep, moist soil; tolerant of alkaline soil; intolerant of desert heat; deer-resistant; cultivars
Hardy	Spring	Foundations, hedges, massing; compact, rounded form; dark green foliage; black fruit; hardier than most cultivars; withstands pruning; moist, acid soils; tolerates clay soils; deer-resistant
Hardy to Zones 4 and 5	Late spring - early summer	Borders, massing; dense, symmetrical becoming loose and open; glossy dark green foliage; cup-shaped flowers in clusters; deadhead; cool, moist, acid, well-drained soil; many cultivars
Hardy to Zones 4 and 5	Spring	Specimen, borders, foundations; irregular, upright; sparsely branched; holly-like foliage opens reddish bronze turning glossy green; flowers in clusters; edible blue-black fruit; moist, well-drained, acid soils; protect from hot, drying winds; may not thrive in Midwest; deer-resistant
Hardy	Early: January - March Mid: March - April Late: April - May	Borders, mass plantings, foundation plantings; rounded to upright; small to large leathery leaves; some blooms fragrant; constantly rich, moist, well-drained, acid soil; intolerant of soil salts; surface roots benefit from acid-rich mulches such as pine needles and oak leaves; do not cultivate soil
Hardy to Zone 4	Spring	Foundations, hedges, screens, massing; erect, broad, narrow or spreading; glossy, dark green, leathery needles; red fruit; moist, sandy, well-drained soil; withstands heavy pruning; many cultivars
Hardy to Zone 5	Spring	Mass plantings, hedges, foundations; upright; purplish-green spiny foliage; must have male and female for showy red fruit; moist, rich, acid soil; protect from drying winter winds; takes pruning well; deer-resistant
Very hardy; wind-, heat-, and drought-tolerant	NA	Accent; densely pyramidal; slow-growing; light green, short needles; moist soil
Very hardy	NA	Screen, hedges, accent; columnar pyramidal; scale-like leaves with good green winter color; single leader; moist, deep, well-drained soil; tolerant of alkaline soils; do not prune; deer-resistant

Peter C. Jones

V
EDIBLE
GARDENS

Vegetables

Herbs

VEGETABLES

Vegetables are among the most gratifying plants. They grow quickly, rewarding your hard work with delicious results. If you are a discriminating cook, try planting exotic and gourmet varieties that are hard to find at local supermarkets. Gardeners committed to an organic diet can control what they eat by using organic seeds, fertilizers and nontoxic pest controls. Plant enthusiasts can grow heirloom vegetables for their delicious flavor and to support genetic diversity. Everyone can enjoy vegetables for their beautiful shapes, texture and colors. But don't grow vegetables to save money. Once you've bought the plants, seeds, soil amendments, fertilizers and tools, and fenced and irrigated the garden, you may find that a head of home-grown lettuce costs more than the gas to go to the store. Grow them instead for their flavor, freshness, beauty, and the sheer pleasure of watching them grow.

Grow Vegetables:
- For sustenance
- For freshness and flavor
- For exotic and gourmet varieties
- For genetic diversity
- To control your consumption of pesticides
- For their shape, color, texture and beauty
- To share with friends
- For pleasure

UNDERSTANDING VEGETABLES

Usually known by the edible part of the plant, vegetables include root crops, such as carrots and beets; leaf vegetables, such as lettuce, spinach, cabbage and Swiss chard; the flower heads of broccoli and cauliflower; the bulbs of onions and garlic; the enlarged stems of rhubarb, turnips and potatoes; the fruit of tomatoes, eggplants and peppers; and the seeds inside the fruit of corn and peas!

Annual Or Perennial?

Most vegetables are annuals and must be replanted each season. However, a few, such as asparagus, rhubarb, horseradish and Jerusalem artichoke, are perennial and should have a special home in the garden where they will not be disturbed.

Vegetable Families

Vegetables, like flowers, trees and shrubs, are grouped together into families of plants with similar characteristics, including growing habits, temperature tolerance, soil preferences, and related pest problems. Understanding the nine major vegetable families will help you plan and rotate your garden, giving your plants what they need to excel.

AMARYLLIDACEAE OR LILIACEAE (The amaryllis or lily family) Includes onion-type vegetables and asparagus. Some, such as onions, are grown for their edible bulbs; others, such as chives, for their edible leaves and flowers. While most seeds require warmth to germinate, those in the lily family prefer a cool weather start in rich, moist, well-drained soil. The longer the bulb grows, the larger it will be.

APIACEAE OR UMBELLIFERAE (Plants with umbel flowers) Includes many fragrant or flavorful herbs, such as parsley and dill, and vegetables, such as carrots, parsnips, and celery. Prefer cool weather and deep, loose soils. All need light, moist soil to germinate.

ASTERACEAE OR COMPOSITAE (The sunflower family) Includes many ornamental plants, such as asters and daisies, and salad plants, including lettuce, endive, and chicory. Prefer cool weather.

BRASSICACEAE OR CRUCIFERAE (The cabbage or mustard family) Includes ornamentals, such as alyssum and candytufts, as well as broccoli, Brussels sprouts, cauliflower, kale, collards, turnips, rutabaga, kohlrabi, watercress and radishes. Prefer cool weather and moist, rich soils. Susceptible to cutworms and cabbage worms.

CHENOPODIACEAE (The goosefoot family) Includes vegetables such as spinach, Swiss chard, beets as well as some herbs and shrubs. Among the most problem-free vegetables except spinach, which bolts in the heat.

CUCURBITACEAE (The gourd or cucumber family) Includes cucumbers, squash, pumpkins, melons and gourds. Tendril vine-growing plants that prefer warm weather and rich, fertile soil. Susceptible to cucumber beetles.

FABACEAE OR LEGUMINOSAE (The legume or pea family, called legumes) Includes ornamentals, trees and vegetables, such as peas, beans, peanuts, soybeans and clover. Cold tolerance varies. Nitrogen-fixing nodules on the roots of these plants convert nitrogen from the air into nitrogen in the soil. This is extremely beneficial to the soil and a boon to plants

rotated to their spot in the garden. Susceptible to diseases that are spread when the leaves are wet.

POACEAE OR GRAMINEAE (The grass family) Includes some of the most important grain crops, such as corn, oats, and wheat, as well as grasses, sugar cane, and bamboo. Many, such as corn, deplete the soil of nutrients and should be rotated annually.

SOLANACEAE (The tobacco or nightshade family) Includes tomatoes, peppers, potatoes and eggplants. Prefer warm weather and rich, moist soil. Crop rotation is important as plants are susceptible to disease. Some are used for medicinal purposes while others have toxic parts.

What's In A Name?

Like people, all plants are given names to differentiate them within their families. Only plants have two different types of names: a botanical name, which is in Latin and universally accepted, and a common name, which may differ from region to region. The Latin name consists of two words. The first is the genus; the second the species. As a species is a subdivision of the genus, you'll find that all plants of a certain genus share common characteristics but differ in at least one habit. For instance, *Allium sativum* is a garlic and *Allium cepa* is an onion. However, while it is becoming an accepted practice to refer to many plants by their Latin names, edible plants are still most often referred to by their common name.

Varieties

Today there are thousands of varieties and cultivars (cultivated varieties), from which to choose. Although they retain most of the characteristics of the species, they may differ slightly in their drought or temperature tolerance, disease resistance, color or fruit size. Open-pollinated varieties reproduce by means of the wind or animals, such as birds and bees, so their fruits and flowers are never exactly alike. Seed companies simply select the best plants from the crop. Many of the heirloom vegetables are grown from open-pollinated seed. As hybrids are grown from seed that has been produced from deliberate cross-pollination, they have more consistent qualities. In the seed catalogs open-pollinated and hybrid names are usually printed within single quotation marks. For instance 'Tall Telephone' (an heirloom pea); 'Early Girl' (a tomato cultivar). Have fun choosing your plants. Experiment! There's bound to be one that's just right for your climate.

VEGETABLES IN YOUR CLIMATE

Vegetables require different amounts of sun and different temperatures to thrive. Begin by mapping out how much sun your property receives and where there's shade at different times of the day. Determine the expected summer temperatures, the length of the growing season and the first and last days of frost.

With your short growing season, from mid-June to late August in parts of Zone 3, it's important to select your vegetables carefully. Some vegetables like cool nights to germinate, while others are tender, preferring warm soil and air temperatures. Some ripen only in full sun all day, while others may bolt in the heat. Know what the plants need, what your climate can provide and plan your garden accordingly.

SUN/SHADE

Sun is the essential ingredient for an abundant crop of healthy vegetables. In Zones 3, 4, and 5, vegetables grow best, and fastest, in full sun all day. However, some vegetables, such as leafy crops and young seedlings, may get too much sun in areas with excessively hot summers and may lose more water to transpiration than they can take up through their roots. Although happiest in early and late summer, given a little shade, they too will thrive through the heat of the summer. If your garden does not receive light shade, you can easily construct a cover.

Blanching

Some vegetables benefit from the denial of sunlight, referred to as "blanching." Blanching produces the colorless heads of cauliflower and makes other vegetables more tender and less bitter. To blanch cauliflower, pull the leaves over the developing flower head and secure them with string.

Day Length

Vegetables are particularly responsive to day length, or the number of daylight hours. The greater the number of daylight hours, the faster the growth; the fewer the daylight hours, the longer the time to ripen. For example, in northern areas with midnight sun, such as Alaska, vegetables grow very large, very fast.

Some plants are more sensitive than others to day length. Onions don't begin to form their bulbs until there are at least sixteen hours of daylight. On the other hand, the heads of cauliflower begin to develop as the days get shorter. Short days when combined with cool temperatures can be beneficial for "holding" leafy vegetables such as lettuce, cole crops such as broccoli and cabbage, and root crops such as carrots.

TEMPERATURE

Temperature controls the life cycle of vegetables. Seeds germinate and vegetables ripen in warm weather; cold weather usually signals the end of a vegetable's life cycle. Gardeners in Zones 3, 4 and 5 can expect warm summer daytime temperatures generally followed by cool nights, a wonderful combination for vegetables. The warm sun produces excellent color and high sugar content, while the cool nights allow the plants to revive, increasing productivity.

Annual Vegetables

Annual vegetables are extremely sensitive to climatic conditions and are categorized by their cold and heat tolerance. The different types of annual vegetables are:

HARDY VEGETABLES Can survive frost. Are successful when sown directly in the vegetable garden, even while cool temperatures prevail. Include broccoli, Brussels sprouts, cabbage, collard, kale, onion, and spinach.

HALF-HARDY VEGETABLES Will take some frost, but not as much as hardy vegetables. Include cauliflower, endive, and lettuce.

TENDER VEGETABLES Cannot tolerate frost. Many of these types need several weeks time in order to reach maturity, so they should be sown early indoors, in cold frames, or outdoors only after danger of frost has past. These can also be purchased as greenhouse-grown seedlings or rooted cuttings. Include cucumber, eggplant, pepper, pumpkin, squash, tomato, watermelon.

Consider the following when selecting vegetables:

- The coldest expected temperatures in the summer
- The highest expected temperatures in the summer
- The average first day of frost
- The average last day of frost
- The crop's germination temperature
- The crop's frost tolerance

Cool- And Warm-season Crops

A vegetable's hardiness influences whether it is a cool-season or warm-season crop. In Zones 3, 4, and 5, the soil and air are late to warm in the spring, making cool-season crops a good choice. Warm-season crops are sensitive to the cold and should be started indoors to give them enough time to mature before the first fall frost.

COOL-SEASON CROPS These hardy and some half-hardy vegetables can tolerate cool weather. Include beets, broccoli, Brussels sprouts, cabbage, cauliflower, greens and spinach, lettuce and salad greens, peas and radishes.

WARM-SEASON CROPS These half-hardy or tender vegetables prefer warm temperatures and warm soil and may show no growth until the soil warms sufficiently. Include beans, corn, cucumber, eggplant, melons, peppers, potatoes, squash and tomatoes.

FULL-SEASON CROPS These vegetables, such as onions, can tolerate cool and warm weather.

It's very important when planning a vegetable garden in your cold zone to have as accurate a date as possible for the last day of frost. Almost all planting calculations depend on it. Check with local gardeners, nurserymen or your Agricultural Extension Service to be sure. Keep a record in your own garden; it will help you zero in on your garden's particular microclimate.

For the best results in the coldest zones, gardeners should include lots of cool-season vegetables, such as frost-hardy kale and Swiss chard, which mature within the short growing season. Avoid sweet potatoes and large watermelons, which need a longer growing season to ripen. One of the biggest challenges for gardeners in Zones 3, 4 and 5 is finding vegetable varieties that ripen before cold weather sets in. Only grow peppers and eggplants if you begin with plants, and get them into the garden as soon as the weather allows. If a late August frost threatens, cover your vegetables with sheets or blankets, row covers made of agricultural fabric, or hot caps so you can take full advantage of the warm September days that are sure to follow. If using sheets, remove them in the morning and allow them to dry before using them again. Row covers can be left in place during most of the growing season. Although they are light and water permeable, row covers do keep out insects. Be sure not to cover plants such as cucumbers when they are in bloom as they rely on bees for cross-pollination.

Some vegetables taste better after the arrival of cool weather and frost. Kale, collards, cabbage, lettuce and other leaf vegetables lose their bitter flavor, while leeks, carrots and beets become more sweet.

WIND

In your cold zone, harsh winds can lower temperatures and cause severe damage to vegetable plants in exposed gardens, especially on the Great Plains and in the prairie states. Protect your garden with a windbreak (see Windbreak Illustration, p.17) or a 4' to 6' high fence installed on the windward side of the garden. A wind barrier will create a microclimate, protecting plants for a distance up to ten or fifteen times its height. Without the windbreak, a Zone 5 garden may in reality be a Zone 4. But be sure the windbreak doesn't shade the plants or block the flow of cold air out of the garden; the goal of vegetable gardeners in Zones 3, 4 and 5 is to warm the garden.

HINT: Keep the soil warm. A plant with warm roots can better combat chilly air.

WATER

Water is essential; without it seeds won't germinate and plants won't grow. Many vegetables consist primarily of water, and consequently grow best when the soil is constantly moist. When you first sow your seeds it's particularly important to keep the soil moist to promote germination. Water the beds lightly early each morning and again during the day if the soil is dry. Water transplants regularly, keeping the soil wet for the first week. Water seedlings and transplants thoroughly but less often once they have begun to grow. Once plants are established, provide about 1" of water whenever the top 2" of soil is dry. The frequency will depend on your soil and microclimate. If you live in a humid area water will evaporate more slowly.

Keep a close eye on the garden. Watch the soil to see how fast it dries; watch the plants for signs of stress. A well-watered plant will have turgid, glossy leaves; a dry plant, dull or wilting leaves. Try never to let plants wilt, but don't overwater either; wilting can also be a sign of overwatering or infestation by borers.

PLANNING YOUR VEGETABLE GARDEN

Choosing The Site

The ideal site for a vegetable garden is healthy for both the plants and for you. Select a site that has full sun all day, good drainage, no competing roots from trees or shrubs and easy access to a water source. In Zones 3, 4 and 5 a gently sloping, south-facing site is ideal, but avoid low sites where water may collect or cold air might settle. Be sure to check the history of the site for any secrets hidden in the soil. Were strong pesticides used nearby? Is it near a garage or driveway where oil or gas may have leaked into the soil? Has flaking lead paint or disintegrating asbestos from an old barn or house contaminated the soil?

> *HINT: To prevent runoff and soil erosion, lay out your rows running across a slope, not up and downhill.*

What Should The Garden Look Like?

The location and purpose of the garden will help determine its style. If the garden is near the house, an ornamental vegetable garden is ideal. Make it a formal, geometric shape, with brick or stone paths, low borders or brick edging, or enclose it with espaliered fruit trees. Use poles, tepees, and tripods to add a vertical element to the garden, bringing vegetables up to eye level.

For an informal garden, design free-form beds and plant them with herbs, flowers and vegetables. When space is limited, intermingle herbs and vegetables with flowers in containers on the deck or terrace. But if you want a workhorse of a garden, or are very busy and won't have the time to keep the garden looking its best, choose a simple design, such as a rectangle, and locate it away from the house, perhaps behind a fence or hedge. But pay attention to the details.

Each decision you make — the type of enclosure, the paths, the edging for the beds and the vertical plant supports — reinforces the style you have selected.

GARDEN DESIGN

There are so many delicious vegetables, it's very tempting to design a big garden. But start small. Select a few useful and easy-to-grow vegetables such as radishes, carrots, green beans, cabbage, leaf lettuce, summer squash, and tomatoes. When making an ornamental vegetable garden, select vegetables for their appearance as well as their flavor. Think of vegetables the way you would perennials. Consider their growth habit, leaf size, color and texture: tall and narrow, short and bushy or vine-like; rosette-shaped heads like lettuce or feathery foliage like carrots and dill. Edge the garden with the beautiful shapes of lettuce or cabbage or intermingle them with herbs and flowers. Weave the fine tufts of carrots or dill through flowers such as dahlias or snapdragons for contrasting textures or add variegated sage or ruby basil for contrasting leaf color.

Including Edible Flowers

Plant vegetables with edible flowers. They are delicious in salads and beautiful as garnishes. Their flavors range from mild, to peppery to sweet:

- *Alcea rosea* (hollyhock) — slightly sweet
- *Antirrhinum majus* (snapdragon) — mild flavor
- *Brassica hirta* (mustard) — warm, subtle mustard flavor
- *Calendula officinalis* (calendula) — tangy flavor
- *Centaurea cyanus* (bachelor's button) — mild flavor
- *Cucurbita* spp. (squash) — make excellent cups for fillings
- *Dianthus caryophyllus* — mild flavor
- *Fuschia* — tart lemon flavor

- *Hemerocallis* (daylily) — mild flavor
- *Hibiscus syriacus* (rose-of-Sharon) — sweet, mild flavor
- *Lavandula* (lavender) — lavender flavor
- *Lonicera* (honeysuckle) — sweet flavor
- *Monarda* (bee balm) — citrus flavor
- *Pelargonium* (scented geranium) — a variety of aromas from coconut to nutmeg
- *Petunia* x *hybrida* — mild, sweet flavor
- *Tagetes* spp. (marigold) — tarragon flavor
- *Tropaeolum majus* (nasturtium) — hot, peppery flavor
- *Rosa* — rose aroma
- *Viola* x *wittrockiana* (pansy) — mild flavor
- *Viola odorata* — sweet flavor

Only eat flowers you know are edible. Do not eat toxic flowers such as buttercups, *Delphinium*, common daisies, *Aconitum* (monkshood), *Narcissus* and *Nerium* (oleander).

Next select a shape for your garden: rectangular, square, round, triangular, crescent or free-form — the choices are as varied as your imagination. The easiest design is rectangular: 20' x 24' for a small garden; 40' x 60' for a large garden. Then decide whether you want to plant in rows or raised beds. Rows give you great design flexibility; raised beds are more permanent but are excellent when starting a garden in poor, shallow or poorly drained soil.

Raised Beds

Raised beds are a cold zone gardener's best friend. Raised above the cold surrounding ground, the soil temperature can be 5-8 degrees Fahrenheit warmer, making it possible to plant earlier in the spring. Use raised beds to improve drainage and amend poor or shallow soils. By raising the soil level above the existing grade with amended soil, you will improve the soil while also increasing its depth and drainage. Corn, cucumbers, melons, potatoes, squash, tomatoes, peppers, pumpkins and eggplants grow better in the well-drained soil of raised beds, while lettuce, spinach, radishes, Swiss chard, carrots, and beets can be planted earlier in the warmth of raised beds. Use brick, bluestone, or 2 x 6 pressure-treated lumber edging to make raised beds. But raised beds are not for every garden. In dry climates they dry out more quickly, requiring additional watering.

> HINT: *When designing raised beds, make them no wider than 4' to 6' allowing you to reach the vegetables in the center.*

(Top to bottom) *Build bottomless enclosures of pressure-treated 2 x 6 lumber and place them on top of the soil, leaving adequate space for paths between them. Dig topsoil out of the paths to fill the beds. Fill the paths with mulch, brick or stone to meet the original grade.*

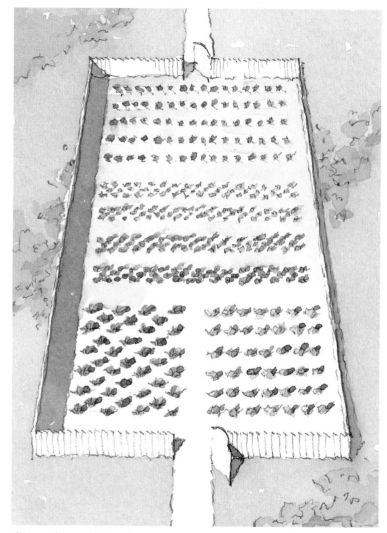

(Top to bottom) Single rows, wide rows, staggered in blocks (bottom left), aligned in blocks (bottom right).

PLANTING PATTERNS

Now comes the fun part, known as the planting pattern, or how you arrange the vegetables within the beds. Planting patterns are integral to the overall design of the garden. Plant your vegetables in rows, blocks or beds.

Planting In Rows

Rows can be either single or several plants wide. Single rows are ideal for vegetables that are picked regularly; however, they take up a lot of valuable space in small gardens. Wide rows are more practical for vegetables that don't need as much attention, such as beets, radishes, carrots and greens.

Rows are easy to mulch and give you the opportunity to create contrasting patterns. Align the rows in different directions, including north-south, east-west and diagonally.

Balance your sunlight by orienting your garden rows on a north-south axis. Place corn and tall plants toward the north end where they will block the wind but not the sunlight. Placed to the south, they will provide welcome shade for cool-season plants.

Planting In Beds And Blocks

Planting in beds and blocks saves space as paths are eliminated between the rows. Within the bed or block, plants are spaced equally in all directions, either in a grid pattern or staggered rows. When the plants are spaced so that they touch, few weeds will grow in their shade. If you like the look of mass planting, organize your plants in blocks or beds. Alternate blocks of different colored lettuces to create a checkerboard effect.

Garden Paths

Formal or informal, all vegetable gardens need paths for easy access to the plants. In small formal gardens use brick, stone, gravel or crushed oyster shells; in large gardens grass is a less expensive alternative, but it needs to be edged and mowed. For

an informal garden lay down a thick layer of mulch such as ground wood chips, loose straw or salt hay. If you have the time to cultivate the soil regularly to prevent weeds, let the paths compact naturally. Make paths at least 2' to 3' wide to accommodate wheel barrows and baskets for weeding or harvesting.

HINT: Stay on the garden paths. Foot traffic can compact the soil and disturb the plants.

Edging
Edging clearly defines the planting beds, emphasizing the design of the garden. Brick or bluestone are beautiful but costly. 2 x 6 pressure-treated lumber makes a fine edge, is easy to install and is much less expensive.

FENCING
Good fences make for abundant harvests; without them, creatures other than you will be enjoying the benefits of your hard work. If you live in an area with deer, rabbits, woodchucks or other voracious eaters, good fences are essential. Make them formal, using white pickets or ornamental metal, or informal, using post-and-rail, split rail or wire. Tailor the fence to the critter. For instance, utilize wire with 1" openings for rabbits and skunks, aviary wire for gophers. If only a decorative wood fence with pickets spaced at 4" will do, add chicken wire on the inside to keep out the smaller animals. Be sure to make your fence high enough: go 3' to 4' for woodchucks and raccoons; 8' to 10' for deer. But don't stop there. Go underground too! Extend chicken wire 6" underground, then make an L, running it horizontally away from the garden for another 6". The garden gate is also a prime entry point. Add a width of chicken wire at the bottom, trying not to leave any gaps between the soil and bottom of the gate.

Extreme Measures
FOR RACCOONS If raccoons are making it over your 4' fence, add another 2' of chicken wire above it. Securely attach the bottom foot of wire to vertical posts, leaving the top foot of wire loose. When a raccoon tries to climb over, the loose wire will bend backward, tossing the masked intruder to the ground.

FOR DEER Because deer like to see where they are going, they rarely go over solid fences. But solid fences are expensive, so new designs are aimed at the deer's inability to jump long distances. Try erecting a double fence: two 4' high fences with a 3' wide space between them. If your vegetable garden is not in view of the house, try a 4' high fence to which a slanting wood-and-wire barrier has been added to the outside. To build the barrier, attach one end of an 8' long 2 x 4 to the top of each post, slant it down to the ground and secure it with a stake. Then run wire between the 2 x 4's, spacing it at 12" intervals. If all else fails, install an electric fence.

For additonal tips on keeping out uninvited guests, see "Pests And Intruders" on p.39.

SPACING
Spacing depends on the growth habit of each plant and the planting pattern you have selected. Remember, seedlings are placed much closer together, and ultimately the weakest plants will be thinned out, leaving the sturdiest to mature. To plan your garden, see the spacing requirements in the vegetable list, then lay out the rows or beds accordingly. In general, space plants as follows:

SINGLE ROWS Align single rows 1' to 4' apart; within the row, space small plants such as carrots 3" to 4" apart; large plants such as tomatoes 1' to 2' apart.

WIDE ROWS Align wide rows 3' to 4' apart; for vines, such as peas, make a single, 4" to 6" wide trench throughout which you can scatter the seeds; for lettuces, carrots, radishes and

beets, make three or four parallel grooves, 4" to 6" apart in each row.

BLOCKS OR BEDS Space all plants equally in all directions according to the required spacing for the individual plant.

Spacing Guidelines

With a roll of string and a few stakes you can easily lay out your rows or divide your beds into equal spaces.

TO PLANT IN ROWS Insert a stake in the first corner of the prepared bed, then measure off the predetermined length of the row and place a second stake at the opposite end. Stretch a string between the two stakes. The string marks the center of the row. Sow your seed or plant your seedlings in line with the string at the appropriate spacing.

TO PLANT IN A BLOCK OR BED For equal spacing, divide the prepared planting area into a grid of squares. First insert stakes at equal distances on all four sides of the bed (stakes should be directly opposite each other). Stretch string between opposite stakes. This will form a grid of squares. Position seeds or seedlings in the center of each square.

SUCCESSION PLANTING

Succession planting uses the garden space efficiently and provides you with a continuous flow of fresh vegetables. Consider your microclimate, the temperature preferences of your vegetables and their growing speed. In the coldest zones, the growing season is too short for successive plantings of most vegetables except lettuce, radishes, spinach, peas and beets. For the best results use the following approaches:

- Plant different varieties of the same vegetable for early, midseason and late harvests.
- Stagger plantings of the same vegetable at two-week intervals for a continuous yield.
- Interplant vegetables that mature at successive intervals.

INTERPLANTING

Interplanting means growing two different vegetables in the same area. Interplanting makes efficient use of the space between slow-growing vegetables, such as corn, tomatoes and peppers, for fast-growing crops, such as lettuce, radishes and carrots. Interplant cool-season vegetables, such as lettuce, with tall-growing vegetables, such as corn and pole beans. The shade of the tall-growing plants will prevent the lettuce from bolting. But not all plants make good neighbors. Some vegetables attract destructive pests; others inhibit the neighboring vegetable's growth. Onions especially can be too much for other vegetables to handle.

VEGETABLE	COMPATIBLE WITH	INCOMPATIBLE WITH
Asparagus	Chard, basil, parsley	Onions, garlic
Bush beans	Marigolds, corn, beets	Onions, garlic
Carrots	Onions, leeks, savory herbs	Dill
Cucumbers	Corn, radishes	Potatoes, sage
Eggplant	Peas	Potatoes
Greens	Cabbages, potatoes	
Lettuce	Corn, tomatoes, broccoli, peppers	
Melons	Corn, cucumbers	Potatoes
Onions	Carrots, lettuce, radishes	Peas, beans
Peas	Carrots, turnips, radishes	Onions
Peppers	Carrots, eggplants, onions, tomatoes	
Radishes	Carrots, lettuce	
Squash	Beans, corn, radishes	
Tomatoes	Onions, parsley, carrots	Brassicas, corn
Turnips	Peas	

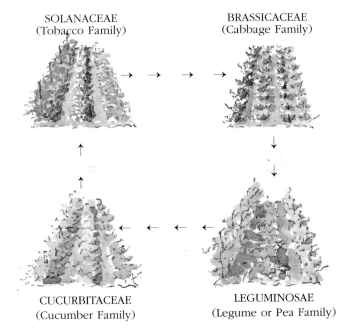

SOLANACEAE
(Tobacco Family)

BRASSICACEAE
(Cabbage Family)

CUCURBITACEAE
(Cucumber Family)

LEGUMINOSAE
(Legume or Pea Family)

CROP ROTATION

When crops are rotated, their location in the garden changes from year to year. Rotate your crops to reduce the level of pests and disease in the garden and to maintain the soil's level of nutrition.

Different pests attack different plants. When you change the plants in a bed, the overwintering larvae will wake up in the late spring to plants that are not their vegetable of choice. Their appetites curbed, the less damage they will do, and the more slowly they will multiply.

Vegetables also have varying nutritional needs. Some, such as cabbage, are heavy feeders and deplete the soil of specific nutrients. Others in the legume family replenish the soil. By rotating your crops you ensure that no one nutrient is depleted.

The key to rotating your crops is to identify the plant family (see p.170). Plant vegetables from the same family, such as cabbage, broccoli and cauliflower, in the same bed the first year; grow them in another bed the following year. The vegetables that benefit most from rotation are the cucumber family, including squash, pumpkins and melons; the legumes, including peas and beans; the cabbage family, including broccoli and cauliflower; and the tobacco or nightshade family, including tomatoes, potatoes and eggplants. Although crop rotation may seem like a lot of work, it will mean less fertilizing, healthier plants and fewer pests.

HINT: Perennial vegetables, such as asparagus, do not have to be rotated.

PLANNING AT A GLANCE:
- Microclimate
- Length of growing season
- Soil
- Water
- Cool-season or warm-season
- Annual or perennial
- Time you have available to garden
- Time required for germination
- Time required from seeding to harvest
- Plant growth habit
- Height and width
- Leaf size, texture and color
- Vegetable family and crop rotation
- Spacing
- Harvest goals
- Time of harvest: one-time or continuous
- Garden style: formal, informal, ornamental
- Planting pattern: rows or beds
- Pest control

BED PREPARATION

To lay out the bed put stakes in the corners and stretch string between them. If the bed is in a lawn area, remove the sod (see "Removing Sod," p.33). Rototill to break up all chunks of soil and expose rocks and other buried surprises. Remove all weeds, with roots intact, and add them to your compost pile. Continue going through the soil until it is loose and free of all rocks and debris.

To get a head start in the fall, spread 3" to 4" of compost and manure over the bed, then work it into the top 8" to 12" of topsoil. Cover it completely with a continuous sheet of black plastic secured with heavy rocks. If this is applied early in the fall, any remaining weeds that try to come up will be frustrated by the darkness, leaving the bed practically weed-free for the spring.

If beginning in the spring, you won't have the benefit of the winter in which to kill weeds. If your new vegetable garden is located in an area where perennial grasses, weeds and/or shrubs were growing, finely rake the top 6" of soil to be sure you have removed all the grass rhizomes and weed roots. If you have a small garden, use a riddle or piece of 1/2" screen to sieve out grubs, cocoons or cutworms as well. This will reduce future weeding and save your seedlings from hungry munchers. Add amendments as recommended by the soil test (p.18).

For small gardens, double digging (see "Double Digging" p.34) will improve the texture and nutrient content of even the most hard, compact garden soil. If you are making a garden near a newly constructed house, there may be little topsoil and the ground may have been compacted by heavy machinery. Double digging will be well worth the effort.

SOIL

Good soil preparation is essential for a bountiful vegetable garden. Consider your soil's composition, pH and fertility.

The best garden soil is a deep loam with loose texture for good aeration. It should retain moisture, yet have good drainage, be free of rocks and weeds, rich in nutrients, microorganisms and earthworms.

A neutral pH level of 6.0 to 6.8 is especially important in your cold zone where you want your plants to grow as quickly as possible. Soil with a neutral pH level makes more nutrients available to plants, helping them to flourish. To check your soil, take a sample and send it to a local Agricultural Extension Service to see which nutrients are lacking and how much you need to adjust your soil's pH level. Even if you are starting on a rocky, barren site, you can make good soil with a little elbow grease, time and lots of organic matter. Or for large areas, use raised beds into which you have placed improved topsoil.

Amending The Soil

Vegetables grow best in a deep loam with a neutral pH (6.0 to 6.8). Add any soil amendments recommended by the results of a soil test (See "Soil" p.18.) Once you know what your soil needs, refer to the organic amendment chart on the next page. Amending your soil may seem like a lot of work, but when your vegetables respond enthusiastically, it will all seem worthwhile.

To raise the pH, add ground limestone. A good rule of thumb is to add seventy pounds to raise the pH one point (from 5.5 to 6.5) over an area of one thousand square feet (a 20' x 50' bed). To lower the pH one point (from 7.5 to 6.5) over the same area, add twenty pounds of agricultural sulfur. Broadcast the limestone or sulfur over the bed, then thoroughly till it into the soil.

HINT: Milorganite is a common organic amendment rich in nitrogen and iron, but as it is made up of sludge, which may contain high levels of metals, such as cadmium, it is not recommended for use on edibles.

Organic Amendments	N	P	K	Comments
Alfalfa Hay	2.5	0.5	2.1	Let rot as mulch first or use alfalfa meal instead. Fast-acting. Also contains trace minerals.
Blood Meal	12.0	1.5	0.6	Strong. Can burn plants. Use carefully as a side-dressing. Medium- to fast-acting. Smelly. Repels deer.
Bone Meal (steamed)	1.0-4.0	10.0-34.0	0	Phosphorus available faster to plants than with rock or colloidal phosphate but still slow- to medium-acting. Good for side-dressing. More expensive.
Canola Meal	6.0	2.0	1.0	Medium- to slow-acting.
Colloidal (soft) Phosphate	0.0	2.0	0	Phosphorus available faster to plants than rock phosphate. Best source of phosphorus for alkaline soil.
Compost (dry)	1.0	1.0	1.0	Good mulch; retains moisture. Slow-acting.
Compost (homemade)	1.5-3.5	0.5-1.0	1.0-2.0	Good mulch; retains moisture. Slow-acting.
Cow Manure (fresh)	0.3	0.2	0.1	May burn plants. Compost, let mellow for 3-4 weeks, or make manure tea. Medium-acting. If taken from manure pit, may be very gloppy. Smelly when wet.
Cornstalks (fresh)	0.3	0.1	0.3	Decomposes slowly. Shred well and compost first.
Cottonseed Meal	6.0	2.5	1.7	Acidic. Good for side-dressing. Slow- to medium-acting.
Fish Meal	10.0	4.0	0	Slow-acting. Smelly.
Grass Clippings (fresh)	1.2	0.3	2.0	Compost with dry material to avoid nutrient loss. Shred for quicker decomposition.
Granite Dust	0.0	0.0	4.0	Also contains silicas.
Greensand	0.0	0.0	5.0	Also contains silicas.
Guano (bat)	5.7	8.6	2.0	Medium-acting.
Guano (seabird)	13.0	11.0	3.0	Medium-acting.
Hoof and Horn Meal	12.0	0.5	0	Slow-acting. May take 4-6 weeks to be effective. Can be smelly.
Horse Manure (fresh)	0.3	0.15	0.5	May burn plants. Compost, let rot for 3-4 weeks, or make manure tea. Medium-acting. Best if horse is grain-fed and forages grasses not weeds.
Dried Kelp	0.9	0.5	4.0-13.0	Apply lightly. Also contains natural growth hormones. Slow-acting.
Leaves (beech and maple)	0.7	0.1	0.7-0.8	Shred and mix with other amendments.
Leaves (oak)	0.7	0.1	0.5	Very acidic. Shred and mix with other amendments.
Pig Manure (fresh)	0.3	0.3	0.3	May burn plants. Compost, let rot for 3-4 weeks, or make manure tea. Medium-acting. If taken from manure pit, may be very gloppy. Smelly when wet.
Mushroom Compost	0.4-0.7	57.0-62.0	0.5-1.5	Slow-acting.

KEY: *Nitrogen (N); phosphorus (P); potassium (K)*

(chart continued on next page)

Organic Amendments	N	P	K	Comments
Pine Needles	0.5	0.1	0.0	Very acidic. Good mulch for acid-loving plants.
Poultry Manure (fresh)	1.5-6.0	1.0-4.0	0.5-3.0	Usually mixed with sawdust. Nutrient value is greater the lower the water content. May burn plants. Compost, let mellow for 3-4 weeks, or make manure tea. Smelly when wet.
Rabbit Manure (fresh)	2.4	1.4	0.6	May burn plants. Compost, let rot for 3-4 weeks, or make manure tea. Smelly.
Rock Phosphate	0.0	3.0	0.0	Slow-release. Long-lasting. Best source of phosphorus in acid soil. Good for side-dressing.
Salt Marsh Hay	1.1	0.3	0.8	Best when well rotted. Use as mulch first. Retains moisture.
Sawdust	4.0	2.0	4.0	Compost first with ammonium phosphate. Very slow-acting.
Sheep Manure (fresh)	0.7	0.3	0.9	May burn plants. Compost, let rot for 3-4 weeks, or make manure tea. Smelly.
Soybean Meal (dry)	6.7	1.6	2.3	Slow- to medium-acting.
Steer Manure (fresh)	0.3	0.2	0.1	May burn plants. Primarily processed grass. Medium-acting. Compost, let mellow for 3-4 weeks, or make manure tea. Widely available in West.
Straw	0.7	0.2	1.2	Best when well rotted. Use as mulch first. Retains moisture.
Wood Ash	0.0	1.5	3.0-7.0	Alkaline. Use with lime to raise pH. Do not apply more than once every 2-3 years. Fast-acting.
Worm Castings	0.5	0.5	0.3	Improves germination of seeds. Good indicators of healthy soil.

HINT: Remember, a soil rich in organic matter will retain moisture better and require less water.

PLANTING
Seeds Or Plants?
When it comes time to plant you have a choice between sowing or transplanting. Consider your climate, length of growing season and time required from sowing to harvest for the vegetables you've selected. In your cold zone your growing season is so short, you will want to get a jump on the season with seedlings (especially warm-season vegetables) you have started indoors or purchased from a local nurseryman. However, with seeds you will find a much wider variety and a number of sources. If an organic garden is your goal, it may be difficult to buy organic seedlings. Whether you opt for seeds or plants, buy disease-resistant varieties whenever possible.

Buying Seeds
Vegetable seeds can be purchased from your local garden center or from a variety of mail order sources (see "Sources"). You will find an enormous selection available through mail-order catalogs, including many improved and old-fashioned varieties, organic, gourmet and exotic seeds. They are available as loose seed in seed packets or in a much more limited selection, as seed tapes and "Seed 'n Start" kits. Seed tapes are actually soluble tapes with seeds imbedded in them for perfect planting in rows! "Seed 'n Start" kits are cell packs filled with a lightweight starting mix and seeds, covered with clear tops to retain the moisture and enhance germination.

In Zones 3 and 4, you'll want to select varieties with the shortest number of days to maturity. Look for seed companies that specialize in seeds for your cold climate. The seeds they provide are generally from plants that are acclimated to your cold temperatures. They will grow faster and produce a better crop within your short growing season. Experiment with different varieties.

Buying Plants
Buying vegetable plants is an easy way to beat the short growing season. The best vegetables to buy as plants are tomatoes, cabbage, broccoli, cauliflower and peppers. Plants are usually available in flats, cell-packs and individual pots. See "Buying Plants" in "Annuals," p.50.

SOWING SEED
Starting Indoors
Seeds need warmth, water, oxygen and light to germinate. Sow seeds in individual pots or plastic trays filled with a sterile, lightweight soil mix. Soilless mixes containing perlite, vermiculite and peat moss also provide excellent results. Follow the instructions for spacing and planting depths for each type of seed. Be sure not to plant them too deep as light must be able to reach the seeds. A good rule of thumb for determining planting depth is to plant seeds three times as deep as they are wide. See the Vegetable List on p.190 and read the back of the seed packets for more specific recommendations.

Water the seeds in well and keep them moist, but do not overwater. Place them in a sunny spot where the temperature is between 60° and 70° Fahrenheit. If you don't have at least six hours of strong sun, a fluorescent light will speed up germination. Within two to three weeks true leaves should appear. This is the time to transplant the seedlings into divided trays or individual pots filled with slightly heavier potting soil.

Damping Off
Damping off is a soilborne disease that attacks seedlings during germination, causing them to wilt. It spreads most easily in warm, moist conditions with poor air circulation. Prevention is the best defense against damping off.

To avoid damping off:
- Use clean pots or trays.
- Use sterilized potting soil.
- Keep seeds moist, but do not overwater.
- Do not crowd seeds; thin them out as necessary.
- Immediately remove infected seedlings from trays.

Timing
To ascertain when to start seeds indoors, determine the date of your last expected spring frost and subtract the number of weeks needed from sowing to transplanting size. The length of time varies with each plant as follows:

10 WEEKS onions, leeks, peppers, eggplant, asparagus.
9 WEEKS parsley.
8 WEEKS early lettuce.
6-8 WEEKS tomatoes, basil.
6-7 WEEKS early cabbage, broccoli, Brussels sprouts, kale, early head lettuce.
5-6 WEEKS late cabbage, early leaf lettuce, cauliflower.
4-5 WEEKS cucumbers, melons, squash, pumpkins, gourds.

Hardening Off
Before transplanting seedlings into the garden, they must be acclimated or "hardened off." Harden off seedlings by first moving them to a cold frame (a box with a light-permeable cover that can be opened and closed depending on the temperature) or a shady, protected spot outdoors. Water them regularly. After three days they should be prepared for their sum-

mer in the garden. If unseasonably cold weather threatens, bring your seedlings back indoors.

In the northernmost areas of Zone 3, it's often tempting to set out transplants during those first warm days in May. But beware, there is sure to be frost into June and sometimes even in July! Only set out hardy transplants early, and keep sheets or other covers on hand for frost protection.

> *HINT: Recycle plastic 32 oz. soft drink bottles and milk jugs to make "hot caps" for your tender transplants. Simply cut off the bottoms, then cut a hole in the top for ventilation and they're ready for action.*

Sowing Seed Outdoors

In your cold zone you are likely to receive lots of rain in the late spring just at sowing time. Cold, wet soil can cause poor germination. For greater success, improve the drainage by using raised beds and planting in hills.

Sow seed outdoors at the recommended depth and spacing for each specific vegetable. Avoid planting seeds too close; they won't grow as well. For small seeds, firm the soil at the appropriate depth and cover with a lightweight or soilless mix. Water seeds gently at the time of planting, keep the soil moist until the seedlings emerge, then water regularly.

> *HINT: If hungry birds are a problem, protect your freshly sown seed by covering the rows with netting.*

Special Hints

CARROT AND RADISH SEEDS are so small it is hard to sow them evenly. An easy solution is to fold the seed packet in half length-wise, tear an opening at the end of the sharp crease, align the seeds in the opening and gently tap out one seed at a time.

PRESPROUT PEAS, BEANS AND CORN to get a jump start on the spring in your cold zone. Place seeds in a sandwich of damp paper towels, wrap them in plastic and put them in a warm, dark spot to germinate. But don't forget them! Check them each morning and plant them outdoors as soon as they have sprouted, usually in two days.

Sowing In Hills

Plant vining plants that require warm, well-drained soil, such as cucumbers, pumpkins and squash, in hills. Use a hoe to form a mound 3" to 4" high and 12" to 18" across. Make a hole 2" to 3" deep in the center of the hill. Place a few seeds in the hole and gently firm the soil over them. Sprinkle the mound gently until it is completely saturated.

Planting in hills, ridges, on the flat and in furrows.

Sowing In Furrows

Furrows are shallow planting trenches, which can vary in depth depending on the size of the seed. Use furrows when you are planting in rows. After you have laid out the row using stakes and string (see "Spacing Guidelines" p.175), form a trench directly beneath the string. Use the corner of a hoe to form deep furrows; the tip of a trowel for shallow furrows. Distribute the seeds evenly, then firm the soil over the furrow using the flat side of a rake. Some gardeners prefer covering seeds with a light, moisture-retentive soilless mix. Gently sprinkle the beds taking care not to wash seed away.

Sowing In Ridges

If planting time is cold and rainy in your area, it may be best to plant in ridges. Ridges will warm up faster and dry out more easily, preventing the seeds from rotting. Using a hoe, form ridges by hilling soil several inches high directly beneath the row guideline. Make a shallow furrow down the center for the seed.

Thinning

When sowing, seeds are often so small it's difficult to space them just right. Several seeds may begin to develop right next to each other. To develop into full, healthy plants, seedlings need enough space in which to grow. Look over your seedlings. Decide which are the most vigorous, then make room for them by thinning out, or pulling out, the less vigorous plants. To prevent disturbance to the remaining seedling, press down on the soil around it with your fingers, while simultaneously pulling out the other.

TRANSPLANTING

Transplant homegrown or purchased plants into rows, ridges or hills. When transplanting, avoid damage to the stems as they are the plant's lifeline, without which they cannot grow. If plants are growing in flats, carefully prick out the seedlings. If plants are in cell packs, push the root ball out from the bottom.

For most vegetables, dig a hole slightly bigger than the root ball. Holding the plant gently by the root ball or leaves, set it in the hole at the same level as it was growing in the container. Hold the seedlings gently by the leaves and carefully smooth the soil in around them. Softly tamp the soil to remove all air pockets, which enables the roots to make good contact with the soil. Water the seedlings in to further settle the soil.

Tomatoes are an exception. They actually benefit from being planted slightly deeper. This encourages them to root along their stems where the additional roots provide greater support and improve moisture absorption.

When you remove a plant from a container, you inevitably injure a few roots, which may cause a slight setback in plant growth. Try these transplanting techniques to reduce stress:

- Plant seedlings immediately after removing them from their containers.
- Transplant on a cloudy day or in the early morning before the heat of the day.
- Water the seedlings before transplanting, gently spraying the leaves to reduce wilting.
- Water transplants thoroughly after planting.
- Shade plants if necessary.

WEEDING

Weeds compete with vegetables for water and nutrition. You'll be off to a good start if you remove as many weeds as possible when you prepare the bed and maintain a good layer of mulch to prevent weed seeds from germinating. Use a hoe to uproot weed seedlings. Pull larger weeds by hand so you can be sure to get all the roots without harming the vegetables. And remember, weeding isn't just for summer. Some weeds are cool-season performers and should be removed whenever you

can work the soil. Add the weeds to your compost pile where they'll be able to do the garden some good!

HINT: Don't use fresh field hay as mulch. It may contain a lot of weed seeds, which would only increase your weeding woes.

CULTIVATING

Cultivate, or break up the soil, to remove weed seedlings and to increase air and moisture penetration. Soil should never be allowed to form a hard crust! Begin prior to mulching, once the seedlings are a few inches high. If your vegetables are planted in rows, cultivate them using a hoe to loosen the soil around the base of the plants, being careful not to break the stems or injure the roots. A three-pronged fork is excellent for hand-cultivating small areas. Don't cultivate very deep; it will bring more weed seeds up to the surface. Cultivate often, if you do not mulch.

FERTILIZING

Nutrient-rich soil produces a bountiful harvest. If your goal is to grow organic vegetables, organic materials such as manure, kelp, compost and/or bone meal can be added to the soil in the necessary amounts to satisfy your soil test. Just keep in mind the nutrient composition and pH of each material. For instance, bone meal is high in phosphorus (2-14-0), and cottonseed meal is very acidic. Making the calculations and spreading the amendments (you need twenty pounds of cow manure to equal the NPK content of one pound of 5-10-5 fertilizer) takes extra time and effort, but many gardeners feel the results are well worth it as the manure is more efficient at delivering its nutrient load. Manure remains in the soil while synthetic fertilizers may evaporate or wash away.

You may opt to use a combination of organic materials and synthetic fertilizers. Synthetic fertilizers will efficiently provide the essential nutrients (NPK) while compost and manure will add the micronutrients and organic matter. Fertilizers are available in a variety of formulations, which benefit specific crops as follows:

5-10-5 For fruiting crops, such as squash and tomatoes
10-10-10 For leafy vegetables, such as lettuce, spinach and cabbage
5-10-10 For peppers and other crops requiring more potash

But as synthetic fertilizers are released more quickly than organic materials, you will have to apply them more often. If you are growing crops such as melons, which take over one hundred days to mature, use a slow-release synthetic fertilizer. But keep in mind that fertilizers are potent. Use them with care. Do not let them come in direct contact with roots or stems and always water them in well. If you are experiencing a dry summer, fertilize with care and only if you can follow up with water.

FOLIAR FEEDING is often beneficial for watering in young transplants and to give sad-looking plants a midseason boost. Spray the liquid fertilizer directly on the leaves. Use a balanced 20-20-20 formula that comes in liquid and crystalline form or organic fertilizers such as seaweed extract and fish emulsion. Be sure to mix it well. For large areas use a hose attachment that automatically mixes the fertilizer at the correct rate. For young transplants use a weaker solution, particularly if you use manure tea. This should be diluted 1:1.

SIDE-DRESSING is a good way to satisfy the special needs of specific vegetables in the garden. It is especially beneficial to vegetables that take more than sixty days to mature. You simply take a handful of the appropriate fertilizer and scratch it into the soil next to the plant several times during the growing season. Side-dress peppers after they have set their first fruits. Broccoli, side-dressed with 10-10-10 fertilizer after you have

picked the primary head, will continue to produce. Bonemeal, blood meal, rock phosphate and cottonseed meal are good organic fertilizers for side-dressing.

Manure Tea

Some manures, such as chicken manure, are too "hot," or potent, to use directly on the garden. Instead they are applied as a "manure tea." All you need to make manure tea is a large (fifty-five gallon) barrel, a burlap bag or cheesecloth, water and manure. Fill the burlap bag with manure (about five gallons worth) and suspend it in a barrel of water. Wait two or three days and serve the nourishing tea to your vegetables. Dilute it further if it looks too strong. If you don't have a large barrel, mix the tea at a rate of two cups manure to one gallon of water.

If you want to use manure directly in the garden, be sure it is well rotted. Fresh manure is smelly and "hot" due to the high ammonia content. Well-rotted manure looks like rich soil, is odorless, and will not burn your plants. You can purchase it packaged from your local nursery or in bulk from a local farmer. Always ask for aged manure. If you have any doubts, let it age for a few weeks before applying it to plants.

MULCH

Mulch your vegetable garden to moderate the soil temperature, retain moisture and reduce weeds. In your cold climate it's important to check the soil temperature before you mulch. You want the soil to be warm to encourage plant growth. If you mulch too early, it won't have a chance to warm up. Covering the beds with black plastic early in the season will warm up the soil faster for a jump start on the growing season.

Once your seedlings are a sturdy height (3" or 4"), apply a fine-textured mulch, such as ground-up leaves or compost, 2" to 3" thick. When the plants are taller, apply a loose mulch of straw or spoiled hay 6" to 8" thick. Straw and spoiled hay are also good on paths in between the rows.

Apply loose mulches in the fall to prevent the soil from freezing, allowing you to leave hardy root crops, such as carrots, in the ground later in the fall. When you're ready to eat them, simply pull aside the mulch, pick what you need, then replace the mulch. In your cold, snowy climate, however, you won't be able to store them in the ground all winter long. Dig them before the ground freezes and the snow flies!

There are varying opinions on mulching vegetables in the coldest zones (Zone 3 and colder). Watch your garden and see how your plants respond. For instance you may find that while cool-season crops, such as peas, beets, cauliflower and broccoli, do well when mulched early in the spring, they take longer to mature, which can pose a problem in your short growing season. Some warm-season crops may mature faster without summertime mulch as the sun's rays are able to reach and heat the soil.

HINT: When using black plastic always spread it on moist, but not soggy, soil, as water will not penetrate it.

EXTENDING THE SEASON

Vegetable gardeners in Zones 3, 4 and 5 really benefit from an extended growing season. With a little help you can enjoy fresh vegetables from early summer to late in the fall. For the most productive vegetable garden, your goal is to control the growing conditions. But careful seed selection is just as important. Cold-climate seed varieties given extended growing seasons will provide cold climate gardeners with bountiful crops. To extend the season:

- Control the soil and air temperature with mulches and plant or row covers.
- Select vegetables that tolerate the cool weather in spring and fall.

- Select vegetables that thrive in the peak summer heat.
- Start seeds indoors, then move the seedlings outdoors to a cold frame until it's warm enough to transplant them into the garden.
- Plant in raised beds.
- Use mulch and plant covers to add weeks at both ends of the growing season.
- Use plastic mulch to warm the soil in the spring (see "Mulch," p.185). Remove the black plastic when the weather is warm, but save it to re-use the following year.
- Use covers like Wall-o-Water for individual plants, such as tomatoes or eggplants, which take a long time to reach maturity. The Wall-o-Water will protect the plants from cold spring winds and release stored heat during the night.
- To extend cool-season crops, such as lettuce, into the summer, select heat-tolerant varieties, then keep them cool by providing shade using shade cloth or lath.
- Plant a second crop of cool-season vegetables, such as carrots, in the summer for harvest in the fall. To protect your tender plants from frost in the fall, cover them with sheets at night or make tunnels of plastic stretched over metal hoops. Be sure to remove the covers if it becomes hot so your vegetables won't cook before you want them to.
- Water regularly and harvest often to keep your garden productive.

HINT: If you want to work your snow-covered garden earlier in the spring, sprinkle it with wood ashes, soil, or sand. The dark color will retain the heat, melting the snow faster.

STAKING AND TRAINING

Staking and training vining plants, such as tomatoes, beans and peas, is a wonderful way to save space in the garden, while providing excellent air circulation around the plants. Tomatoes that are staked are less likely to rot and will ripen faster and more evenly. Use stakes, tripods, trellises, netting, wire cages and even sturdy twigs for support. The climbing habit of the plant will determine the type of support required.

HINT: Many gardeners underestimate the strength they need from their supports. Plan ahead for the mature weight of tomatoes, pole beans, gourds and melons. They can get heavy!

FOR INDIVIDUAL PLANTS, SUCH AS TOMATOES Use sturdy stakes or caging. Place the stake on the windward side to counter the force of the wind. Loosely tie the plant to the stake using green plastic tape or soft strips of cloth, such as old sheets or similar materials. Wire cages require less work as tomatoes grow freely without tying. Make a cage out of sturdy turkey wire supported by two or three stakes or buy a ready-made cage.

FOR CLIMBERS, SUCH AS POLE BEANS AND CUCUMBERS Use poles, tepees, netting, trellis or wire mesh. Attach the mesh to A-frames or 8' posts sunk 24" into the ground. When the seedlings are tall enough to reach the mesh, wrap them around the mesh to show them the way to grow.

FOR TENDRIL CLIMBERS, SUCH AS PEAS Use the structures for climbers or use brush stakes. Stick a branch from a twiggy bush in the ground next to seedlings in the spring and let them grow up through it.

FOR LOW, RUNNING PLANTS SUCH AS MELONS Use a pole supported horizontally about 8" to 12" above the ground. The fruit or vegetables will be suspended until large and heavy enough to rest on the ground.

PESTS AND COMPANION PLANTS
Prevention is the best practice when it comes to pests in the vegetable garden. Avoid pests and disease by rotating your crops, keeping a clean garden and enclosing your garden with a fence. Do not use pesticides on anything you are going to eat. See "Pests And Intruders," p.39.

> *HINT: Plant companion plants to deter pests. Marigolds repel rabbits and nematodes; radishes repel the squash vine borer; onions and garlic repel just about everything.*

HARVESTING VEGETABLES
The harvest is your big payoff! After weeks of hard work, you are finally able to savor your bounty.
- Harvest vegetables as soon as they are ready. As with flowers that go to seed, if left too long, an unpicked vegetable will start to shut down, reducing its productivity.
- Keep a close eye on lettuce, broccoli and other vegetables that may have to be picked daily so they do not pass their prime.
- Regularly harvest plants that produce over a long period of time, such as peas and beans.
- Plan ahead for your harvest. If you are going to be away, select vegetables that ripen either before or after your trip and plant them at the appropriate time. Or let a favorite neighbor enjoy your rewards.

SEASONAL CLEANUP
Seasonal cleanup is important for a healthy, productive vegetable garden. Pull out all plants as soon as the crop is finished. Continue to weed so that weeds are removed before they set seed. Pull out all stakes and temporary structures, such as tomato cages, and clean them before storing them for the winter. Cultivate all beds except those planted with perennial vegetables. Apply mulch over the entire garden but especially to protect your perennial vegetables. This will prevent soil erosion and weed seed germination. If you have time, instead of mulching, you can plant a cover crop such as clover, oats or winter rye. In the Midwest, where there is little snow cover, cover crops are especially beneficial. They not only prevent erosion, but, when they are turned under in the spring, also enrich the soil. Ask your local Agricultural Cooperative Extension Service for the best cover crop for your soil and climate.

Vegetables... *For Your Garden*

Common Name / Botanical Name	Key	Sun/Shade	Microclimate	Height	Depth	Spacing
Asparagus / *Asparagus officinalis*	P	○	Hardy; cool-season	3-6'	Root crowns 6-8"	18-24"
Bean (pole snap) / *Phaseolus vulgaris*	A	○	Tender; warm-season	6-10'	1 1/2-2"	6"
Bean (bush snap) / *Phaseolus vulgaris* var. *humilis*	A	○	Tender; warm-season	10-24"	1"	sow 2" apart in rows; thin to 6"; space hills 1' apart
Beets / *Beta vulgaris*	B/A	○	Hardy; cool-season	6-12"	1/4"	sow 2" apart; thin to 4-6"
Broccoli / *Brassica oleracea* (Botrytis group)	B/A	○	Hardy; cool-season	1 1/2-3'	1/4 - 1/2"	18-24" apart
Cabbage / *Brassica oleracea* (Capitata group)	A	○	Hardy; cool-season	12-15"	1/4-1/2"	10-24"
Carrot / *Daucus carota* var. *sativus*	B/A	○	Hardy; cool-season	8-12"	1/4-1/2"	sow 1" apart; thin to 3-4"
Cauliflower / *Brassica oleracea* (Botrytis group)	B/A	○	Hardy; cool-season	18-24"	1/4-1/2"	18-24"
Corn (sweet) / *Zea mays* var. *rugosa*	A	○	Tender; warm-season	4-7'	1"	sow 3" apart; thin to 9-12"
Cucumber (slicing) / *Cucumis sativus*	A	○	Tender; warm-season	4-6'	1/2"	sow 3" apart; thin to 6-9"
Eggplant / *Solanum melongena* var. *esculentum*	P/A	○	Tender; warm-season	1 1/2-2'	1/4-1/2"	18-24"
Endive / *Chicorium endiva*	A	○ ◑	Hardy; heat-tolerant	8-14"	1/4-1/2"	8-15"
Garlic / *Allium sativum*	B	○	Hardy; full-season	1-3'	1-2"	4-6"
Kale / *Brassica oleracea* (Acephala group)	A	○ ◑	Hardy; cool-season	1-1 1/2'	1/2"	sow 6" apart; thin to 2'

Key: Annual (A); Biennial (B); Biennial, grown as annual (B/A); Perennial (P); Perennial, grown as annual (P/A)

Row Spacing	Time to Harvest	Comments
4'	3rd year, then annually in spring	Rich, moist, well-drained soil; prepare bed as for perennial flowers; plant divisions in trenches or sow seeds after last frost; male and female root crowns; male plants produce more spears; mulch in fall
4'	55-75 days	Rich, well-drained, sandy soil; pH 6.0-7.0; sow seed successively outdoors 3 weeks after last frost; do not apply nitrogen fertilizer; provide support
2-3'	50-70 days	Rich, well-drained soil; pH 6.5-7.0; sow seed outdoors 2 weeks after last frost at 3-week intervals; plant in hills or rows; do not apply nitrogen fertilizer
2-3'	45-65 days	Rich, well-drained, sandy but rock-free soil; pH 6.0-6.8; prone to rot in wet soils; amend clay soils with compost and gypsum; sow seed outdoors 2-3 weeks before last frost in succession until hot weather; do not apply high-nitrogen fertilizers
18-30"	70-95 days	Moist, loose, well-drained soil; pH 6.0-6.8; for fall harvest sow seed outdoors 10-12 weeks before first fall frost; provide light shade in hot weather and protection from insects with row covers; harvest center head first to allow smaller heads to form
2-3 1/2'	65-125 days	Moist, well-drained soil; pH 6.0-6.8; transplant outdoors 2-4 weeks before last frost; plant deeper than originally growing; sow outdoors 10-12 weeks before first frost for fall harvest; avoid midsummer heat; harvest before bolt in summer heat and before hard freeze in fall
12-15"	55-75 days	Well-drained, deep, sandy but rock-free soil; pH 6.0-6.8; sow outdoors 2-3 weeks before last frost at 2-3 week intervals; use raised beds for improved drainage; to prevent splitting, water regularly during dry periods; may become bitter in hot weather
2-3'	50-90 days	Moist, well-drained neutral to alkaline soil; add lime as necessary; sow seed indoors 6-8 weeks before last frost for early harvest; transplant outdoors when days are above 50°F; blanch when heads are golf ball-size
2-3'	85-115 days	Well-drained, moist soil; pH 6.5-7.0; sow seed outdoors when soil reaches a minimum of 55°F or ideally 65°F; in Zone 3, sow just after last frost; plant in blocks for best pollination; select quick-maturing cultivars
5-6'	50-70 days	Rich, loose, well-drained soil; pH 6.0-6.5; sow seed outdoors when soil is min. 65°F; water evenly for well-formed fruit; provide windbreaks in windy areas to allow for pollination; provide supports; harvest when flower falls off fruit
2-4'	60-85 days	Rich, moist, well-drained soil; pH 6.0-6.8; transplant outdoors when soil temperature is above 65°F and night temperatures are above 50°F; use black plastic mulch to raise soil temperature; harvest regularly; do not damage fruit
12-18"	60-85 days	Moist, well-drained soil; pH 6.5-6.8; sow seed outdoors in succession from 2-4 weeks before last frost; transplant outdoors after last frost; blanch or buy self-blanching cultivars; use raised beds for good drainage; better than lettuce in hot weather; flavor improves with light frost
12-15"	90-100 days	Moist, rich, well-drained soil; pH 6.0-6.8; plant sets (small bulbs) 4-6 weeks before first frost; pinch flowers in following summer; harvest in fall; look for cultivars adapted to your region
2-4'	60-70 days	Rich, well-drained, evenly moist soil; pH 6.0-6.8; for fall harvest sow outdoors in midsummer when evening temperatures drop; flavor improves with frost

Vegetables...*For Your Garden*

Common Name Botanical Name	Key	Sun/Shade	Microclimate	Height	Depth	Spacing
Lettuce *Lactuca sativa*	A	○ ◑	Half-hardy; cool-season	6-12"	1/4-1/2"	6-9"
Melons *Cucumis melo*	A	○	Tender; warm-season	1-2'	1/2"	2-8'
Onion (bulb and globe) (Cepa group)	B/A	○	Half-hardy; full-season	1-4'	1/2" for seeds; 1" for sets	sow seeds 1/2" apart; thin to 3-8"
Pea (shelling) *Pisum sativum* var. *sativum*	A	○ ◑	Hardy; cool-season	1 1/2-5' vines	1/2-1"	3-4"
Pepper (sweet or bell) *Capsicum annuum* (Grossum group)	P/A	○	Tender; warm-season; intolerant of cool, wet climates	2-3'	1/4"	1-2'
Potato *Solanum tuberosum*	P/A	○	Half-hardy; warm-season	12-30"	3-4"	10-12"
Pumpkin *Cucurbita pepo* var. *pepo*	A	○	Tender; warm-season	12-18' vines	3/4-1"	18-24"
Radish *Raphanus sativus*	B/A	○ ◑	Half-hardy; cool- to full-season	6-12"	1/2"	1-2"
Rhubarb *Rheum rhabarbarum*	P	○ ◑	Hardy; cool-season	2-3'	2"	30-36"
Spinach *Spinacia oleracea*	A	○ ◑	Hardy; cool-season	6-12"	1/2"	6-9"
Summer squash and zucchini *Cucurbita pepo* var. *melopepo*	A	○	Tender; warm-season	1-4'	1/2-1"	24-30"
Sunflower *Helianthus annus*	A	○	Tender; warm-season	5-10'	3/4-1"	2-3'
Tomato *Lycopersicon esculentum*	P/A	○	Tender; warm-season	4-10'	1/2"	2-3'
Tomato (cherry) *Lycopersicon esculentum* var. *cerasiforme*	P/A	○	Tender; warm-season	2-4'	1/2"	2-3'

Key: Annual (A); Biennial (B); Biennial, grown as annual (B/A); Perennial (P); Perennial, grown as annual (P/A)

Row Spacing	Time to Harvest	Comments
1-1 1/2'	50-80 days; 90-100 for crisp head	Moist, well-drained soil; pH 6.5-6.8; sow seed outdoors successively from early spring; transplant outdoors after last frost; best flavor in good soil and temperatures between 60-65°F; use raised beds for good drainage; provide in peak summer heat; harvest before bolting
5-7'	65-100 days	Rich, loose, well-drained soil; pH 6.0-6.5; sow seed outdoors in hills after last frost; provide extra water initially; reduce water as they ripen to avoid watery fruit; harvest when they achieve true color and are easily removed from stem
1-1 1/2'	75-120 days	Well-drained, sandy soil; pH 6.0-6.8; sow seed outdoors when soil reaches 45°F; plant sets (bulbs) outdoors 2 weeks before last frost; wait until tops yellow to harvest; let dry with good air circulation for 3-4 days; look for long-day onions
2-3'	55-70 days	Deep, rich, moist, well-drained soil; pH 6.0-6.8; sow seed treated with a fungicide at 2-week intervals as soon as the ground can be worked in the spring until July 4; provide support
2 1/2-3'	50-75 days	Well-drained soil; pH 6.0-6.8; transplant outdoors 4 weeks after last frost; use black plastic mulch to raise soil temperature before planting; overhead watering may prevent pollination; provide supports, such as wire cages
2-3'	90-120 days	Rich, well-drained, sandy soil; pH 6.0-7.0; plant certified disease-free "seed potatoes" or "spud buds" with at least 2 eyes after last frost; hill loose soil around growing plants to provide sun protection for tubers
6-8'	90-115 days	Rich, well-drained soil; pH 6.0-7.0; water evenly; sow seed in hills outdoors after last frost; use black plastic mulch to raise soil temperature before planting
1'	27-35 days	Loose, moist, well-drained soil; pH 6.0-6.8; avoid heavy clay soil; sow seed in succession outdoors in early spring until summer; sow fall radishes 30-40 days before first fall frost; harvest before heavy frost
3'	2nd year from spring - midsummer	Rich, well-drained, moist soil; plant root cuttings in spring; no fertilizing necessary
1-1 1/2'	45-55 days	Rich, well-drained soil; pH 6.0-6.8; sow seed in succession outdoors as soon as ground can be worked; for fall harvest sow outdoors when evenings become cooler; more tender in cool weather
3-5'	50-55 days	Rich, loose, well-drained soil; pH 6.0-7.0; sow seed indoors in Zones 3,4,5; sow seeds outdoors when soil reaches 60°F; use black plastic mulch to raise soil temperature before planting; transplant seedlings with true leaves outdoors after last frost; provide support for vines
6-8'	70-90 days	Average, loose, well-drained soil; sow seed outdoors in early spring
3-6'	55-95 days	Rich, well-drained soil; pH 6.0-7.0; water evenly to prevent cracks; transplant outdoors when soil reaches 70°F and night temperatures minimum 55°F; look for disease-resistant varieties; use cutworm collars; provide supports such as wire cages
2 1/2-3'	50-75 days	Rich, well-drained soil; pH 6.0-7.0; water evenly to prevent cracks; transplant outdoors when soil reaches 70°F and night temperatures of minimum 55°F; look for disease-resistant varieties; use cutworm collars; provide supports such as wire cages

Peter C. Jones

HERBS

Thymus vulgaris

Grown for their flowers as well as their leaves, herbs are among the most useful plants in the garden. Powerful healers, herbs form the foundation of modern medicine. Let them soothe and satisfy the senses. Use them as ornamentals in the herbaceous border, to edge a flower bed or in pots on the terrace or deck where their foliage adds color, texture and fragrance. Plant herbs between the stones in a terrace or path where their fragrance will be released with each step. Topiaries of rosemary are elegant additions to any garden.

Grow herbs you use regularly in cooking near the kitchen door where you'll be able to step outside and quickly snip a few stems when preparing dinner. Use them to flavor food, make teas, infuse oils or flavor vinegars. Plant large blocks of annual herbs in the vegetable garden; freeze or dry your harvest to last you all winter long. Or interplant them with your vegetables to save space and repel pests.

Grow Herbs:

- For cooking
- For healing
- For their fragrance
- For freshness and flavor
- For exotic and gourmet varieties
- To control your consumption of pesticides
- As ornamentals
- In terraces and paths
- For their shape, color and texture
- To share with friends
- For pleasure

SUN/SHADE

Most herbs prefer full sun. Some tolerate partial shade, including bee balm, bay, catmint, chamomile, lemon balm, lovage, parsley, mint, tarragon, thyme and violets.

TEMPERATURE

Some herbs, such as dill, basil, chervil and coriander, are annual; parsley is a biennial and tarragon, sage, chives, lavender, mint, oregano and thyme are all perennials. Like other plants their tolerance of heat and cold controls their life cycles. Warm weather encourages germination of most seeds and produces lush, leafy growth; cold weather usually signals the end of an annual herb's life cycle and the beginning of dormancy for perennial herbs.

Annual Herbs

Annual herbs are extremely sensitive to climatic conditions and are categorized by their cold and heat tolerance. Herbs generally thrive in warm, sunny weather, so hardy herbs are your best bet in your cold zones. The different types of annual herbs are:

HARDY HERBS Can survive frost. Are successful when sown directly in the garden, even while cool temperatures prevail. Include dill and chervil.

HALF-HARDY ANNUALS Will take some frost, but not as much as hardy herbs. Include anise.

TENDER HERBS Cannot tolerate frost. Many of these types need several weeks in order to reach maturity, and should be sown early indoors, in cold frames, or outdoors only after danger of frost has past. These can also be purchased as greenhouse grown seedlings or rooted cuttings. Include basil.

Perennial Herbs

Perennial herbs are also sensitive to both cold and warm temperatures. Look for plants that are cold hardy in your zone. But don't shy away from the best-loved herbs, such as rosemary and bay, which are tender perennials. Pot them up in the fall and bring them inside for the winter.

Consider the following when selecting herbs:

- The lowest expected temperatures in the summer
- The highest expected temperatures in the summer
- The average last day of frost
- The average first day of frost

SOIL

While many herbs, such as dill, rosemary and thyme, tolerate poor, dry soils, all herbs do better in well-drained, fertile soil with an average pH (5.5 to 7.0). If drainage is a problem, plant your herbs in raised beds. Herbs that tolerate wet, but not water-logged, soils, include borage, lovage and mint. Others, such as marjoram, oregano, rosemary, sage, santolina, tarragon, thyme and winter savory, tolerate quick-draining, dry soils. To increase the fertility, soil texture and water retention, amend the soil with organic matter. See "Soil," p.18.

WATER

Most herbs prefer moist, well-drained soil. When planting new herbs, always water deeply and thoroughly. Provide regular moisture during the growing season as the amount of rain you receive will affect the flavor of your herbs. During hot, dry summers, herbs left unwatered may become stunted and their flavor more intensely concentrated. During rainy summers, the flavor may be diluted.

CHOOSING THE SITE

The ideal site for an herb garden has full sun all day, good drainage, no competition from the roots of trees or shrubs and easy access to a water source. In Zones 3 and 4, a gently sloping, south-facing site is ideal, but avoid low sites where water may collect or cold air may settle. Locate heat-loving herbs, such as lavender, in sunny, sheltered gardens. As for all edible gardens, investigate the history of the site for contamination of the soil from pesticides, oil or gas, disintegrating asbestos and flaking lead paint.

DESIGNING THE HERB GARDEN

For a traditional, formal herb garden design a garden with geometric beds within the view of the house. Make the paths of brick or stone; clearly define the beds with decorative edging or a low hedge of boxwood or santolina. Add a focal point such as a bench, birdbath, sundial or sculpture. Ambitious gardeners may want to try making a traditional knot garden with low-growing herbs such as thyme and green and grey santolina grown in neatly trimmed, continuous bands or hedges that are interwoven in intricate patterns to define the edges of the beds. Fill the areas in between the bands with creeping herbs, flowers or colored stone.

Make an ornamental herb garden near the house, mixing flowers with the herbs and adding decorative pots, topiaries

Geometric designs provide ideal frameworks in which to plant formal herb gardens. Use the individual beds to create blocks of contrasting colors and texture.

and arbors. For a cottage garden, design free-form beds filled with herbs, flowers, roses and shrubs.

Planting Patterns

Planting patterns are integral to the overall design as they establish the planting order within the beds. Plant your herbs in rows, blocks or beds as in "Vegetables," p.168, or plan the bed as if you were planning a perennial border.

Spacing

The general rule of thumb for spacing annuals is to allow one half their mature height between plants. For perennial herbs allow at least 6" to 12" between plants. See the herb list for more specific spacing.

PLANNING AT A GLANCE:
- Microclimate
- Soil
- Water
- Annual or perennial
- Time you have available to garden
- Time required for germination
- Time required from seeding to harvest
- Plant growth habit
- Height and width
- Leaf size, texture and color
- Spacing
- Harvest goals
- Time of harvest: one-time or continuous
- Garden style: formal, informal, ornamental
- Planting pattern: rows or beds
- Pest control

HINT: Only plant herbs and flowers with the same cultural needs in the same beds.

SEEDS OR PLANTS?

When it comes time to plant you have a choice between sowing seeds directly or transplanting. Most annual herbs are grown from seed; perennials from seed or transplants. Consider your climate, length of growing season and time required from sowing to harvest for the herbs you've selected. As annuals take a long time to reach maturity, in your cold zones it is best to start seedlings indoors or purchase them from a local nurseryman. Start off with the largest transplants you can afford especially if you are growing low herb hedges. Use small plants to cover areas quickly in stone paths, terraces and other places where there might be competition from weeds. If you are just beginning, try easy-to-grow herbs such as parsley, sage, oregano, winter savory and chives. For tips on selecting healthy plants, refer to "Buying Annuals" and "Buying Perennials" before purchasing your herbs.

PLANTING AND MAINTAINING

For bed preparation, planting, weeding, cultivating and mulch see "Annuals" and "Perennials" in Chapter 3.

FERTILIZING

Most herbs are such enthusiastic growers, they won't need much encouragement at all. But all herbs benefit from a weak liquid fertilizer at planting time. Fertilize established perennial herbs in the spring, but do not fertilize them in the fall. Perennial herbs grown in cold zones need time to harden off before winter.

CONTROLLING RAMPANT HERBS

Perennial herbs can grow out of control. Mint is such a vigorous grower that without containment it will engulf its tame neighbors by midsummer. Plant vigorous growers in clearly defined beds, surrounded by lawns, embraced by stone or brick paths or edged with stone, brick or 2 x 6 pressure treat-

ed lumber. Impermeable mulches, such as 1" layers of news-paper covered with attractive mulches, will also curb their spread. If all else fails, plant invasive herbs in sunken containers with holes drilled in the bottom for drainage.

PESTS

Although herbs are generally pest-free, they aren't immune. In hot, humid areas, good air circulation will keep fungal diseases to a minimum. Remove pests by hand whenever possible, use insecticidal soap or only grow those varieties which are pest-free in your area. Do not use pesticides on any herbs you plan to eat. See "Pests And Intruders" on p.39.

HARVESTING HERBS

Allow your herbs to become well established before you begin to harvest them. Perennials, such as chives and tarragon, need a full year before you pick more than just a few leaves. Once they've begun growing vigorously, pick continuously without guilt or save your harvest until the late summer.

Although herbs picked early in the morning will last longer, there's nothing quite like herbs picked fresh just as you need them for cooking. Pick them as you would a flower, just above a node for branching herbs, such as rosemary or dill; at the base of the stem for single-stemmed herbs, such as parsley and chives. Always harvest the outside, or older, stems of parsley first to allow the inside stems to develop. Enjoy your basil before the leaves turn tough and bitter. Regularly cut annual herbs grown for their leaves to prevent them from going to seed; cut back perennials for a bushier plant. Pick annuals right up to the first frost, but stop picking perennial herbs three weeks prior to your first expected frost date.

PRESERVING HERBS

When harvesting herbs, your goal is to preserve the essential oils that provide the fragrance and flavor in their leaves and flowers.

Wash herbs only if absolutely necessary, then dry them thoroughly. Avoid overdrying — the essential oils evaporate quickly. For the best flavor preserve herbs immediately after picking.

FOR FRESH HERBS Store them up to ten days between layers of paper towels in resealable plastic bags in the refrigerator. Make sure they are not wet as they will not last as long.

FOR DRIED HERBS Spread them in a single layer on screens or hang them upside down to air dry. If they are not dry in a week, dry them in an oven set at 100° Fahrenheit until they are crispy. Store them in airtight bottles.

TO FREEZE HERBS Place herbs in resealable plastic bags in the freezer. Pulverize herbs such as basil and freeze the mix in ice-cube trays. It is not necessary to add liquid to the puree.

FOR HERB SEEDS Pick the entire herb branches when the seeds are light brown or grey. Enclose the seed heads in plastic bags and hang them upside down to dry. When partially dry, shake the seeds loose and continue to dry them on screens. Separate the hulls by blowing on them or putting the seeds through a colander.

FOR HERB VINEGARS Place several stems of your favorite herbs in bottles. Warm the vinegar and pour it over the herbs. Set the bottles in a warm, sunny spot for two weeks to let the herbs steep.

SEASONAL CLEANUP

Pull out all annuals as soon as the crop is finished. Continue to weed, making sure all weeds are removed before they set seed. Cultivate all beds except those planted with perennials. Apply mulch over the entire garden but especially to protect your perennial herbs. In areas with little snow cover, perennial herbs will benefit from an additional covering of evergreen boughs. To block harsh winter winds especially in the Midwest and on the Great Plains, erect a windscreen of burlap stretched between wood stakes.

Herbs

Best Bets For Your Garden

Common Name Botanical Name	Key	Sun/ Shade	Microclimate	
Basil *Ocimum basilicum*	A	○	Tender; warm-season; best in Zones 4 and 5	
Bay *Laurus nobilis*	P/A	○ ◑	Half hardy	
Borage *Borago officinalis*	A	○	Hardy; cool-season	
Chamomile *Chamaemelum nobile*	P	○ ◑	Hardy to Zone 6	
Chervil *Anthriscus cerefolium*	A	○ ◑	Hardy; cool-season	
Chives *Allium schoenoprasum*	P	○	Very hardy	
Coriander *Coriandrum sativum*	A	○ ◑	Very hardy; cool-season	
Dill *Anethum graveolens*	A	○	Hardy; cool-season	
Fennel *Foenicumum vulgare*	P/A	○	Cool-season	
Lovage *Levisiticum officinale*	P	○ ◑	Hardy to Zone 5; cool-season	
Marjoram *Origanum majorana*	P/A	○	Tender; heat- and drought-tolerant	
Mint *Mentha spp.*	P	○ ◑	Hardy to Zone 5	
Oregano *Origanum vulgare*	P	○ ◑	Hardy to Zone 5; drought-tolerant	
Parsley (curly) *Petroselinum crispum*	B/A	○ ◑	Hardy to Zone 5	
Rosemary *Rosmarinus officinalis*	P/A	○ ◑	Half-hardy shrub	
Sage *Salvia officinalis*	P	○ ◑	Hardy to Zones 4 and 5; heat- and drought-tolerant	
Savory (summer) *Satureja hortensis*	A	○	Warm-season; heat- and drought-tolerant	
Tarragon *Artemisia dracunculus*	P	○ ◑	Hardy to Zones 4 and 5	
Thyme *Thymus vulgaris*	P	○ ◑	Hardy to Zone 5; drought-tolerant	

Key: Annual (A); Perennial (P); Biennial grown as an annual (B/A);

Height	Seed Depth	Plant Spacing	Comments
10-36"	1/8"	Thin to 5-6"	Rich soil; pH 5.5-7.7; sow seed indoors in early spring or outdoors when soil is warm
6-30'	Transplants	3'-10'	Rich, well-drained soil; pH 6.0-7.0; evergreen shrub; plant in protected area; grows well in containers that can be overwintered indoors
12-18"	1-2"	6-8" apart	Light, well-drained soils; pH 6.0-7.0; sow seed outdoors after last frost; self-sows
6-9"	Transplants	6"	Light, moist soil; pH 6.7-7.3; sow seed indoors or outdoors when soil warms above 55° Fahrenheit; transplant in spring
1-2'	1/8"	Thinning unnecessary	Rich, moist, soil; pH 6.0-6.7; sow seed successively outdoors in early spring; goes to seed in extremely hot, dry weather
10"	Transplants	6" apart; thin every 2 years	Rich, well-drained soil; pH 6.0-7.0; sow seed indoors in late winter; transplant outdoors or divide in early spring; do not pick during first year
3'	1/2"	Thin to 4-5"	Rich, well-drained soil; pH 6.0-6.7; sow seed successively outdoors in spring; self-sows; also known as cilantro
3'	1/8"	Thin to 6-8" apart	Rich, well-drained soil; pH 6.0-6.7; sow seed successively outdoors in early spring; may not transplant well; self-sows; separate from fennel to prevent cross-pollination
18-24"	1/8"	8-10" apart	Average, well-drained soil; pH 6.0-6.7; sow seed outdoors in warm soil or transplant in late spring
4-6'	1/8"	Thin to 2' apart	Rich, moist, well-drained soil; pH 6.0-7.0; sow seed outdoors in late summer to early fall; transplant in spring or fall
1-2'	1/8"	8-10"	Light, well-drained soil; pH 6.7-7.0; sow seed indoors in early spring; transplant after last frost; grows well in containers that can be overwintered indoors
3-36"	Transplants	6-12"	Rich, moist, well-drained soil; pH 6.0-7.0; transplant spring or fall; keep flowers picked for best flavor; benefits from pruning; very invasive
12-30"	1/8"	8-10"	Average, well-drained soil; pH 6.0-7.0; sow seed early indoors or outdoors when soil warms above 45° Fahrenheit; transplant in spring
8-12"	1/8"	5-6"	Rich, moist soil; pH 5.5-6.7; sow seed successively outdoors from early spring to midsummer; transplant early spring; Italian parsley var. neapolitanum is more flavorful
2-3'	Transplants	1-2'	Light, well-drained soil; pH 6.0-6.7; transplant outdoors when soil warms; evergreen shrub; grows well in containers that can be overwintered indoors
1-2'	1/8"	8-10"	Light, sandy, well-drained soil; pH 6.0-6.7; sow seed indoors in late winter or outdoors in late spring; transplant spring or fall
12-18"	1/8"	Thin to 3-4" apart	Light, well-drained soil; pH 6.5-7.0; sow seed outdoors when soil warms; may self-sow
18-24"	Transplants	8-12"	Average, well-drained soil; pH 6.0-7.3; sterile, so cannot be grown from seed; transplant outdoors in spring
6-15"	1/8"	6-10"	Sandy, well-drained soil; pH 6.0-6.7; good air circulation; evergreen sub-shrub; sow seed outdoors in spring; transplant in spring

Perennial grown as an annual (P/A)

Michael H. Dodge

VI
SUREFIRE
GARDENS

Annuals

Ageratum houstonianam (Ageratum)
Begonia x *semperflorens* (Wax begonia)
Calendula officinalis (Calendula)
Gaillardia pulchella (Blanket flower)
Impatiens balsamina (Balsam)
Lobelia erinus (Lobelia)
Lobularia maritima (Sweet alyssum)
Matthiola incana (Stock)
Nicotiana alata (Flowering tobacco)
Pelargonium peltatum (Ivy geranium)
Pelargonium x *domesticum* (Fancy geranium)
Phlox drummundii (Annual phlox)
Salvia splendens (Salvia)
Scabiosa atropurpurea (Sweet scabious)
Tagetes spp. (Marigold)
Tithonia rotundifolia (Mexican sunflower)
Verbena x *hybrida* (Verbena)

Biennials

Daucus carota (Queen Anne's lace)
Dianthus barbatus (Sweet William)
Digitalis purpurea (Foxglove)

Perennials

Achillea spp. (Yarrow)
Chrysanthemum parthenium (Feverfew)
Cimicifuga racemosa (Snakeroot)
Coreopsis verticillata (Threadleaf coreopsis)
Echinacea purpurea (Purple coneflower)
Echinops humilis (Globe thistle)
Gaillardia x *grandiflora* (Blanket flower)
Gypsophila paniculata (Baby's breath)

Heliopsis helianthoides (False sunflower)
Hemerocallis spp. (Daylily)
Heuchera x *brizoides* (Coral bells)
Hibiscus moscheutos (Rose mallow)
Iris spp. (Iris)
Limonium latifolium (Sea lavender)
Malva moschata (Musk mallow)
Nepeta x *faassenii* (Catmint)
Oenothera spp. (Evening primrose)
Perovskia hybrids (Russian sage)
Platycodon grandiflorus (Balloon flower)
Rudbeckia spp. (Black-eyed Susan)
Solidago hybrids (Goldenrod)
Veronica spicata (Speedwell)
Yucca filamentosa (Adam's needle)

Roses

Rosa rugosa (Rugosa rose)

Bulbs, Rhizomes And Tubers

Allium (Ornamental onion)
Chionadoxa luciliae (Glory-of-the-snow)
Crocus (Crocus)
Galanthus nivalis (Snowdrop)
Muscari armeniacum (Grape hyacinth)
Narcissus spp. (Daffodil)
Scilla siberica (Squill)
Tulipa spp. (Tulip)

Groundcovers

Cerastium tomentosum (Snow-in-summer)
Euonymus fortunei radicans (Wintercreeper)
Hemerocallis spp. (Daylily)

Vines

Campsis radicans x *tagliabuana* 'Madame Galen' (Trumpet vine)
Clematis x *Jackmanii* (Large-flowered clematis, cultivars)
Clematis paniculata (Sweet autumn clematis)
Lathyrus latifolius (Everlasting sweet pea)
Parthenocissus quinquefolia (Virginia creeper)
Polygonum aubertii (Silver lace vine)
Wisteria sinensis (Chinese wisteria, many selections)

Ornamental Grasses

Chasmanthium latifolium (Inland sea oats)
Panicum virgatum (Switch grass)

Shrubs

Berberis thunbergii 'Atropurpurea' (Barberry)
Buddleia davidii (Butterfly bush)
Buxus sempervirens 'Suffructicosa' (True dwarf boxwood)
Clethra alnifolia (Sweet pepper bush)
Cotoneaster horizontalis (Rockspray cotoneaster)
Juniperus horizontalis (Creeping juniper, cultivars)
Spiraea vanhouttei (Vanhoutte spirea)
Viburnum carlesii (Korean spice bush)

All plants on this list have moderate salt tolerance.

Philadelphus coronarius

THE HEAVY CLAY SOIL GARDEN
Annuals
Gomphrena globosa (Globe amaranth)
Helianthus annuus (Sunflower)
Ipomea alba (Moonflower)
Ipomoea purpurea (Morning glory)

Biennials
Digitalis purpurea (Foxglove)

Perennials
Aruncus dioicus (Goatsbeard)
Asclepias tuberosa (Butterfly weed)
Astilbe x *arendsii* (Astilbe)
Boltonia asteroides 'Snowbank'
  (Snowbank boltonia)
Echinacea purpurea (Purple coneflower)
Hemerocallis spp. (Daylily)
Hosta spp. (Hosta)
Monarda didyma (Bee balm)
Solidago spp. (Goldenrod)

Vines
Polygonum aubertii (Silver lace vine)
Campsis radicans (Trumpet creeper)

Shrubs
Berberis spp. (Barberry)
Chaenomeles spp. (Flowering quince)
Clethra alnifolia (Sweet pepper bush)
Cotoneaster spp. (Cotoneaster)
Forsythia spp.(Forsythia)
Lonicera spp. (Honeysuckle)
Philadelphus coronarius (Mock orange)

Asclepias tuberosa 'Gay Butterflies'

THE POOR, SANDY SOIL GARDEN
Annuals
Calendula officinalis (Pot marigold)
Centaurea cyanus (Batchelor's button)
Coreopsis tinctoria (Golden coreopsis)
Cosmos bipinnatus (Cosmos)
Eschscholzia californica (California poppy)
Gaillardia pulchella (Blanket flower)

Helianthus annuus (Sunflower)
Impatiens balsamina (Balsam)
Lobularia maritima (Sweet alyssum)
Papaver rhoeas (Shirley poppy)
Tagetes spp. (Marigold)
Tithonia rotundifolia (Mexican sunflower)
Tropaeolum majus (Nasturtium)
Verbena x *hybrida* (Verbena)

Perennials
Achillea spp. (Yarrow)
Alchemilla mollis (Lady's mantle)
Armeria maritima (Sea pink)
Asclepias tuberosa (Butterfly weed)
Baptisia australis (Wild blue indigo)
Canna x *generalis* (Canna)
Centranthus ruber (Red valerian)
Echinops humilis (Globe thistle)
Gaillardia x *grandiflora* (Blanket flower)
Hemerocallis spp. (Daylily)
Limonium latifolium (Sea lavender)
Nepeta x *faassenii* (Catmint)
Rudbeckia hirta (Black-eyed Susan)
Salvia spp. (Perennial salvia)
Yucca filamentosa (Adam's needle)

Shrubs
Berberis spp. (Barberry)
Cotoneaster spp. (Cotoneaster)
Hypericum spp. (Saint John's-wort)
Juniperus spp. (Juniper)

THE SPECIAL SOIL GARDEN

THE ALKALINE SOIL GARDEN
Annuals
Ageratum houstonianum (Ageratum)
Antirrhinum majus (Snapdragon)
Brassica oleracea (Ornamental cabbage)
Calendula officinalis (Pot marigold)
Callistephus chinensis (China aster)
Cosmos bipinnatus (Cosmos)
Eschscholzia californica (California poppy)
Gaillardia pulchella (Blanket flower)
Gomphrena globosa (Globe amaranth)
Matthiola incana (Stock)
Phlox drummondii (Annual Phlox)
Tagetes spp. (Marigold)
Tithonia rotundifolia (Mexican sunflower)
Zinnia elegans (Zinnia)

Perennials
Achillea spp.(Yarrow)
Aquilegia canadensis (Native columbine)
Bergenia cordifolia (Bergenia)
Centranthus ruber (Red valerian)
Dianthus spp. (Pinks)
Dicentra spp. (Bleeding heart)
Echinacea purpurea (Purple coneflower)
Geranium spp. (Hardy geranium)
Gypsophila paniculata (Baby's breath)
Helenium autumnale (Sneezeweed)
Heuchera x *brizoides* (Coral bells)
Iberis sempervirens (Candytuft)
Paeonia lactiflora (Peony)
Rudbeckia hirta 'Gloriosa Daisy'
   (Gloriosa daisy)
Scabiosa caucasica (Scabiosa)
Veronica spicata (Speedwell)

Bulbs
Leucojum aestivum (Leucojum)
Lilium candidum (Madonna lily)
Narcissus jonquilla (Jonquil)

Vines
Actinidia kolomitka (Male) (Arctic beauty kiwi)
Akebia quinata (Five-leaf akebia)
Campsis x *tagliabuana* 'Madame Galen'
   (Trumpet creeper)
Euonymus fortunei radicans (Wintercreeper)
Hydrangea anomala petiolaris (Climbing
   hydrangea)
Wisteria sinensis (Chinese wisteria)

Groundcovers
Adiantum pedatum (Maidenhair fern)
Ajuga reptans (Bugleweed)
Euonymus fortunei radicans (Wintercreeper)
Hedera helix (English ivy)
Hemerocallis spp. (Daylily)
Lamium maculatum (Dead nettle)
Pachysandra terminalis (Japanese pachysandra)
Vinca minor (Common periwinkle)

Shrubs
Buddleia davidii and cvs. (Buddleia)
Buxus microphylla 'Koreana' (Wintergreen
   boxwood)
Buxus sempervirens 'Suffructicosa' (True
   dwarf boxwood)
Cotoneaster spp. (Cotoneaster)
Deutzia gracilis (Slender deutzia)
Euonymus alatus compacta (Burning bush)
Forsythia ovata 'Northern Gold' (Northern
   gold forsythia)
Ligustrum vulgare 'Cheyenne' (Cheyenne
   privet)
Ligustrum obtusifolium regelianum (Regal
   border privet)
Lonicera spp. (Honeysuckle)
Potentilla fruticosa varieties (Cinquefoil)
Rosa rugosa (Rugosa rose)

Rhododendron

THE ACID SOIL GARDEN
Shrubs
Arctostaphylos uva-ursi (Bearberry)
Clethra alnifolia (Sweet pepper bush)
Enkianthus campanulatus (Redvein
   enkianthus)
Fothergilla spp. (Fothergilla)
Kalmia latifolia (Mountain laurel)
Rhododendron spp. (Rhododendron)

Annuals

Brassica oleracea (Ornamental cabbage)
Calendula officinalis (Pot marigold)
Callistephus chinensis (China aster)
Impatiens balsamina (Balsam)
Impatiens wallerana (Impatiens)
Matthiola incana (Stock)
Nicotiana alata (Flowering tobacco)
Thunbergia alata (Black-eyed Susan vine)
Viola x *wittrockiana* (Pansy)

Biennials

Myosotis 'Blue Ball' (Forget-me-not)

Perennials

Aruncus dioicus (Goatsbeard)
Aster novae-angliae (New England aster)
Aster novi-belgi (New York aster)
Astilbe spp. (Astilbe)
Eupatorium purpureum (Joe-Pye weed)
Filipendula rubra (Queen of the prairie)
Hemerocallis spp. (Daylily)
Hibiscus moscheutos (Rose mallow)
Hosta spp. (Plantation lily)
Iris spp. (Iris)
Lobelia siphilitica (Great blue lobelia)
Monarda didyma (Bee balm)

Groundcovers

Euonymus fortunei 'Colorata' (Wintercreeper)
Pachysandra terminalis (Japanese
  pachysandra)
Vinca minor (Common periwinkle)

Shrubs

Chaenomeles spp. (Flowering quince)
Clethra alnifolia and cvs. (Sweet pepper
  bush)
Cornus alba and cvs. (Dogwood)
Deutzia spp. (Deutzia)
Forsythia spp. (Forsythia)
Hamamelis (Witch hazel)

Ilex, deciduous types (Holly)
Kalmia latifolia (Mountain laurel)
Ligustrum spp. (Privet)
Symphoricarpos x *chenaultii* 'Hancock'
  (Chenault coralberry)
Thuja occidentalis (Arborvitae)
Viburnum dentatum (Arrowwood)

Annuals
Ageratum houstonianum (Ageratum)
Catharanthus roseus (Vinca)
Celosia cristata (Cockscomb)
Cleome hasslerana (Spiderflower)
Gomphrena globosa (Globe amaranth)
Lavatera trimestris (Annual mallow)
Nierembergia hippomanica (Nierembergia)
Tithonia rotundifolia (Mexican sunflower)

Perennials
Achillea spp. (Yarrow)
Anaphalis margaritacea (Common pearly everlasting)
Asclepias tuberosa (Butterfly weed)
Coreopsis verticillata (Threadleaf coreopsis)
Echinops humilis (Globe thistle)
Nepeta x *faassenii* (Catmint)
Perovskia hybrids (Russian sage)
Rudbeckia spp. (Black-eyed Susan)
Salvia spp. (Perennial salvia)
Sedum spectabile (Showy stonecrop)
Solidago hybrids (Goldenrod hybrids)
Yucca filamentosa (Adam's needle)

Groundcovers
Cerastium tomentosum (Snow-in-summer)
Hedera helix (English ivy)
Hemerocallis spp. (Daylily)
Sedum kamtschaticum (Sedum)

Vines
Polygonum aubertii (Silver lace vine)

Ornamental Grasses
Calamagrostis acutiflora 'Stricta' (Feather reed grass)
Carex morrowii 'Variegata' (Variegated Japanese sedge)
Panicum virgatum 'Haense Herms' (Switch grass)
Sesleria autumnalis (Autumn moor grass)

Shrubs
Berberis thunbergii and cultivars (Barberry)
Buddleia alternifolia (Butterfly bush)
Caragana arborescens and cultivars (Siberian pea)
Chaenomeles spp. (Flowering quince)
Cotoneaster spp. (Cotoneaster)
Fothergilla major (Fothergilla)
Juniper spp. (Juniper)
Ligustrum spp. (Privet)
Myrica pensylvanica (Bayberry)
Potentilla spp. (Cinquefoil)
Rhus typhina 'Laciniata' (Laceleaf staghorn sumac)
Rosa rugosa cultivars (Rugosa rose)
Yucca filamentosa (Adam's Needle)

Herbs
Origanum majorana (Marjoram)
Origanum vulgare (Oregano)
Salvia officinalis (Sage)
Santolina chamaecyparissus (Santolina)
Satureja hortensis (Summer savory)
Satureja montana (Winter savory)

All drought-tolerant plants require water until they are established and most prefer regular water.

Annuals
Begonia x *semperflorens* (Wax begonia)
Impatiens balsamina (Balsam)
Impatiens wallerana (Impatiens)

Perennials
Dicentra spectabilis (Bleeding heart)
Hosta spp. (Plantain lily)

Bulbs
Lilium hybrids (Lily hybrids)

Groundcovers
Ajuga reptans (Bugleweed)

Athyrium filix-femina (Lady fern)
Convallaria majalis (Lily-of-the-valley)
Dennstaedtia punctilobula (Hay-scented fern)
Epimedium grandiflorum (Bishop's hats)
Euonymus fortunei and cvs. (Wintercreeper)
Galium odoratum (Sweet woodruff)
Hedera helix and cvs. (English ivy)
Osmunda cinnamomea (Cinnamon fern)
Pachysandra terminalis and cvs. (Japanese pachysandra)

Vines
Vinca minor (Common periwinkle)

Shrubs
Clethra alnifolia and cvs. (Sweet pepper bush)
Euonymus alatus 'Compacta' (Burning bush)
Hamamelis spp. (Witch hazel)
Hydrangea quercifolia (Oakleaf hydrangea)
Ilex (Holly)
Kalmia latifolia and cvs. (Mountain laurel)
Mahonia aquifolium (Mahonia)
Rhododendron maximum (Rhododendron)
Viburnum, most (Viburnum)

Plants on this list thrive in full shade.

THE CUTTING AND FRAGRANT GARDENS

THE CUTTING GARDEN

Annuals

Antirrhinum majus (Snapdragon)
Callistephus chinensis (China aster)
Centaurea cyanus (Bachelor's button)
Cleome hasslerana (Spiderflower)
Consolida spp. (Annual larkspur)
Cosmos bipinnatus (Mexican aster)
Cynoglossum amabile (Chinese forget-me-not)
Gomphrena globosa (Globe amaranth)
Gypsophila elegans (Baby's breath)
Helianthus annuus (Sunflower)
Lathyrus odoratus (Sweet pea)
Matthiola incana (Stock)
Phlox drummondii (Annual phlox)
Scabiosa atropurpurea (Sweet scabious)
Zinnia elegans (Zinnia)

Biennials

Campanula medium (Canterbury bells)
Daucus carota (Queen Anne's lace)
Dianthus barbatus (Sweet William)
Digitalis purpurea (Foxglove)
Myosotis 'Blue Ball' (Forget-me-not)

Perennials

Alchemilla mollis (Lady's mantle)
Aster novae-angliae (New England aster)
Aster novi-belgi (New York aster)
Baptisia australis (False indigo)
Campanula persicifolia (Bellflower)
Centranthus ruber (Red valerian)
Coreopsis verticillata (Threadleaf coreopsis)
Dahlia (Dahlia)
Delphinium elatum (Delphinium)
Echinops humilis (Globe thistle)
Gaillardia x *grandiflora* (Blanket flower)
Gypsophila paniculata (Baby's breath)
Liatris spicata (Gayfeather)
Limonium latifolium (Sea lavender)
Perovskia hybrids (Russian sage)
Physotegia virginiana (False dragonhead)
Rudbeckia spp. (Black-eyed Susan)
Salvia spp. (Perennial salvia)
Scabiosa caucasica (Scabiosa)
Solidago hybrids (Goldenrod)

Roses

Many roses

Bulbs, Rhizomes And Tubers

Gladiolus spp.
Iris (All irises)
Lilium (All lilies)
Narcissus spp. (Daffodil)
Tulipa spp. (Tulip)

THE FRAGRANT GARDEN

Annuals

Lathyrus odoratus (Sweet pea)
Lobularia maritima (Sweet alyssum)
Matthiola incana (Stock)
Nicotiana alata (Nicotiana) — Night fragrance
Verbena x *hybrida* (Verbena)

Biennials

Dianthus barbatus (Sweet William)

Perennials

Monarda didyma (Bee balm)
Nepeta x *faassenii* (Catmint)
Oenothera spp. (Evening primrose) — Night fragrance
Paeonia spp. (Peony)
Phlox spp. (Phlox) — Night fragrance
Viola odorata (Sweet violet)

Herbs

Many herbs have fragrant foliage

Bulbs And Tubers

Hyacinthus spp. (Hyacinth)
Lilium spp. (Lily)
Narcissus spp. (Narcissus)

Vines

Clematis paniculata (Sweet autumn clematis)
Lonicera spp. (Honeysuckle)
Wisteria floribunda (Wisteria)
Wisteria sinensis (Chinese wisteria)

Groundcovers

Convallaria majalis (Lily-of-the-valley)

Shrubs

Buddleia davidii (Butterfly bush)
Buxus sempervirens (Boxwood) — fragrant foliage
Clethra alnifolia (Sweet pepper bush)
Lonicera spp. (Honeysuckle)
Rhododendron arborescens (Sweet azalea)
Rosa spp. (Rose)
Viburnum x *burkwoodii* (Burkwood viburnum)
Viburnum carlesii (Korean spice bush)

Annuals
Ageratum houstonianum (Ageratum)
Antirrhinum majus (Snapdragon)
Coreopsis tinctoria (Golden coreopsis)
Cosmos bipinnatus (Cosmos)
Gaillardia pulchella (Blanket flower)
Impatiens balsamina (Balsam)
Nicotiana alata (Nicotiana)*
Scabiosa atropurpurea (Sweet scabious)
Tagetes patula (French marigold)
Tithonia rotundifolia (Mexican sunflower)
Verbena x *hybrida* (Garden verbena)
Zinnia elegans (Zinnia)

Perennials
Achillea spp. (Yarrow)
Asclepias tuberosa (Butterfly weed)*
Aster spp. (Aster)
Centhranthus ruber (Red valerian)
Coreopsis verticillata (Threadleaf coreopsis)
Echinacea purpurea (Purple coneflower)
Echinops humilis (Globe thistle)
Helenium autumnale (Sneezeweed)
Hesperis matronalis (Dame's rocket)
Liatris spicata (Gayfeather)
Monarda didyma (Bee balm)*
Phlox spp. (Phlox)
Physostegia virginiana (Obedient plant)

Rudbeckia hirta (Black-eyed Susan)
Scabiosa caucasica (Scabiosa)
Sedum spectabile (Sedum)
Solidago spp. (Goldenrod)

Bulbs
Allium spp (Ornamental onion)
Lilium spp. (Lily)*

Shrubs
Buddleia davidii (Butterfly bush)*
Clethra alnifolia (Sweet pepper bush)

Attracts hummingbirds

Annuals

Ageratum houstonianum (Ageratum)
Antirrhinum majus (Snapdragon)
Begonia x *semperflorens* (Wax begonia)
Calendula officinalis (Pot marigold)
Consolida spp. (Larkspur)
Cynoglossum amabile (Chinese forget-me-not)
Iberis umbellata (Candytuft)
Ipomea purpurea (Morning glory)
Lobelia erinus (Lobelia)
Lobularia maritima (Alyssum)
Matthiola incana (Stock)
Salvia splendens (Salvia)
Tagetes spp. (Marigold)
Tithonia rotundifolia (Mexican sunflower)
Tropaeolum majus (Nasturtium)

Biennials

Digitalis purpurea (Foxglove)
Myosotis 'Blue Ball' (Forget-me-not)

Perennials

Alchemilla mollis (Lady's mantle)
Aquilegia spp. (Columbine)
Asclepias tuberosa (Butterfly weed)
Aster novae-angliae (New England aster)
Aster novi-belgi (New York aster)
Astilbe x *arendsii* (Astilbe)
Bergenia cordifolia (Bergenia)
Boltonia asteroides 'Snowbank' (Snowbank boltonia)
Centranthus ruber (Red valerian)
Cimicifuga racemosa (Snakeroot)

Coreopsis verticillata (Threadleaf coreopsis)
Dianthus x *allwoodii* (Cottage pink)
Echinacea purpurea (Purple coneflower)
Geranium spp. (Cranesbill)
Helenium autumnale (Sneezeweed)
Hibiscus moscheutos (Rose mallow)
Iris spp. (Iris)
Monarda didyma (Bee balm)
Perovskia hybrids (Russian sage)
Phlox paniculata (Border phlox)
Rudbeckia spp. (Black-eyed Susan)
Salvia spp. (Perennial salvia)
Sedum spectabile (Showy stonecrop)
Solidago hybrids (Goldenrod)
Veronica spicata (Speedwell)
Viola odorata (Violet)

Bulbs

Allium spp. (Flowering onion)
Chiondoxa luciliae (Glory-of-the-snow)
Crocus spp. (Crocus)
Galanthus nivalis (Snowdrop)
Leucojum vernum (Snowflake)
Muscari armeniacum (Grape hyacinth)
Narcissus (Daffodil, Narcissus, Jonquil)
Scilla siberica (Squill)

Groundcovers

Ajuga reptans (Bugleweed)
Arctostaphylos uva-ursi (Bearberry)
Cerastium tomentosum (Snow-in-summer)
Convallaria majalis (Lily-of-the-valley)
Cotoneaster spp. (Cotoneaster)
Epimedium spp. (Bishop's hats)

Galium odoratum (Sweet woodruff)
Juniperus spp. (Juniper)
Lamium maculatum (Dead nettle)
Pachysandra terminalis (Japanese pachysandra)
Sedum spp. (Sedum)
Vinca minor (Myrtle)

Vines

Akebia quinata (Five-leaf akebia)
Clematis spp. (Clematis)
Euonymus fortunei radicans (Wintercreeper)
Hedera helix (English ivy)
Lonicera spp. (Honeysuckle)
Parthenocissus quinquefolia (Virginia creeper)
Parthenocissus tricuspidata (Boston ivy)
Polygonum aubertii (Silver lace vine)
Wisteria spp. (Wisteria)

Shrubs

Berberis spp. (Barberry)
Buddleia davidii (Butterfly bush)
Buxus spp. (Boxwood)
Cotoneaster spp. (Cotoneaster)
Forsythia spp. (Forsythia)
Ilex spp. (Holly)
Juniperus spp. (Juniper)
Mahonia aquifolium (Oregon holly grape)
Syringa vulgaris (Lilac)
Thuja spp. (Arborvitae)

Deer will browse almost any plant if starving, but these plants are at the bottom of their wish list in most parts of the country.

Peter C. Jones

GLOSSARY

ACID SOIL Soil that has a pH below 7

ALKALINE SOIL Soil that has a pH above 7

AMENDMENT Material other than fertilizer that is added to improve the soil

ANNUAL PLANT A plant that completes its life cycle within one growing season

BALLED-AND-BURLAPPED Plants with their root balls wrapped in burlap for transplanting

BARE-ROOT Plants transplanted during dormancy without soil around their roots

BIENNIAL PLANT A plant that completes its life cycle within two growing seasons

BIODEGRADABLE Made of materials that decompose naturally

BLUING The turning blue of red and pink rose petals in intense heat and sunlight

BORDER A narrow planting bed that edges a path, wall, fence or hedge

BROAD-LEAFED EVERGREEN Evergreens that have broad, flat leaves, not needles, and do not bear cones

CALICHE A concrete-like material under the soil's surface composed of calcium carbonate

CANDLE New shoots at the tips of evergreen branches that send out new needles

CANE On roses, major woody stems with pithy centers

CLAY SOIL Soil with a greater percentage of clay particles than silt or sand

COMPOST Decomposed organic matter, such as leaves and grass clippings, used to amend the soil

CONIFER Cone-bearing shrubs and trees, which are usually evergreen with needled foliage

CONTAINER-GROWN Plants grown in, not transplanted into, the containers they are sold in

CULTIVAR A cultivated variety

CULTIVATION The working of soil with tools, such as hoes, to break it up for improved aeration and weed control

DAMPING OFF A fungal disease carried in the soil that kills seedlings

DEADHEAD The removal of spent blossoms to encourage new blooms

DECIDUOUS Plants that are not evergreen and lose their leaves at season's end

DIEBACK The dying of woody plants in a downward direction

DIVISION The dividing of plants that reproduce vegetatively, such as perennials, into two or more clumps

DOUBLE Roses that have fifteen to thirty petals

DORMANCY Period usually triggered by extreme heat or cold in which plant growth processes slow down

DRIPLINE The outermost limits of a tree's canopy from which water drips

EVERGREEN Plants that retain their foliage year-round

FAMILY A category of plants sharing similar characteristics that is comprised of related *genera*

FERTILE Capable of producing viable seed

FOLIAR FEEDING The application of liquid fertilizer by spraying plant leaves

FREEZE-THAW CYCLE Alternating hard freezes and rapid thaws that can cause severe damage to plants

FULLY DOUBLE Roses that have more than thirty petals

GENUS Class of related plants that comprise plant families

GERMINATION The chemical and physical processes in which plants develop from seed

GLAUCOUS Blue in color

GROUNDCOVER Low-growing shrubs, roses, perennials, succulents or vines, which cover the ground quickly and thoroughly

HALF-HARDY Plants that will take some frost, but not as much cold as hardy plants

HARDENING OFF The acclimatization of seedlings raised under cover to outdoor conditions

HARDPAN A hard, often densely compacted layer of soil, impermeable to water and air

HARDY Plants that survive cold winter temperatures

HEELING IN The temporary planting of bare-root plants

HERBACEOUS Having soft, not woody, stems

HYBRID A plant resulting from the crossing of two different species

INFLORESCENCE The flower of an ornamental grass

INTEGRATED PEST MANAGEMENT (IPM) Pest management by intelligent plant selection, biological and nontoxic controls with the use of pesticides only as a last resort

LIME Calcium carbonate, a soil amendment for reducing acid levels

LOAM Soil containing a good balance of sand, silt and clay

MASS PLANTINGS Similar plants installed in large masses to form a bold, uncluttered statement in the landscape

MICROCLIMATE A small area where growing conditions differ from the overall climate

MICRONUTRIENTS Trace elements important for a plant's health, including boron, chlorine, copper, iron, manganese, molybdenum and zinc

MULCH Organic or inorganic materials spread over the soil's surface to conserve moisture, moderate temperature and control weeds

NEMATODE A threadlike worm living in the soil that feeds upon plant roots, bulbs and leaves

NEUTRAL SOIL Soil with a pH of 7, neither acid nor alkaline

PERENNIAL Plant that lives for more than two growing seasons

pH The expression of a soil's relative acidity or alkalinity

PINCHING The removal of a plant's growing tip to encourage the growth of side branches

RESPIRATION The chemical process in which a plant uses oxygen to break down carbohydrates to create energy, carbon dioxide and water

SALINE SOIL Soil that contains a level of soluble salts damaging to plants

SEMIDOUBLE Roses that have eight to fourteen petals

SEMIEVERGREEN A plant that retains its leaves for most of the winter

SIDE-DRESSING The application of fertilizer close to individual plants

SINGLE Roses that have four to seven petals

SPECIES A group of plants with similar characteristics, represented by the second word in a plant's botanical name

SPECIMEN PLANT A plant with special characteristics in perfect condition that, like a sculpture, is placed to be viewed

SPIT The depth of a spade's blade, a means of measuring a trench's depth when digging

TENDER Plants that cannot tolerate frost

TOPIARY The art of clipping and training plants into decorative shapes

USDA HARDINESS MAP United States Department of Agriculture's map, which illustrates eleven different climate zones delineated by average minimum annual temperatures

VARIETIES Plants that retain most of the characteristics of the species, but may differ slightly in their drought or temperature tolerance, disease resistance, color or fruit size

WATER TABLE The upper limit of ground water

WINTER KILL The dying back of plants due to severe winter conditions

XERISCAPE GARDENING Water-efficient gardening, which incorporates plants compatible with the microclimate and the natural level of rainfall

G L O S S A R Y

AGRICULTURAL COOPERATIVE EXTENSION SERVICES

Alaska Cooperative Extension
University of Alaska, Fairbanks
P.O. Box 756180
Fairbanks, AK 99775-6180

Cooperative Extension Service
Colorado State University
1 Administration Building
Fort Collins, CO 80523

Cooperative Extension System
University of Idaho
Agricultural Science Building
Moscow, ID 83843

Cooperative Extension Service
University of Illinois
122 Mumford Hall
1301 West Gregory Drive
Urbana, IL 61801

Cooperative Extension Service
Iowa State University
315 Beardshear Hall
Ames, IA 50011

Cooperative Extension Service
Kansas State University
123 Umberger Hall
Manhattan, KS 66506-3401

Cooperative Extension Service
University of Maine
5741 Libby Hall
Orono, ME 04469-5741

Cooperative Extension Service
University of Massachusetts
Stockbridge Hall
Room 117
Amherst, MA 01003

Cooperative Extension Service
Michigan State University
106 Agriculture Hall
East Lansing, MI 48824

Minnesota Extension Service
University of Minnesota
200 Coffey Hall
1420 Eckles Avenue
St. Paul, MN 55108

Cooperative Extension Service
University of Missouri
309 University Hall
Columbia, MO 65211

Cooperative Extension Service
Montana State University
212 Montana Hall
Bozeman, MT 59717

Cooperative Extension
University of Nebraska
211 Agriculture Hall
Lincoln, NE 68583-0703

Nevada Cooperative Extension
University of Nevada, Reno
Mail Stop 189
Reno, NV 89557-0106

UNH Cooperative Extension
59 College Road
103 Taylor Hall
Durham, NH 03824-3587

Cooperative Extension Service
New Mexico State University
Box 3AE
Las Cruces, NM 88003

Cooperative Extension Service
Cornell University
276 Roberts Hall
Ithaca, NY 14853-4203

NDSU Extension Service
North Dakota State University
315 Morrill Hall
Fargo, ND 58105-5437

Ohio State University Extension
2120 Fyffe Road
Columbus, OH 43210

Cooperative Extension Service
Oregon State University
Ballard Extension Hall
Corvallis, OR 97331

Cooperative Extension Service
The Pennsylvania State
University
201 Agriculture Administration
Building
University Park, PA 16802-2600

Cooperative Extension Service
South Dakota State University
Agriculture Hall 154
P.O. Box 2207D
Brookings, SD 57007-9988

Cooperative Extension Service
Utah State University
Agricultural Science Building
Logan, UT 84322-4900

University of Vermont
Extension System
601 Main Street
Burlington, VT 05401-3439

Cooperative Extension Service
Washington State University
421 Hulbert Hall
Pullman, WA 99164-6242

Cooperative Extension Service
University of Wisconsin
Extension
432 N. Lake Street
Room 601 Extension Building
Madison, WI 53706

Cooperative Extension Service
University of Wyoming
College of Agriculture
P.O. Box 3354
Laramie, WY 82071-3354

S O U R C E S

PERENNIALS AND PLANTS

Klehm Nursery
4210 N. Duncan Road
Champaign, IL 61821
(217) 359-2888 FAX 373-8403
Perennials

Kurt Bluemel, Inc.
2740 Greene Lane
Baldwin, MD 21013
(410) 557-7229 FAX 557-9785
Ornamental grasses

Milaeger's Gardens
4838 Douglas Avenue
Racine, WI 53402-2498
(414) 639-2371 FAX 639-1855

Plants of the Southwest
Route 6, Box 11A, Agua Fria
Santa Fe, NM 87501
(800) 788-7333

Wayside Gardens
P.O. Box 1
Hodges, SC 29695-0001
(800) 845-1124
*Perennials, grasses, shrubs,
roses and bulbs*

White Flower Farm
Route 63
Litchfield, CT 06759-0050
(203) 496-9600 FAX 496-1418
*Perennials, grasses, shrubs,
roses and bulbs*

ROSES

High Country Rosarium
1717 Downing Street
Denver, CO 80226
(303) 832-4026 FAX same
Hardy roses

Royal River Roses/Forever
Green Farm
70 New Gloucester Road
North Yarmouth, ME 04097
(207) 829-5830 FAX 829-6512
Old-fashioned and hardy roses

The Roseraie at Bayfields
P.O. Box R
Waldoboro, ME 04572
(207) 832-6330
Old, modern, and hardy roses

Vintage Gardens
3003 Pleasant Hill Road
Sebastopol, CA 95472
(707) 829-5342
Old and modern roses

BULBS

Dutch Gardens, Inc.
P.O. Box 200
Adelphia, NJ 07710
(908) 780-2713 FAX 780-7720

John Scheepers, Inc.
23 Tulip Drive
Bantam, CT 06750
(203) 567-5323

SEEDS

The Cook's Garden
P.O. Box 535
Moffits Bridge
Londonderry, VT 05148
(802) 824-3400 or 3406
FAX 824-3027
*Vegetable, herb and flower
seeds*

High Altitude Gardens
P.O. Box 1048
308 S. River
Hailey, ID 83333
(208) 788-4363 FAX 788-3452
Seeds for cold, short seasons

Shepherd's Garden Seeds
30 Irene Street
Torrington, CT 06790
(203) 482-3638
*Heirloom vegetable, herb, and
flower seeds*

W. Atlee Burpee Company
300 Park Avenue
Warminster, PA 18974
(215) 674-4900, (800) 888-1447

SUPPLIES

Gardens Alive!
5100 Schenley Place
Lawrenceburg, IN 47025
(812) 537-8650 FAX 537-8660
*Natural insect and disease
control*

The Natural Gardening
  Company
217 San Anselmo Avenue
San Anselmo, CA 94960
(415) 456-5060 FAX 721-0642
Organic gardening supplies

Peaceful Valley Farm Supply
P.O. Box 2209
Grass Valley, CA 95945
(916) 272-4769 FAX 272-4794
*Organic growing supplies, soil
testing*

TOOLS

A.M. Leonard, Inc.
P.O. Box 816
6665 Spiker Road
Piqua, OH 45356-0816
(513) 773-2694, (800) 543-8955

Gardener's Eden
Box 7307
San Francisco, CA 94120-7307
(800) 822-9600
Tools, equipment and gadgets

Gardener's Supply Company
128 Intervale Road
Burlington, VT 05401
(802) 660-3500 FAX 660-3501
Tools and equipment

Smith & Hawken
117 East Strawberry Drive
Mill Valley, CA 94941
(800) 776-3336
*Tools, equipment and
ornaments*